STUDY GUIDE

Microeconomic Principles & Policies

SIXTH EDITION

RYAN C. AMACHER
HOLLEY H. ULBRICH

Prepared by
PATRICIA PANDO
Houston Baptist University

SOUTH-WESTERN College Publishing

An International Thomson Publishing Company

Acquisitions Editor: Jack C. Calhoun
Developmental Editor: Alice C. Denny, Dennis Hanseman
Production Editors: Sue Ellen Brown, Rebecca Roby
Production House: Shepherd, Inc.
Cover Design: Sandy Weinstein/Tin Box Studio
Cover Illustration: Jane Sterrett

HB67FD2
Copyright © 1995
by South-Western College Publishing
Cincinnati, Ohio

ALL RIGHTS RESERVED
The text of this publication, or any part thereof, may not be reproduced or transmitted in any form or by any means, electronic or mechanical, including photocopying, recording, storage in any information retrieval system, or otherwise, without prior written permission from the publisher.

ISBN: 0-538-83853-1
   3 4 5 6 7 MZ 0 9 8 7 6 5
Printed in the United States of America

 This book is printed on acid-free paper that meets Environmental Protection Agency standards for recycled paper.

International Thomson Publishing

South-Western College Publishing is an ITP Company. The ITP trademark is used under license.

PREFACE

This *Study Guide* is your guide to the basics of economics; it is meant to be used. You may have read a travel guidebook before you took a vacation. A travel guide points out important things you should see and explains details you might not have known or understood. However, reading the guidebook is not the same thing as taking the trip!

In the same manner, this *Study Guide* will help you get the most out of your study of economics. You should refer to it and work in it often. However, it is not a substitute for reading the text book or going to class; it is a complement to those activities. Students who have done well in introductory economics courses frequently report that they reviewed each chapter in the Study Guide before the material was presented in class. Because the students were already familiar with the material, they were able to ask questions about troublesome parts while the chapter was being discussed in class. If you try this, you should find your grades improving.

Each Chapter of the *Study Guide* is divided into several parts:

Checking In summarizes the important points of each chapter in a few paragraphs. You may want to read this section before you read the chapter in the text, and you will certainly want to read it before your instructor discusses the material in class.

Trying Out the Terms allows you to match the new terms from each chapter with their definitions. Do this as soon as you finish reading the textbook chapter. Understanding all the terms will make the questions and problems easier for you..

Testing Yourself lets you check how well you understand each chapter. You should complete this part after you have mastered the new terms. This section contains true/false statements, multiple choice questions, and problems. Many problems are numerical applications of theories discussed in the textbook, and working with them will make the theories easier to understand. If you have difficulty with any part of this section, ask your instructor to review the material. If you are a member of a study group, your group can use these questions as a review and as a springboard for discussion. You will want to rework this section before your examination.

Taking Another Look presents a new application of or a different way of looking at some of the timely issues discussed in the textbook. This section does not appear in every chapter.

Checking Out gives you a last look at the important topics in each chapter. Use this section as a self-test; if you cannot explain an item, go back and review it in your text or class notes. This section is a good place to begin your review for an examination.

Answers to the Trying Out the Terms and Testing Yourself sections follow Checking Out.

Exercises end each chapter. Your instructor may assign the exercises as homework or as an in-class activity. If they are not assigned, you can complete them as a review. Ask you instructor for a copy of the solutions.

The *Study Guide* was prepared with you in mind. Its purpose is to help you understand and enjoy economics and also to help you earn a better grade. If, in your studies, you find some parts of the Study Guide more helpful than others, or if you come up with new methods of studying that you think will help others, please let us know. We will try to incorporate your suggestions when the Study Guide is revised.
Good luck!

Patricia N. Pando
Ryan C. Amacher
Holley H. Ulbrich

CONTENTS

Chapter	1	Economics, Economic Methods and Economic Policy	1
Chapter	2	Markets, Governments and Nations: The Organization of Economic Activity	19
Chapter	3	Supply and Demand: The Basics of Economic Analysis	33
Chapter	4	Policy Applications of Supply and Demand	49
Chapter	5	Elasticity: The Measure of Responsiveness	63
Chapter	6	Demand and Consumer Choice	79
Chapter	7	Firms and Production	99
Chapter	8	Costs and Profits	115
Chapter	9	Perfect Competition	129
Chapter	10	Monopoly	145
Chapter	11	Monopolistic Competition and Oligopoly	163
Chapter	12	Regulation, Deregulation and Antitrust Policy	177
Chapter	13	Marginal Productivity Theory and Labor Markets	191
Chapter	14	Organized Labor in the United States	203
Chapter	15	Rent, Interest and Profit	221
Chapter	16	Poverty, Inequality, and Income Redistribution Policies	235
Chapter	17	Market Failure and Government Intervention Policies	247
Chapter	18	Government Failure and Public Choice	261
Chapter	19	Policy Studies: Cities, the Environment, and Health Care	273
Chapter	20	Trade Among Nations	283
Chapter	21	International Finance and Exchange Rates	295
Chapter	22	Economies in Transition	311

STUDY GUIDE FOR

MICROECONOMIC PRINCIPLES & POLICIES

CHAPTER 1

ECONOMICS, ECONOMIC METHODS, AND ECONOMIC POLICY

CHECKING IN

You are about to begin the very interesting subject of economics. Economics is the study of the ways in which people and institutions make decisions about producing and consuming goods and services, or how they face the problems caused by scarcity.

The study of economics is generally divided into two parts; both are concerned with these problems of scarcity. Microeconomics considers the interactions of producers and consumers in individual markets. Macroeconomics looks at the economy as a whole; it is concerned with aggregates, or quantities whose values are determined by adding up values for all of the individual markets.

Economics is usually classified as a social science. Economic theory is an abstract way of thinking that allows the development of models and tools that can be used to study social problems.

Resources are finite, but human wants are unlimited. In dealing with the problem of scarcity, people must make choices. They cannot produce everything, so in order to get more of one thing, they must give up something else. The value of the alternative given up is the opportunity cost. The principle of increasing opportunity cost says that the more of one good people have, the greater the amount of other goods they must sacrifice to obtain one more unit of that good.

The importance of opportunity cost is illustrated by the production possibilities curve. This model not only demonstrates the importance of opportunity cost, but also is useful in describing unemployment, economic growth, and the benefits of specialization and exchange.

The approach that most economists take is to make positive statements rather than normative ones. Normative statements suggest what *should* be done. Positive statements say "if this is done, then that will happen," without saying whether it *ought* to be done.

Economists assume that people act out of self-interest: that people always try to make themselves (or their firms or institutions) as well off as possible. Economics stresses how individuals respond to incentives (self-interest), so economists tend to rely on the market to solve many problems that they analyze. They attempt to clarify the options available to the decision maker and consider all possible costs. Economists also consider alternatives or substitutes that are available.

Chapter 1   Economics, Economic Methods, and Economic Policy   *1*

Policy analysis involves five steps: stating the problem, applying the relevant economic model, identifying solutions, evaluating solutions, and choosing and implementing solutions. Most economists' disagreements are over policy choices rather than economic theory. In general, economists agree much more than they disagree.

Economists depend on graphs and algebra to assist in their analysis. The Appendix to this chapter reviews some techniques you will be using in your study of economics.

TRYING OUT THE TERMS

Match each of the following terms with its definition, and then check your answers. If you are having trouble, go back to the text and find the definition there.

Part I

_____ 1. microeconomics   _____ 10. resources

_____ 2. self-interested behavior   _____ 11. macroeconomics

_____ 3. testable hypothesis   _____ 12. aggregates

_____ 4. model   _____ 13. economics

_____ 5. theory   _____ 14. *ceteris paribus* assumption

_____ 6. normative statements   _____ 15. social science

_____ 7. increasing opportunity cost   _____ 16. opportunity cost

_____ 8. unlimited wants   _____ 17. positive statements

_____ 9. scarcity   _____ 18. production possibilities curve

A. The study of how people and institutions make decisions about production and consumption and how they face the problem of scarcity.

B. The study of individual market interactions, focusing on production and consumption by the individual consumer, firm, or industry.

C. The study of the economy as a whole or of economic aggregates, such as the level of employment and the growth of total output.

D. An academic field that studies the behavior of human beings, individually and in groups, and examines their interactions.

E. Quantities whose values are determined by adding across many markets.

F. The central economic problem that there are not enough resources to produce everything that individuals want.

Chapter 1   Economics, Economic Methods, and Economic Policy

G. The needs and desires of human beings, which can never be completely satisfied.

H. The value of the other alternatives given up in order to enjoy a particular good or service.

I. A graph that depicts the various combinations of two goods that can be produced in an economy with the available resources.

J. The principle that as production of one good rises, larger and larger sacrifices of another are required.

K. A set of principles that can be used to make inferences about the world.

L. An inference from a theory that can be subjected to real-world testing.

M. A set of assumptions and hypotheses that is a simplified description of reality.

N. The assumption that everything else will remain constant, used for most economic models.

O. A basic assumption of economic theory that individual decision makers do what is best for themselves.

P. A set of propositions about what is, rather than what ought to be.

Q. A set of propositions about what ought to be (also called value judgments).

R. Inputs used to produce goods and services.

Part II

These terms are found in the Appendix to the chapter.

_____	1. coordinates	_____ 9. pie chart
_____	2. *y*-axis	_____ 10. minimum
_____	3. scatter diagram	_____ 11. origin
_____	4. tangent line	_____ 12. positive relationship
_____	5. *x*-axis	_____ 13. 45° line
_____	6. bar chart	_____ 14. negative relationship
_____	7. independent variable	_____ 15. maximum
_____	8. slope	_____ 16. dependent variable

A. The upright line in a coordinate system that shows the values of the dependent variable; the vertical axis.

B. The horizontal line in a coordinate system that shows the values of the independent variable; the horizontal axis.

C. The intersection of the vertical and horizontal axes of a coordinate system, at which the values of both the x-variable and the y-variable are zero.

D. The variable, usually plotted on the horizontal axis, that affects or influences the other variable.

E. The variable, usually plotted on the vertical axis, that is affected or influenced by the other variable.

F. The values of x and y that define the location of a point in a coordinate system.

G. A graph that plots actual pairs of values of two variables to determine whether there appears to be any consistent relationship between them.

H. A relationship between two variables in which an increase in one is associated with an increase in the other and a decrease in one is associated with a decrease in the other.

I. A relationship between two variables in which an increase in the value of one is associated with a decrease in the value of the other.

J. The ratio of the change in the dependent variable (y) to the change in the independent variable (x).

K. A straight line just touching a curve (nonlinear graphic relationship) at a single point. The slope of the line is equal to the slope of the curve at that point.

L. The point on a graph at which the y-variable, or dependent variable, reaches its highest value.

M. The point on the graph at which the y-variable, or dependent variable, reaches its lowest value.

N. A line in the first quadrant, passing through the origin, with a slope of +1, which divides the quadrant in half. If the scales on the axes are the same, the value of the x-variable is equal to the value of the y-variable along this line.

O. A graphic representation in the shape of a pie that expresses actual economic data as parts of a whole. The sizes of the slices of the pie correspond to the percentage shares of the components.

P. A graphic representation that expresses data using columns of different heights.

4   Chapter 1   Economics, Economic Methods, and Economic Policy

TESTING YOURSELF

In the next three sections, you will answer questions and work problems that are based on information in the text. Master all of the terms before you begin these sections. Work each section without referring to your notes or the text, and then check your answers.

Part I: True or False

Mark each statement as true or false. Whenever you mark a statement as false, jot down a sentence stating why it is false. Statements 11–14 are based on material in the Appendix.

_____ 1. The study of economics is concerned with how people react to changing income and prices.

_____ 2. The level of employment in the economy is a macroeconomic issue.

_____ 3. Microeconomics is concerned with the interactions of producers and consumers in individual markets.

_____ 4. Opportunity cost is always measured in monetary terms.

_____ 5. When some of a society's resources are unemployed, the society is operating at a point inside the production possibilities curve.

_____ 6. The typical production possibilities curve has a bowed-out shape because of increasing opportunity costs.

_____ 7. When the Vietnam War began, the United States was operating at a point inside its production possibilities curve.

Chapter 1   Economics, Economic Methods, and Economic Policy   5

_____ 8. The question, "What will happen to the price of corn in a year when there is both a flood and a fall in the price of fertilizer?" observes the *ceteris paribus* assumption.

_____ 9. An economics teacher tells her class that all transfer payments to veterans should be eliminated. This is an example of a positive economic statement.

_____ 10. The self-interest assumption holds that all people are selfish.

_____ 11. If for every increase in x, y increases by 2, 3, or 4 units, the graph of the equation will be a straight line.

_____ 12. If two variables are negatively (inversely) related, then one variable will increase in value as the other variable decreases.

_____ 13. The slope of a curve at a particular point is equal to the slope of the straight line tangent to that point.

_____ 14. If the numbers reported are accurate, statistical reports always give an undistorted view of reality.

Part II: Problems

Problem 3 is based on the Appendix.

1. You are given the following data for a small country that can produce either bread or tractors.

Bread	Tractors
70	0
60	2
50	4
40	6
30	8
20	10
10	12
0	14

   a. On the graph below, plot the production possibilities curve.

   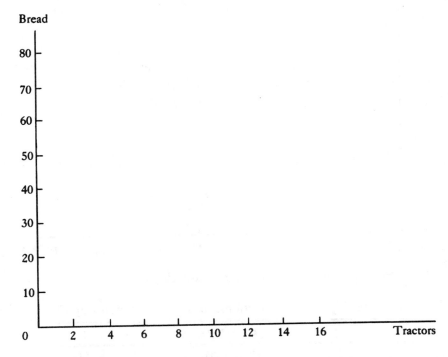

   b. What is the opportunity cost of increasing production of bread from 10 units to 20 units? From 40 units to 50 units?

Chapter 1   Economics, Economic Methods, and Economic Policy

c. What role do increasing opportunity costs play in this model?

d. On your graph, mark the point representing the production of 45 units of bread and 8 tractors. Will this economy ever produce at this point? Why or why not?

2. On the graph below, plot the sales of a typical retail store during the months of October through February. It is not necessary to use exact values; simply graph the relationship.

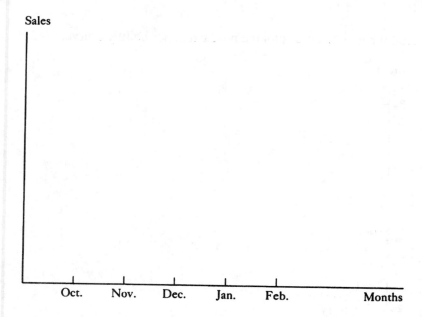

3. Consider each of the following relationships:

Relationship A		Relationship B		Relationship C	
x	y	x	y	x	y
1	5	10	20	100	90
2	4	12	15	125	100
3	3	14	10	150	110
4	2	16	5	175	120

a. Which of these relationships is/are positive? How can you tell?

b. What is the slope of each relationship?

c. In the graph provided below, plot relationship B.

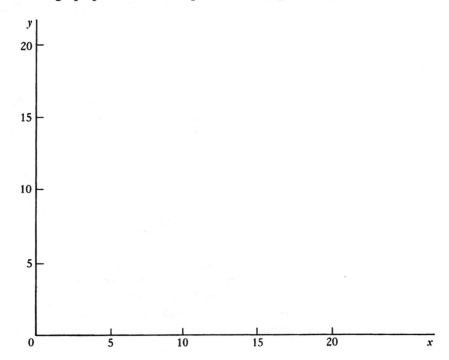

Part III: Multiple Choice

Questions 13–15 are based on the Appendix.

_____ 1. Economics can be defined as the
   a. study of money and commerce.
   b. science of behavior modification.
   c. study of how people and institutions respond to the problems of scarcity.
   d. study of how labor and product markets are related.

_____ 2. The study of the overall price level and the levels of unemployment and output is called
   a. macroeconomics.
   b. microeconomics.
   c. decision science.
   d. global economics.

_____ 3. In microeconomics we would expect to study
   a. the effects of inflation.
   b. the tax policies of the federal government.
   c. changes in the consumer price index.
   d. the determination of the price of corn.

Use this graph to answer Questions 4–6.

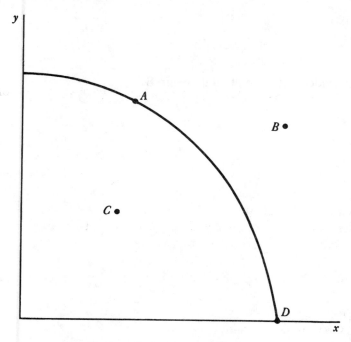

_____ 4. If the economy is producing at point C,
   a. there is considerable unemployment in the economy.
   b. the economy is operating at full employment.
   c. there is excessive production of Good x.
   d. The point is unattainable.

_____ 5. In this economy, the opportunity cost of an additional unit of y in terms of unit x will
   a. increase as more y is produced.
   b. increase as more x is produced.
   c. remain constant at all levels of production.
   d. increase at a low level of production of y and then become constant.

_____ 6. If the economy is operating at full employment and producing some of both Good x and Good y, it is at point
   a. A.
   b. B.
   c. C.
   d. D.

_____ 7. When an individual makes decisions based on a comparison of costs and benefits, economists say that this individual is acting
   a. selfishly.
   b. out of self-interest.
   c. uneconomically.
   d. in a way that will minimize the general welfare.

Chapter 1   *Economics, Economic Methods, and Economic Policy*

8. Economists tend to think of the basic decision-making unit as the
   a. government.
   b. firm.
   c. individual.
   d. institution (bank, church, etc.).

9. Economists prefer market solutions to economic problems because market solutions are
   a. fairer.
   b. more efficient.
   c. faster.
   d. easier to understand.

10. Economic models are used
    a. because economists don't really understand the way markets work.
    b. because they explain all of the economy at one specific time.
    c. to predict behavior under specific circumstances.
    d. to give accurate and explicit forecasts of the future.

11. Employment is a macroeconomic issue
    a. because everyone is likely to be unemployed at some time.
    b. because unemployed workers represent lost potential output.
    c. because unemployment benefits are spent on consumer goods.
    d. because employment takes place in labor markets.

12. Economist Milton Friedman maintains that the best test of the usefulness of a theory is
    a. the strength of its assumptions.
    b. if it makes accurate predictions.
    c. its logical correctness.
    d. if it demonstrates market behavior.

13. If for every increase of 5 units in the x-variable, the y-variable increases by 10 units, a graph of the equation
    a. has a slope of 1/2.
    b. has a slope of 2.
    c. has no slope.
    d. would show a negative slope, reach a minimum, and then become positive.

14. If for every increase of 10 units in the x-variable, the y-variable decreases by 15 units, a graph of the equation
    a. has a slope of 0.666.
    b. has a negative slope.
    c. is a straight line.
    d. is a straight line with a negative slope.

Chapter 1   Economics, Economic Methods, and Economic Policy   *11*

_____ 15. A straight line that cuts through the origin and divides Quadrant 1 into two equal sections
  a. is called the 45° line.
  b. has a slope of +1.
  c. measures equal values of both the *x*- and *y*-variables.
  d. All of the above.

CHECKING OUT

Now that you have finished studying this chapter, you should be able to:

1. Define economics, and discuss how it is related to other social sciences.

2. Recognize the value of studying economics.

3. Explain the relationship between scarcity and choice, and the role of opportunity costs.

4. Use the production possibilities model to identify unemployment of resources and to explain the concept of economic growth.

5. Recognize the difference between theories, hypotheses, and models.

6. List the elements of the economic approach to policy analysis.

7. Understand and develop the steps followed in policy analysis.

ANSWERS

Trying Out the Terms

Part I

1. B	5. K	9. F	13. A	17. P
2. O	6. Q	10. R	14. N	18. I
3. L	7. J	11. C	15. D	
4. M	8. G	12. E	16. H	

Part II

1. F	5. B	9. O	13. N
2. A	6. P	10. M	14. I
3. G	7. D	11. C	15. L
4. K	8. J	12. H	16. E

Testing Yourself

Part I: True or False

1. false. Economics is concerned with how people make choices when resources are scarce.
2. true
3. true
4. false. Opportunity cost is the value of the next-best alternatives given up in order to enjoy a particular activity or service. It may or may not be stated in monetary terms.
5. true
6. true
7. false. There was very little unemployment. The economy was on its production possibilities curve.
8. false. The *ceteris paribus* assumption means that we are assuming only one thing will change: either the weather or the price of fertilizer.
9. false. This is a normative statement.
10. false. The self-interest assumption holds that individuals make decisions by comparing costs and benefits and then doing what is best for themselves.
11. false. When the graph of an equation is a straight line, y always responds with the same change. For example, for every change in x, y increases by 2.
12. true
13. true
14. false. The way in which accurate numbers are reported (scale, use of averages, etc.) can easily distort reality.

Part II: Problems

1. a.

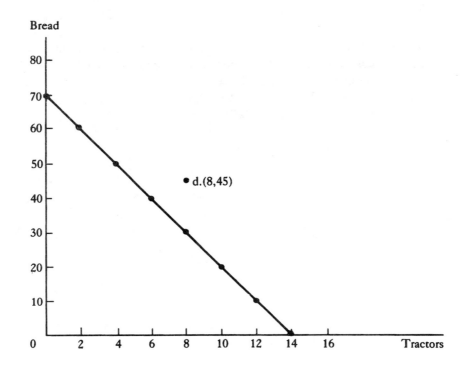

Chapter 1   Economics, Economic Methods, and Economic Policy

b. The opportunity cost of increasing bread production from 10 units to 20 units is 2 tractors. The opportunity cost of increasing bread production from 40 units to 50 units is also 2 tractors.

c. In this case, costs are not increasing. The opportunity cost of 1 unit of bread is always 1/5 of a tractor. In other words, the opportunity cost of 1 tractor is always 5 units of bread.

d. This economy will never be able to produce 45 units of bread and 8 tractors, because that combination is beyond the production possibilities curve.

2. We would expect sales to increase during the fall months, peak in December, fall off dramatically in January, and then level off in February.

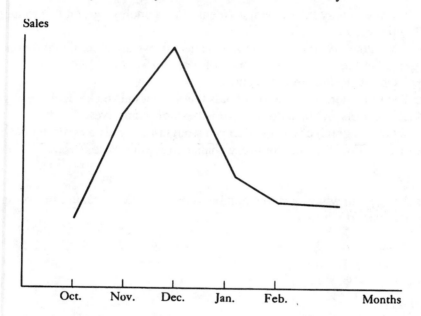

3. a. Relationship C is positive. The two variables change in the same direction; when x increases, so does y. The other relationships are negative.

 b. Relationship A: slope = –1/1 = –1
 Relationship B: slope = –5/2 = –2.5
 Relationship C: slope = 10/25 = 0.4

c.

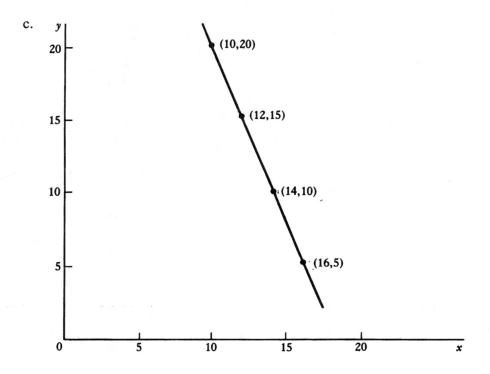

Part III: Multiple Choice

1. c
2. a
3. d
4. a
5. a
6. a
7. b
8. c
9. b
10. c
11. b
12. b
13. b
14. d
15. d

Name _____

CHAPTER 1 EXERCISES

1. List and describe, in one sentence each, the five steps for using economic methods in policy analysis.

    a.

    b.

    c.

    d.

    e.

Chapter 1   Economics, Economic Methods, and Economic Policy   *17*

2. You are given this information about a country's ability to produce toys and typewriters.

Toys	Typewriters	Opportunity Cost of 5 Additional Typewriters
75	0	
68	5	_____
58	10	_____
44	15	_____
25	20	_____
0	25	_____

a. Fill in the opportunity cost of 5 additional typewriters in terms of toys.

b. Plot the production possibilities curve on the graph below.

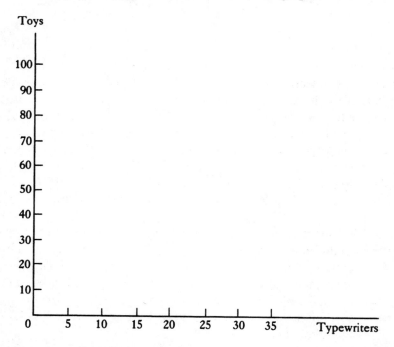

c. Suppose that this country experiences 10 years of peace, prosperity, and economic growth. At the end of those 10 years, it can produce more of all goods. Draw a new production possibilities curve on your graph. Label it *Good Times*.

d. Now suppose that this country has 10 years of war, famine, and disaster. At the end of those 10 years, it has fewer productive resources than it did 10 years earlier. Draw this production possibilities curve and label it *Bad Times*.

CHAPTER 2

MARKETS, GOVERNMENTS, AND NATIONS: THE ORGANIZATION OF ECONOMIC ACTIVITY

CHECKING IN

From Chapter 1, you learned that scarcity is the inescapable economic problem. Regardless of their levels of wealth and types of economic organization, all economies must face and attempt to solve this problem. Because resources are limited, economies must decide how they are to be used by answering three basic questions: *What* will be produced? *How* shall it be produced? *Who* gets a share of what is produced? All of these are questions about how an economy decides to use its resources. *Productive resources* can be divided into four general groups: labor (which receives the payment of wages), land (which receives the payment of rent), capital (which receives the payment of interest), and enterprise (which receives profit).

Although all economies must answer the three basic questions, different economies go about doing so in different ways. The three general ways are tradition, command, and the market. Most countries use a combination of these methods, with one predominating. The majority of Western industrial nations, including the United States, use a mixed economy that relies heavily on the market but allows some government intervention in certain areas. A simple but useful model of the idealized market economy is the circular flow model. We will use this model throughout the rest of the course.

A mixed economy depends both on the market and on the government to answer the basic economic questions. This is because the market either does not perform or does not perform very well some necessary functions. For markets to function at all, we must have clearly defined and protected property rights. There are some goods that markets simply do not provide or provide in the wrong amounts. Markets do answer the question of who is to receive production, but they sometimes answer this question in very uneven ways. Governments often make adjustments in this distribution. Governments also attempt to stabilize the economy.

Whenever government produces a public good or participates in activities that affect private decisions about production and consumption, it is affecting the allocation of resources. Some other ways in which government affects allocation are through taxes, subsidies, and regulation. Government can directly change the market distribution of income by redistributing it through taxes and transfer payments. However, any other action of government

Chapter 2   Markets, Governments, and Nations: The Organization of Economic Activity   **19**

(allocation or stabilization, for example) will also have an effect on the distribution of income. The newest function of government is stabilization. Government uses its ability to tax, spend, and regulate to attempt to bring about full employment, stable prices, and real economic growth.

One way individuals and nations alleviate the problem of scarcity is by specializing in producing goods with low opportunity costs and trading for goods with higher opportunity costs. This principle is known as comparative advantage. International trade in goods, services, and resources benefits both trading partners. Although some workers and firms in a nation may experience losses because of foreign competition, the gains for the nation as a whole will usually exceed such losses.

TRYING OUT THE TERMS

Match each of the following terms with its definition, and then check your answers. If you are having trouble, go back to the text and find the definition there.

Part I

_____	1.	resources	_____	9. circular flow model
_____	2.	positive externalities	_____	10. land
_____	3.	enterprise	_____	11. command economy
_____	4.	resource market	_____	12. human capital
_____	5.	capital	_____	13. allocation
_____	6.	property rights	_____	14. product market
_____	7.	market	_____	15. market economy
_____	8.	labor	_____	16. mixed economy

A. Set of markets in which owners of productive resources sell these to producers.

B. The inputs of land, labor, capital, and enterprise that a firm uses to produce outputs.

C. A place where buyers and sellers meet to exchange goods, services, and productive resources.

D. An economy in which the three basic questions are answered through the market, by relying on self-interested behavior and incentives.

E. An economy in which the three basic questions are answered partly by market forces and partly through government.

F. The physical and mental exertion that human beings put into production activities.

20   *Chapter 2   Markets, Governments, and Nations: The Organization of Economic Activity*

G. Natural resources that can be used as inputs to production.

H. Any activities by government or its agents that affect the distribution of resources and the combination of goods and services produced.

I. The durable inputs into the production process created by people; machines, tools, and buildings are examples.

J. A visual representation of the relationships between the resource market (in which income is obtained) and the product market (in which income is used to purchase goods and services).

K. An economy in which the three basic questions are answered through central planning and control (also called a planned economy).

L. The input to the production process that involves organizing, innovation, and risk taking.

M. The investment made to improve the quality of people's labor skills through education, training, health care, and so on.

N. Spillover benefits to third parties (free riders) that result from production or consumption of certain goods.

O. Set of markets in which goods and services produced by firms are sold.

P. The legal rights to a specific piece of property, including the rights to own, buy, sell, or use in specific ways. Markets can exist and exchanges can occur only if individuals have property rights to goods, services, and productive resources.

Part II

_____ 1. negative externalities

_____ 2. public goods

_____ 3. free riders

_____ 4. investment

_____ 5. profit

_____ 6. rent

_____ 7. specialization

_____ 8. redistribution

_____ 9. wages

_____ 10. public bads

_____ 11. traditional economy

_____ 12. principle of comparative advantage

_____ 13. interest

_____ 14. stabilization

Chapter 2   Markets, Governments, and Nations: The Organization of Economic Activity   21

A. Negative external effects of production or consumption that impact a large number of individuals—for example, acid rain.

B. Goods that are nonrival in consumption and not subject to exclusion.

C. The return to enterprise, one of the productive resources of production; profit is whatever remains after all other resources have been paid.

D. The idea that output will be maximized if people specialize in producing those goods or services for which their opportunity costs are lowest and engage in exchange to obtain other things they want.

E. Actions by government that transfer income from one group to another.

F. The return to land, one of the productive resources.

G. Limiting production activities to one or a few goods and services that one produces best in order to exchange for other goods.

H. An economy in which the three basic questions are answered by custom, or how things have been done in the past.

I. People or business firms who consume collective goods without contributing to the cost of their production.

J. Harmful spillovers to third parties that result from production or consumption of certain goods.

K. The return to labor, one of the productive resources.

L. The return to capital, one of the productive resources.

M. Purchase of real tangible assets, such as machines, factories, or inventories, that are used to produce goods and services.

N. Actions by the government to reduce changes in output, employment, and prices.

TESTING YOURSELF

In the next three sections, you will answer questions and work problems that are based on information in the text. Master all of the terms before you begin these sections. Work each section without referring to your notes or the text, and then check your answers.

Part I: True or False

Mark each statement as true or false. Whenever you mark a statement as false, jot down a sentence stating why it is false.

_____ 1. People are forced to make economic choices only when their wants are greater than their resources.

_____ 2. The salary of a college professor represents wages, the payment to labor, as well as interest, the payment to investment.

_____ 3. The productive resources include land, labor, capital, and enterprise.

_____ 4. Common stocks are a good example of economic capital.

_____ 5. If a farmer leases a farm and all of the equipment on the farm, her payment to the owner of the farm is considered as both a payment to land (rent) and a payment to capital (interest).

_____ 6. The basic economic questions are what, how, and when.

_____ 7. In a traditional economy, distribution of economic resources is determined primarily by an individual's contribution to society.

Chapter 2   Markets, Governments, and Nations: The Organization of Economic Activity   23

_____ 8. A command economy answers the basic economic questions through central planning and control.

_____ 9. A market economy depends on a combination of tradition, planning, and incentives to answer the basic economic questions.

_____ 10. Property rights must be clearly established for a market economy to function.

_____ 11. A mixed economy may have elements of traditional and planned economies, but a traditional economy never incorporates elements of the market.

_____ 12. The circular flow model illustrates the relationship between product markets and resource markets.

_____ 13. When specialization and trade are taking place, people become more dependent on one another.

_____ 14. Specialization can increase the variety of goods produced, but it cannot increase total production.

_____ 15. Although economists frequently disagree, they generally agree that a country benefits from free trade policies.

Part II: Problems

1. Classify each of the following ways of answering the basic economic questions (market, command, or tradition).

    a. The New York Stock Exchange

    b. Gun registration

    c. Going to Fort Lauderdale every year for spring break

    d. Going to Padre Island for spring break because it is cheaper

    e. Cuban students spending spring break harvesting sugar cane as part of the privilege of attending college

    f. Football scholarships at major universities

2. Classify each of the following government actions as being primarily allocation, stabilization, or redistribution.

    a. Raising taxes to control inflation

    b. Cutting out food stamps as a form of welfare payment

    c. Buying a new airplane for the vice president

    d. Holding the annual Easter Egg Roll on the White House lawn

    e. Reinstituting the GI Bill to pay college tuition for veterans

f.   Bailing out the savings and loan industry

3.   Bob and Pat work at a service station. Bob can change 6 tires or do 6 oil changes in an hour. Pat can change 8 tires or do 4 oil changes in an hour. On Saturday morning at 8:00, they are told that they can leave as soon as they have changed 40 tires and done 30 oil changes. Neither can leave until both have finished working.

a.   If Bob and Pat split the work, each doing half of the tire changes and half of the oil changes, when will they leave?

b.   If Bob and Pat specialize, using the principle of comparative advantage, when will they leave?

Part III: Multiple Choice

1.   The productive resources include
a.   land, labor, and services.
b.   enterprise and goods.
c.   labor, goods, and services.
d.   enterprise, capital, and labor.

2.   Which is *not* one of the basic economic questions?
a.   For whom?
b.   What?
c.   How much?
d.   How?

3.   Which of the following would be defined by an economist as embodying enterprise?
a.   A doctor
b.   A professor
c.   The owner of a dry-cleaning business
d.   A coal miner

4.   A planned economy answers the basic economic questions
a.   in the same way economies did in the past.
b.   through a central board or commission.
c.   by relying on the market system and incentives.
d.   by a combination of government regulation and markets.

_____ 5. Sylvia's parents are both doctors, but she decides to study accounting because she thinks it offers better career opportunities. This is an example of what kind of economic decision making?
   a. Command
   b. Rebellion
   c. Market
   d. Anti-tradition

_____ 6. The economies of the United States and Canada are generally thought of as
   a. market economies.
   b. free-trade economies.
   c. mixed economies.
   d. planned economies.

_____ 7. In the simplified pure market economy described by the two-sector circular flow model, the participants are
   a. domestic and foreign countries.
   b. households and government.
   c. commercial institutions and government institutions.
   d. households and firms.

_____ 8. In the pure market economy described by the two-sector circular flow model,
   a. the flow of income to households is equal to the flow of payments to firms.
   b. the flow of income to households is less than the flow of payments to firms.
   c. households are permitted to save, but firms are not.
   d. total production that is not sold becomes investment.

_____ 9. The redistributive function of government is most likely to be answering the economic question of
   a. for whom?
   b. what?
   c. how?
   d. both how and what?

_____ 10. Which of the following is not an economic function of the government?
   a. Redistribution
   b. Optimization
   c. Stablization
   d. Allocation

_____ 11. A public library provides an example of
   a. provision of a nearly public good.
   b. public provision of a private good.
   c. the redistributive function of government.
   d. the stabilization function of government.

Chapter 2   Markets, Governments, and Nations: The Organization of Economic Activity   27

_____ 12. If Ralph Elliott, after refusing to contribute to the neighborhood park fund, spends every Saturday picnicking in the park, we could call him a
   a. tax avoider.
   b. public consumer.
   c. free rider.
   d. cheater.

_____ 13. The stabilization function of government has as a goal
   a. consumer protection.
   b. market equilibrium.
   c. national defense.
   d. stable prices.

_____ 14. Who is generally regarded as the founder of modern economics?
   a. Milton Friedman
   b. Francois Quesnay
   c. Benjamin Franklin
   d. Adam Smith

_____ 15. The transfer of government assets and/or activities to the private sector is called
   a. pro-market implementation.
   b. deficit financing.
   c. privatization.
   d. private sector initiative.

TAKING ANOTHER LOOK

I

We think of the United States as depending strongly on the market to answer the basic economic questions. However, some market decisions are viewed unfavorably. For example, who will get limited experimental medical care? Usually we rely on medical institutions to funnel the care evenly to those who will benefit the most, but often there are more eligible patients than there is treatment.

Lately, some hospitals have developed what they refer to as _patient-funded research._ They offer scarce experimental treatments to those patients who are willing to pay for them. Some people view this practice as unfair and perhaps unethical. Others (generally, the patients receiving the treatment) say that it is simply the market at work and that they have as much right to purchase medical treatment that they can afford as they do to purchase an expensive car or a mansion.

II

Could you open an accounting practice in your extra bedroom or a barber shop in your garage? In most cities, you would run into trouble with the zoning commission. _Zoning_ is government regulation of land use in a municipality. Most commercial activity is prohibited in residential areas. The only large city in the United States that does not have zoning is Houston, Texas. In Houston, land can be purchased anywhere and put to any use the new owner wishes. In some residential areas, there are deed restrictions that limit land use to

28   Chapter 2   _Markets, Governments, and Nations: The Organization of Economic Activity_

single-family residences, but the city does not enforce these restrictions; it is up to the other owners to make sure that they are observed. Visitors can easily tell if they are in Houston or one of its zoned suburbs. In the suburbs, even the busy streets are residential, and commercial activity tends to be concentrated in shopping centers and along major thoroughfares. As soon as visitors enter Houston, they find liquor stores, dry cleaners, video shops, and hardware stores scattered along the streets among the homes.

CHECKING OUT

Now that you have finished studying this chapter, you should be able to:

1. List the three basic economic questions that must be addressed by every economic system.

2. Analyze how traditional, command, and market economies answer the three basic economic questions.

3. Identify the productive resources and use a circular flow model to show the relationships between firms and households in product markets and in resource markets in a market economy.

4. Explain and give examples of the basic economic functions of government.

5. Evaluate the benefits of specialization and exchange based on comparative advantage.

ANSWERS

Trying Out the Terms

Part I

1. B	5. I	9. J	13. H
2. N	6. P	10. G	14. O
3. L	7. C	11. K	15. D
4. A	8. F	12. M	16. E

Part II

1. J	5. C	9. K	13. L
2. B	6. F	10. A	14. N
3. I	7. G	11. H	
4. M	8. E	12. D	

Testing Yourself

Part I: True or False

1. false. All people are forced to economize because resources are limited and have many possible uses.

Chapter 2   Markets, Governments, and Nations: The Organization of Economic Activity   29

2. false. The entire salary is considered a wage; however, because the professor chose to invest in human capital, his wage may be higher than if he had not gone to college.
3. true
4. false. In economics, capital refers to *real* goods, such as factories, tractors, and machines.
5. true
6. false. They are what, how, and for whom?
7. false. In a traditional economy, distribution is generally determined by a person's position in the hierarchy.
8. true
9. false. A market economy relies entirely on incentives and the self-interested behavior of individuals to answer the economic questions.
10. true
11. false. Even the most traditional economies will exhibit some market behavior.
12. true
13. true
14. false. Specialization can increase total output using the same amount of resources.
15. true

Part II: Problems

1. a. market
   b. command
   c. tradition
   d. market
   e. command
   f. market

2. a. stabilization
   b. redistribution
   c. allocation
   d. allocation (with some redistribution of fun to the kids)
   e. redistribution
   f. redistribution

3. a. They will leave at 2:15. Bob will finish his work in 5.83 hours. It will take him 2.5 hours to do the oil changes (15/6) and 3.33 hours to change the tires (20/6). However, he can't leave until Pat finishes. Pat will take 6.25 hours: 3.75 hours to do the oil changes (15/4) and 2.5 hours to change the tires (20/8).
   b. They will leave at 1:00. Bob will do all the oil changes in 5 hours (30/6), and Pat will change all the tires in 5 hours (40/8).

Part III: Multiple Choice

1. d	5. c	9. a	13. d
2. c	6. c	10. b	14. d
3. c	7. d	11. a	15. c
4. b	8. a	12. c	

30   *Chapter 2   Markets, Governments, and Nations: The Organization of Economic Activity*

Name _____

CHAPTER 2 EXERCISES

_____ 1. The most basic economic function of government is
   a. providing public goods.
   b. providing public education.
   c. defining and enforcing property rights.
   d. defining and enforcing contract law.

_____ 2. Which is *not* an example of a transfer payment?
   a. The salary of a public school teacher
   b. The payment of an agricultural subsidy to a dairy farmer
   c. An unemployment check
   d. A Medicare payment

_____ 3. Which function of government affects the answer to the question of what goods to produce?
   a. Stabilization
   b. Redistribution
   c. Allocation
   d. Fiscal federalism

_____ 4. Without government intervention, a market economy will provide
   a. too many public goods.
   b. too few private goods.
   c. too many public bads.
   d. the proper amount of all goods.

_____ 5. Which government function is usually executed by state and local governments?
   a. Stabilization
   b. Redistribution
   c. Allocation
   d. All three are carried out at the state and local levels.

6. Identify each of the following as belonging in the factor market or the product market, and state by whom it is supplied or demanded.

	Market	Supplier	Demander
Land	_____	_____	_____
Goods	_____	_____	_____
Enterprise	_____	_____	_____
Labor	_____	_____	_____
Services	_____	_____	_____
Capital	_____	_____	_____

Chapter 2   Markets, Governments, and Nations: The Organization of Economic Activity   31

7. Fill in the two-sector circular flow model below.

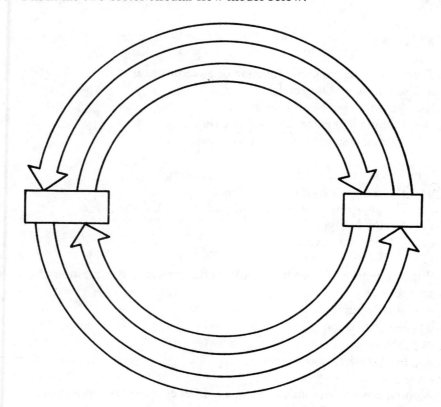

CHAPTER 3

SUPPLY AND DEMAND: THE BASICS OF ECONOMIC ANALYSIS

CHECKING IN

A mixed economy depends on the market to solve many economic problems. This chapter explains the workings of the most basic model of economics: supply and demand, the forces that move markets. This model is one of the most powerful and useful economic tools. Supply and demand are concepts that explain the behavior of market participants during a specified time period. In order to understand the interactions of supply and demand, we must look first at each separately.

Demand is the desire and ability to purchase certain quantities at various prices during a particular time period. In the product market, demand depends on many things: the current price of the good or service, the size of the group demanding the good, the tastes of the group demanding the good, the income and wealth of that group, the prices of related goods and services, and expectations concerning the future. Usually demand·is analyzed by holding all but one of these determinants constant (*ceteris paribus*) and then examining how changes in one determinant can affect demand.

The law of demand states that, *ceteris paribus,* the quantity demanded of a good or service is negatively related to its price. This relationship can be illustrated for specific cases through demand schedules and demand curves. When price changes, the quantity demanded changes in the opposite direction and there is movement along the demand schedule or demand curve.

A change in one of the *ceteris paribus* conditions affecting demand will cause a *change in demand,* resulting in a whole new demand curve or schedule. For example, an increase in income will cause demand for some goods (normal goods) to increase and demand for other goods (inferior goods) to decrease. If two goods are complementary, when the price of one goes up, demand for the other will decrease. If two goods are substitutes for each other, when the price of one goes up, demand for the other will increase.

Supply refers to what firms are willing and able to offer for sale over a period of time at various prices. Supply, like demand, depends on a number of variables: the current price of the good or service, the prices of the factors of production, the level of technology, the price of other goods that could be produced, the number of suppliers, and expectations. The (not quite) law of supply states that the quantity supplied of a good or service is usually a

Chapter 3 Supply and Demand: The Basics of Economic Analysis 33

positive function of price, *ceteris paribus*. Just as with demand, this relationship can be illustrated through supply schedules and supply curves. When price changes, the quantity supplied changes in the same direction and there is movement along the supply schedule or supply curve.

A change in one of the *ceteris paribus* conditions affecting supply will cause a *change in supply,* resulting in a new supply schedule or curve. If technology improves, we would expect to see an increase in supply at every possible price. Likewise, a decrease in the cost of resources would cause supply to increase; an increase in the cost of resources would cause supply to decrease.

Market price and quantity are determined by the interaction of supply and demand. The market is said to be in equilibrium when the quantity supplied is equal to the quantity demanded. The price and quantity at which quantity supplied equals quantity demanded are the equilibrium price and the equilibrium quantity. The equilibrium price is also called the *market-clearing price*. If the quantity supplied is greater than the quantity demanded, a surplus is present. This surplus places downward pressure on the market price, which will fall until it reaches the market-clearing level. When the quantity demanded is greater than the quantity supplied, a shortage exists. This shortage places upward pressure on the market price, which will rise until it reaches the market-clearing level. Price and quantity are endogenous variables of the supply and demand model. Variables that are determined outside of the model but that influence it, such as taste and expectations, are exogenous variables.

Marginal analysis is used with the supply and demand model, as well as with other economic models. It focuses on decisions about the next unit purchased or sold, rather than on aggregate decisions.

Because prices change in response to changes in demand, they perform important functions by informing, directing, and motivating consumers and producers. Markets maximize individual freedom by allowing individuals to pursue their own self-interest. Markets also provide for the efficient allocation of resources, as they answer the basic economic questions.

Although markets are efficient and useful, they are not without shortcomings. Organizing, negotiating, and searching for market opportunities all take time and cause both suppliers and demanders to incur transactions costs. When transactions costs exist, different people often pay different prices for the same product. Market transactions can also affect those who are neither suppliers nor demanders (oil spills on supplies of public drinking water, for example); in such cases, the allocation of resources is inefficient.

Some will argue that a market economy is unstable and that markets do not function well if they are not highly competitive. Often, market shortcomings lead to circumvention of the market; the solutions to economic problems are then provided by the government. Government intervention does not mean that the problems of allocation are avoided; it means only that they are solved by means other than the market.

34   Chapter 3   Supply and Demand: The Basics of Economic Analysis

TRYING OUT THE TERMS

Match each of the following terms with its definition, and then check your answers. If you are having trouble, go back to the text and find the definition there.

Part I

_____ 1. endogenous variables   _____ 8. decrease in demand

_____ 2. expectations   _____ 9. decrease in supply

_____ 3. marginal analysis   _____ 10. law of demand

_____ 4. complementary goods   _____ 11. increase in demand

_____ 5. demand   _____ 12. demand schedule

_____ 6. exogenous variables   _____ 13. demand curve

_____ 7. inferior good

A. Goods that are jointly consumed. The consumption of one enhances the consumption of the other.

B. A shift in the demand curve indicating that at every price, consumers demand a smaller amount than before.

C. A shift in the supply curve indicating that at every price, a smaller quantity will be offered for sale than before.

D. The desire and ability to consume certain quantities of a good at various prices over a certain period of time.

E. A graph representing a demand schedule and showing the quantity demanded at various prices in a certain time period.

F. Variables that are explained or determined within a model.

G. Variables that are determined outside a model and affect endogenous variables.

H. A table that shows quantities demanded at various prices during a specific time period.

I. Feelings that individuals have about future conditions.

J. A shift in the demand curve indicating that at every price, a larger quantity will be offered for sale than before.

K. A good for which demand decreases as income increases.

L. The quantity demanded of a good or service is negatively related to its price, _ceteris paribus_.

M. A technique for analyzing problems by examining the results of small changes.

Chapter 3   Supply and Demand: The Basics of Economic Analysis   35

Part II

_____ 1. secondary effects

_____ 2. market supply curve

_____ 3. normal good

_____ 4. substitute goods

_____ 5. comparative statics

_____ 6. supply curve

_____ 7. (not quite) law of supply

_____ 8. market equilibrium

_____ 9. supply

_____ 10. transaction costs

_____ 11. market-clearing price

_____ 12. primary effect

_____ 13. supply schedule

_____ 14. increase in supply

_____ 15. market demand curve

A. The equilibrium price, which clears the market because there are no frustrated consumers or suppliers.

B. The sum of all of the individual demand curves; it shows what quantities will be demanded by all consumers in a specific time frame in a certain market at various prices.

C. A point at which quantity demanded by consumers is equal to quantity supplied by producers. The price at which this occurs is the equilibrium price, or market-clearing price.

D. The sum of all of the individual supply curves; it shows what quantities will be supplied by all firms at various prices during a specific time period.

E. The quantity supplied of a good or service is usually a positive function of price, _ceteris paribus_.

F. The dominant or immediate effect of a change in an economic variable.

G. Effects indirectly related to the immediate effect, often smaller and felt after some time.

H. Goods that can be interchanged. The consumption of one replaces the consumption of the other.

I. The quantity of a good offered for sale at various prices during a certain time period.

J. A graph representing a supply schedule and showing the quantities supplied at various prices in a certain time period.

K. A table that shows quantities offered for sale at various prices over a particular time period.

L. A good for which demand increases as income increases.

M. A technique of comparing two equilibrium positions to determine the changing relationships between variables.

N. A shift in the supply curve indicating that at every price, a larger quantity will be offered for sale than before.

O. Costs associated with gathering information about markets (prices and quantities supplied) for consuming or producing.

TESTING YOURSELF

In the next three sections, you will answer questions and work problems that are based on information in the text. Master all of the terms before you begin these sections. Work each section without referring to your notes or the text, and then check your answers.

Part I: True or False

Mark each statement as true or false. Whenever you mark a statement as false, jot down a sentence stating why it is false.

_____ 1. A demand curve has a positive slope.

_____ 2. If income increases, the quantity demanded will increase.

_____ 3. If people expect the price of automobiles to increase drastically next year, it is likely that the demand curve for this year's automobiles will shift to the right.

_____ 4. Assume that the demand curve for soft drinks is downward sloping. If the price of a case of soft drinks falls from $7 to $6, we would expect the quantity demanded of soft drinks to increase.

_____ 5. An increase in price would cause the supply curve to shift to the right.

Chapter 3   Supply and Demand: The Basics of Economic Analysis   *37*

_____ 6. If an earthquake destroys most of the steel mills in a country, then the supply curve of steel will shift to the left.

_____ 7. Market supply can be found by adding together all of the individual supply schedules.

_____ 8. The quantity demanded is always equal to the quantity supplied.

_____ 9. If the quantity demanded exceeds the quantity supplied, we would expect the price to increase.

_____ 10. The equilibrium price is the market-clearing price.

_____ 11. If the quantity supplied exceeds the quantity demanded, prices will rise.

_____ 12. If supply of a product decreases and demand is unchanged, we would expect equilibrium price to rise and equilibrium quantity to fall.

_____ 13. If supply of a product decreases at the same time the demand for the product increases, both equilibrium price and equilibrium quantity will increase. (Hint: draw a graph.)

_____ 14. If airports charged higher fees at popular times, airport congestion would be relieved.

_____ 15. Prices of automobiles made in the United States are currently higher than they would be if imports were restricted.

38   _Chapter 3 Supply and Demand: The Basics of Economic Analysis_

Part II: Problems

1. Consider the following information about the market for cable TV hook-ups.

Schedule A		Schedule B	
Price (P)	Hook-ups per Month (Q)	Price (P)	Hook-ups per Month (Q)
$50	95	$50	50
45	90	45	60
40	85	40	70
35	80	35	80
30	75	30	90
25	70	25	100
20	65	20	110
15	60	15	120

a. Which schedule represents the demand schedule? How did you make this determination?

b. Plot the two schedules on the following graph. Label each one, and mark the equilibrium or market-clearing price and quantity.

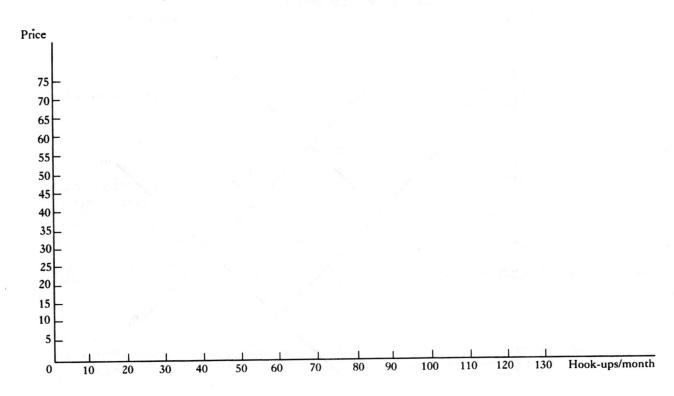

Chapter 3 Supply and Demand: The Basics of Economic Analysis   39

c. What conditions will prevail in the market if the price is $25? What would you expect to happen?

d. What conditions will prevail in the market if the price is $45? What would you expect to happen?

2. Consider the market shown in the graph below. The original supply and demand curves are labeled S_0 and D_0.

   a. For the original supply and demand curves (S_0 and D_0), what are the equilibrium price and quantity?

   b. If demand increases from D_0 to D_1 while supply is unchanged, what will be the resulting equilibrium price and quantity?

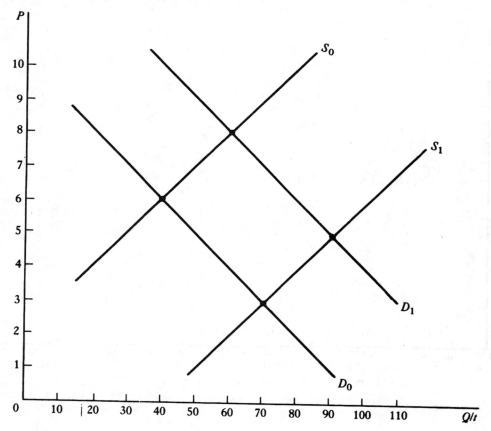

40   Chapter 3   *Supply and Demand: The Basics of Economic Analysis*

c. If supply increases from S_0 to S_1 while demand remains at D_0, what will be the resulting equilibrium price and quantity?

d. If supply and demand increase to S_1 and D_1 respectively, what will be the resulting equilibrium price and quantity?

In Problems 3 and 4, identify the effects listed as primary (P) or secondary (S).

3. Consumers decide to buy American-made cars rather than imported cars.

_____ a. Sales of American cars increase.

_____ b. Wages of U.S. auto workers increase.

_____ c. Consumption of TV sets in Japan decreases.

_____ d. The prices of American cars increase.

4. The price of hay falls dramatically.

_____ a. Beef prices fall.

_____ b. Farmers buy more hay to feed to cattle.

_____ c. Sales of feed corn fall.

_____ d. People eat less chicken.

Part III: Multiple Choice

_____ 1. Demand relates the various amounts that consumers are willing to buy over a specified time period
a. at various prices.
b. as their incomes change.
c. as their tastes change.
d. when prices increase.

_____ 2. The law of demand states that, *ceteris paribus*,
a. as price increases, the quantity demanded increases.
b. as price increases, the quantity demanded decreases.
c. as price decreases, demand decreases.
d. demand responds to changes in supply but not to changes in prices.

Chapter 3   Supply and Demand: The Basics of Economic Analysis   *41*

_____ 3. A demand curve
   a. slopes upward.
   b. is a graph of the demand schedule.
   c. shifts in response to shifts in the supply curve.
   d. holds price constant and allows income to vary.

_____ 4. Price per unit is measured along a demand curve. What is the other variable measured along a demand curve?
   a. Income over a period of time
   b. Tastes over a period of time
   c. Expectations over a period of time
   d. Quantity demanded over a period of time

_____ 5. Which of the following would cause an increase in the quantity demanded of Rich Kid sweatshirts?
   a. An increase in the under 10 population
   b. An increase in the price of Super Baby sweatshirts
   c. A decrease in the price of Rich Kid sweatshirts
   d. A decrease in the supply of Rich Kid sweatshirts

_____ 6. If caviar is a normal good, a decrease in income will
   a. cause the price of caviar to increase.
   b. shift the demand curve for caviar to the left.
   c. shift the demand curve for caviar to the right.
   d. increase the production of caviar.

_____ 7. A rightward shift of an entire demand curve could be the result of an increase in
   a. income, if the good is inferior.
   b. the quantity demanded.
   c. the price of a complement.
   d. the price of a substitute.

_____ 8. Which of the following will cause a change in supply?
   a. An increase in the cost of production
   b. An increase in the price of the product
   c. An increase in the number of demanders in the market
   d. A change in consumers' tastes

_____ 9. There is an increase in the demand for aspirin at the same time that workers in the aspirin industry receive a substantial pay increase. We would expect equilibrium
   a. price and quantity to increase.
   b. price to decrease and quantity to increase.
   c. price to increase and quantity to increase, decrease, or stay the same.
   d. price to be uncertain and quantity to decrease.

_____ 10. If supply remains unchanged, an increase in demand will be followed by _____ equilibrium price and _____ equilibrium quantity.
a. higher; higher
b. higher; lower
c. lower; higher
d. unchanged; higher

_____ 11. Which of the following is *not* a function of price in the market system?
a. Informing
b. Motivating
c. Producing
d. Directing

_____ 12. The directing function of prices ensures that
a. consumers and business participate in proper markets.
b. production will increase for goods with relatively more intense demands.
c. prices move in the right direction.
d. consumers know how to get correct market information.

_____ 13. When the goods most desired by society are produced, we have
a. basic allocation.
b. income inequity.
c. technical optimization.
d. efficiency.

_____ 14. Which of the following is *not* a drawback of the market system?
a. The presence of negative external costs
b. Economic instability
c. Allocation by pricing
d. Uneven distribution of income

_____ 15. The fact that different people often pay different prices for the same good may be due to the presence of
a. transactions costs.
b. market direction.
c. market allocation.
d. consumer disinterest.

TAKING ANOTHER LOOK

One recent Christmas, the owner of a holiday decorations store in Nebraska had a real supply and demand problem. Too many people wanted to come in and see the lavish Christmas displays; long lines formed and kept serious shoppers from making their purchases. The owner applied a market solution to her problem by charging everyone $1 to come in and look around. The lines quickly got shorter. She refunded the dollar to anyone who made a purchase. Was this the spirit of Christmas at work, or had she simply found a way to charge noncustomers for looking around?

Chapter 3   Supply and Demand: The Basics of Economic Analysis   43

CHECKING OUT

Now that you have finished studying this chapter, you should be able to:

1. Define demand and list the factors influencing demand. Show how changes in the *ceteris paribus* conditions affect demand.

2. Define supply, and list the factors influencing supply. Show how changes in the *ceteris paribus* conditions affect supply.

3. Explain how market equilibrium is reached and what disequilibrium and equilibrium mean.

4. Use the supply and demand model to illustrate comparative statics, endogenous and exogenous variables, and marginal analysis.

5. Evaluate the functions of prices in a free market and assess how interference with the market distorts its allocative mechanism.

ANSWERS

Trying Out the Terms

Part I

1. F	5. D	9. C	13. E
2. I	6. G	10. L	
3. M	7. K	11. J	
4. A	8. B	12. H	

Part II

1. G	5. M	9. I	13. K
2. D	6. J	10. O	14. N
3. L	7. E	11. A	15. B
4. H	8. C	12. F	

Testing Yourself

Part I: True or False

1. false. A demand curve has a negative slope. This illustrates the law of demand, which states that as price declines, the quantity demanded will increase.
2. false. This will cause a change in demand (a shift of the demand curve).
3. true
4. true
5. false. It would cause a movement along and up the supply curve. This is a change in the quantity supplied.
6. true
7. true

44   *Chapter 3   Supply and Demand: The Basics of Economic Analysis*

8. false. This is true only when the market is in equilibrium; however, the amount bought is always equal to the amount sold.
9. true
10. true
11. false. Prices will fall.
12. true
13. false. The equilibrium price will increase, but the effect on quantity is uncertain.
14. true
15. false. The presence of foreign-made automobiles increases the available supply and therefore causes prices to be lower.

Part II: Problems

1. a. The demand curve is shown by schedule B. As the price decreases, the quantity demanded increases.

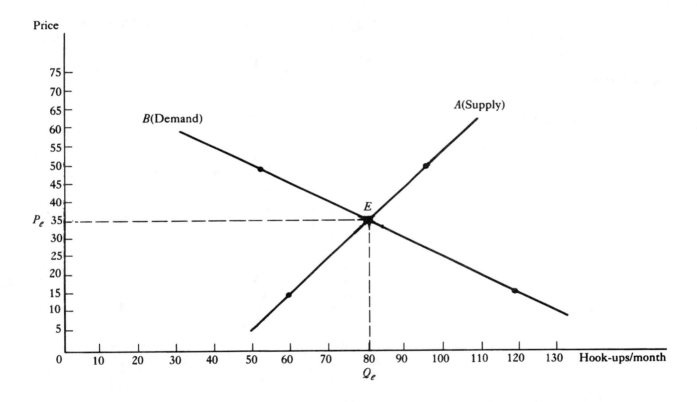

c. At $25, there is a shortage of 30 units. The quantity demanded is greater than the quantity supplied. The price will rise until the market clears at the equilibrium price of $35 and the equilibrium quantity of 80.
d. At $45, there is a surplus of 30 units. The quantity supplied is greater than the quantity demanded. The price will fall until the market clears at the equilibrium price of $35 and the equilibrium quantity of 80.

2. a. $6, 40
   b. $8, 60
   c. $3, 70
   d. $5, 90

3. a. Primary
   b. Secondary
   c. Secondary
   d. Primary

4. a. Secondary
   b. Primary
   c. Secondary
   d. Secondary

Part III: Multiple Choice

1. a	5. c	9. c	13. d
2. b	6. b	10. a	14. c
3. b	7. d	11. c	15. a
4. d	8. a	12. b	

Name _____

CHAPTER 3 EXERCISES

1. Listed below are the *ceteris paribus* factors for supply and demand. Indicate what each factor affects by writing "supply," "demand," or "both" in the space provided.

   a. tastes   _____

   b. technology   _____

   c. number of consumers   _____

   d. price of factors of production   _____

   e. expectations   _____

   f. price of other goods   _____

   g. income and/or wealth   _____

   h. number of producers   _____

2. The markets shown on the next page are in equilibrium. A change affecting each of these markets is listed below. Draw either a new supply curve or a new demand curve on each graph to show the effect of the specified change on equilibrium.

   a. There is a drought in North Carolina, and rosebush suppliers lose most of their stock.

   b. The leading home magazine indicates that the "in" flower to grow this year is the rose.

   c. The price of beef falls.

   d. An enormous snowstorm blankets the entire country, as far south as Miami.

   e. The snowstorm that hit the South killed all of this year's cotton crop.

   f. An announcement is made that the 2000 Republican National Convention will be held in Omaha.

Chapter 3   Supply and Demand: The Basics of Economic Analysis   **47**

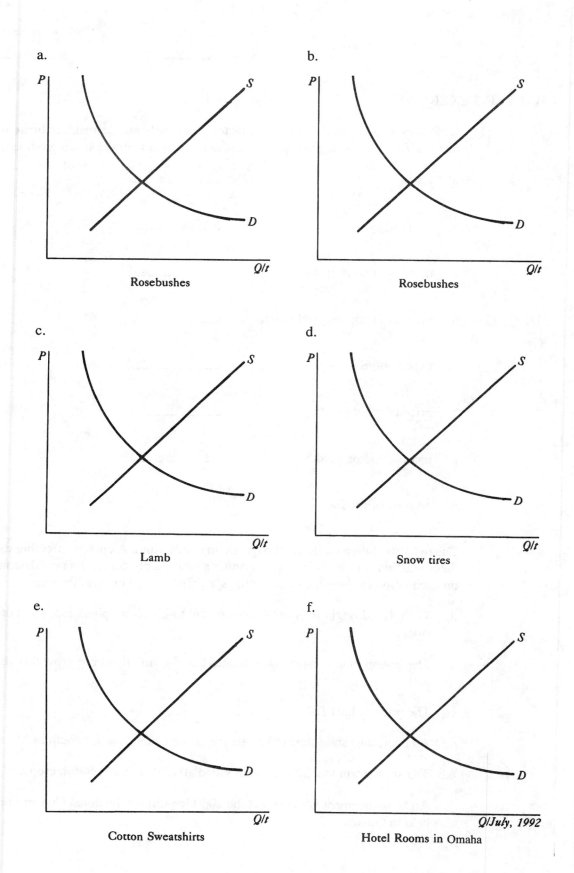

CHAPTER 4

POLICY APPLICATIONS OF SUPPLY AND DEMAND

CHECKING IN

This chapter demonstrates how economic and social issues are analyzed. You get a chance to practice applying the basic supply and demand model from Chapter 3 before going on to new microeconomic challenges. This model gives you the tools to explain how the market works and, sometimes, doesn't work.

People typically weigh costs and benefits before undertaking an action, even when that action is illegal. If the costs of committing a crime are raised by increasing the penalty or the probability of apprehension or if the benefits of committing a crime are reduced, then crime will decrease. This is true whether the crime is littering or treason.

When a market is allowed to function freely, it will reach an equilibrium price and quantity. This was the important lesson of Chapter 3. At times, an equilibrium price doesn't seem fair to everybody, and attempts are made to set either a price floor (above the equilibrium price) or a price ceiling (below the equilibrium price) to make things better. The price does change then, but other interesting things occur, because the price controls interfere with market allocation. We observe surpluses, shortages, or black markets. These situations arise frequently. Rent control is an example of a price ceiling. Minimum wage laws and agricultural supports are examples of price floors.

Over the last century, farmers in the United States have become highly productive. So productive, in fact, that they have produced too much. Agricultural prices have fallen, and farmers have found it difficult to remain in business. In addition to this long-run problem of increased productivity, farmers face short-run problems of strong competition, highly inelastic demand, and unpredictable weather.

The federal government and, to a limited extent, state governments have undertaken a variety of programs to aid the agricultural industry; most of these are pointed toward retaining jobs in agriculture and preserving family farms. Although most of these programs are designed to reduce supply, some are intended to increase the demand for agricultural products. Because there are many programs initiated over a long period of time, it is hard to measure the success of U.S. agricultural policy.

TRYING OUT THE TERMS

Match each of the following terms with its definition, and then check your answers. If you are having trouble, go back to the text and find the definition there.

_____	1.	agricultural support program
_____	2.	soil bank program
_____	3.	price ceilings
_____	4.	target prices
_____	5.	rent control
_____	6.	parity
_____	7.	marketing orders
_____	8.	price floors
_____	9.	Commodity Credit Corporation (CCC)
_____	10.	payment in kind (PIK) program

_____	11.	black markets
_____	12.	Food Security Act
_____	13.	minimum wage
_____	14.	Soil Conservation Service
_____	15.	shortage
_____	16.	surplus
_____	17.	support prices
_____	18.	acreage allotment
_____	19.	Conservation Reserve Program (CRP)

A. Markets in which people illegally buy and sell goods and services at prices above government-imposed price ceilings.

B. Upper limits on prices imposed by a governmental unit. The ceiling is a price that cannot be exceeded.

C. Minimum limits on prices established by a governmental unit. The floor is a price that cannot be undercut.

D. The amount by which the quantity consumers wish to purchase at some price exceeds the quantity suppliers wish to supply at that price. A shortage can occur on a lasting basis only when a price ceiling is in effect.

E. A price ceiling imposed by a governmental unit on housing rents.

F. The amount by which the quantity suppliers wish to supply at some price exceeds the quantity consumers wish to purchase at that price. A surplus can occur on a lasting basis only when a price floor is in effect.

G. A U.S. government agency that makes loans to farmers as part of federal price support programs.

H. A price floor imposed by the federal government in the labor market.

50   Chapter 4   Policy Applications of Supply and Demand

I. Attempts by the federal government to achieve parity for farmers through the use of price supports.

J. A one-to-one ratio between the average prices of farm products and the prices of what farmers buy.

K. Price floors for agricultural products maintained by the government, which purchases any surplus to keep the price from falling.

L. A limit set by the government on the number of acres that can be used to produce a specific crop, based on past production levels.

M. A federal program that pays farmers to remove land from production for ten years or more.

N. A federal program that establishes producer cartels that control the supply of certain agricultural products not subject to price supports.

O. A federal agricultural program beginning in the 1950s under which farmers were paid to let their land lie idle in order to reduce their supply of farm products.

P. A federal program under which grants were given to encourage farmers to contract production by fallowing fields, contour plowing, and other conservation techniques.

Q. Prices the government considers to be fair for farmers, used to determine subsidy payments.

R. A federal agricultural program similar to the soil bank program, but with payments made in surplus commodities rather than in money.

S. A 1985 federal law that sets target prices and requires farmers to agree to keep part of their land idle.

TESTING YOURSELF

In the next three sections, you will answer questions and work problems that are based on information in the text. Master all of the terms before you begin these sections. Work each section without referring to your notes or the text, and then check your answers.

Part I: True or False

Mark each statement as true or false. Whenever you mark a statement as false, jot down a sentence stating why it is false.

_____   1. Tax-financed victim compensation would be an effective deterrent to crime.

_____ 2. The death penalty is an effective deterrent to crime because it increases the expected cost of committing death-penalty crimes.

_____ 3. Models that indicate the outcome or consequence of a policy action are called subjective models.

_____ 4. If a traffic ticket costs $50 and you believe that your chances of getting caught are one in two (50 percent), the estimated cost of the ticket is $50.

_____ 5. If a price ceiling is set below the equilibrium market price, a shortage will occur.

_____ 6. Surpluses are caused by setting a price floor below the equilibrium market price.

_____ 7. If the equilibrium price of compact discs is $12 but a price ceiling of $9 is imposed, there is likely to be a surplus of compact discs.

_____ 8. If the equilibrium price of compact discs is $12 but a price ceiling of $9 is imposed, we are likely to see a black market arise for compact discs.

_____ 9. Whenever a good is scarce, there will be a shortage.

_____ 10. Price floors are imposed to raise the market price above the equilibrium level.

52   _Chapter 4   Policy Applications of Supply and Demand_

_____ 11. According to some studies, an increase in the minimum wage will lead to a decrease in the level of unemployment.

_____ 12. Most U.S. farm policies are designed to increase agricultural efficiency.

_____ 13. A bumper crop may mean lower revenues for farmers.

_____ 14. Increasing farm output may provide the key to solving the farm problem.

_____ 15. If one state passes restrictive farm ownership laws, its neighboring states stand to gain.

Part II: Problems

1. Consider the following supply and demand schedules for cloth.

Quantity Demanded (in yds.)	Price (per yd.)	Quantity Supplied (in yds.)
100	$10.00	3,100
300	9.00	2,800
500	8.00	2,500
700	7.00	2,200
900	6.00	1,900
1,100	5.00	1,600
1,300	4.00	1,300
1,500	3.00	1,000
1,700	2.00	700
1,900	1.00	400

1. a. If the market is allowed to function without interference, what quantity will be traded? What will the price be?

Chapter 4   Policy Applications of Supply and Demand   53

b. Suppose the government decides to make clothing readily available to poverty-level school children by imposing a price ceiling of $3. What will happen?

c. Suppose the government decides to protect the income of poverty-level cotton farmers by setting a price floor at $8. What will happen?

d. In the figure below, graph the situation described in Exercise 1c. Label any surplus or shortage.

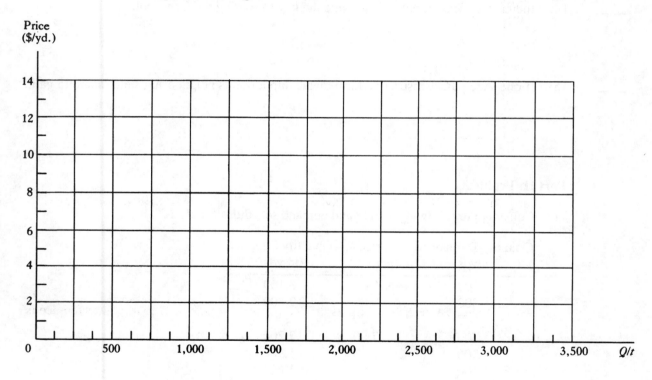

54   Chapter 4   Policy Applications of Supply and Demand

2. Consider the market for croissants, illustrated in the figure below.

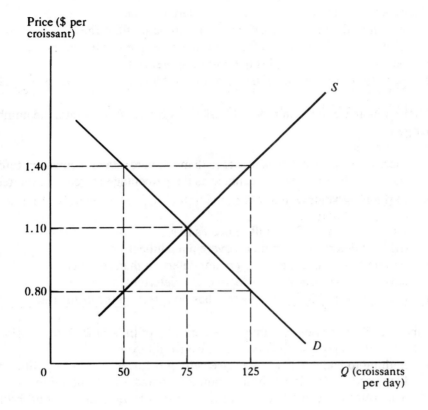

a. At a price of $0.80, how many croissants will be sold? Is there a shortage or a surplus?

b. If there is a persistent surplus of 75 croissants, what sort of market interference is occurring?

c. If the market is operating freely and without interference, what quantity will be traded? What will the price be?

Chapter 4 Policy Applications of Supply and Demand

Part III: Multiple Choice

_____ 1. The expected cost of a crime can be measured by the
   a. length of the prison sentence plus the amount of the fine.
   b. average penalty assessed for that crime over the last ten years.
   c. penalty for the crime plus the cost of apprehension.
   d. penalty for the crime adjusted for the probability of apprehension and conviction.

_____ 2. After an increase in the number of basketball referees in a game, the number of fouls per game
   a. decreased.
   b. increased by a smaller percentage than the percentage increase in referees.
   c. increased by the same percentage as the percentage increase in referees.
   d. was unchanged.

_____ 3. The work of William Trumbull indicates that
   a. the best deterrent to crime is severe punishment.
   b. certainty of punishment is a greater deterrent than severity.
   c. severe punishment is not effective as a deterrent.
   d. the presence of legal alternatives has no effect on the crime rate.

_____ 4. If the equilibrium price (with no price controls) of milk is $0.75 per gallon and a price ceiling of $0.60 per gallon is imposed, we would expect
   a. nothing to happen, since the price ceiling is lower than the equilibrium price.
   b. increased production of milk, leading to increased consumption.
   c. a shortage to occur, since the price ceiling is lower than the equilibrium price.
   d. a surplus to occur, since there is an increased incentive to suppliers.

_____ 5. Black markets usually arise when
   a. goods are scarce.
   b. there is a price ceiling.
   c. there is a price floor.
   d. goods are in excess supply.

_____ 6. A good example of a price floor is
   a. rent control on apartments in major cities.
   b. general admission tickets to concerts.
   c. the minimum wage law.
   d. food stamp regulations.

_____ 7. The economic model of supply and demand indicates that an increase in the minimum wage would lead to
   a. increased incomes.
   b. higher employment among workers over twenty five.
   c. higher teenage unemployment.
   d. no change in the unemployment rate.

8. At the equilibrium price of $3.50 a bushel, with no price controls, 10,000 bushels of oats are sold. If the government imposes a price floor of $4.50, we would expect
   a. nothing to happen, since the price floor is above the equilibrium price.
   b. farmers to continue to supply 10,000 bushels of oats.
   c. the quantity of oats sold to consumers to fall below 10,000 bushels.
   d. a shortage of oats to exist.

9. Government programs to assist the farming industry
   a. cause farmers to grow more and thus cause surpluses to accumulate.
   b. restrict the supply of food in order to raise prices.
   c. require that surpluses of certain agricultural products be destroyed.
   d. All of the above

10. The government has attempted to manage agricultural production in the United States by setting
    a. minimum prices.
    b. acreage allotments.
    c. target prices.
    d. All of the above

11. Most state regulation of agriculture is designed to
    a. encourage increased production.
    b. help farmers decide which crop to plant.
    c. preserve family farms.
    d. encourage the development of new agricultural industries.

12. In 1993, the budget costs for federal agricultural programs were
    a. the smallest in two decades.
    b. more than $1,000 for every nonfarm family in the United States.
    c. more than $1,500 for every nonfarm family in the United States.
    d. smaller than the off-budget transfers to farmers.

13. Government agricultural programs result in a transfer of income from
    a. taxpayers to farmers.
    b. foreigners to farmers.
    c. farmers to city dwellers.
    d. farmers to the government.

14. European Community agricultural policy focuses on
    a. payment for production.
    b. acreage reduction.
    c. output restrictions.
    d. direct welfare payments to farmers.

15. After post-World War II price restrictions were relaxed in Germany
    a. black markets increased.
    b. farm families moved to the city.
    c. railroad travel decreased.
    d. food prices fell.

Chapter 4   Policy Applications of Supply and Demand   57

TAKING ANOTHER LOOK

The text states that black markets spring up almost inevitably when price ceilings are imposed. We frequently hear about black markets for goods that are prohibited by law: marijuana and other controlled substances; alcoholic beverages during the 1920s, or even today in certain areas of the country; medicines not approved by the FDA, such as cancer cures and diet pills. How do these black markets relate to price ceilings?

They relate exactly the same way as black markets for other goods, except that now the ceiling price is equal to zero. People are prohibited from selling such a good at any price. The result is a huge shortage at $0.00 and lots of incentive for illegal sales. In the graph shown below, the equilibrium price is the one that would prevail in a legal market. The black market price would likely be even higher, since the black marketeer would insist on being compensated for the risk involved in this operation. (Remember the costs and benefits of crime in the first section of this chapter?)

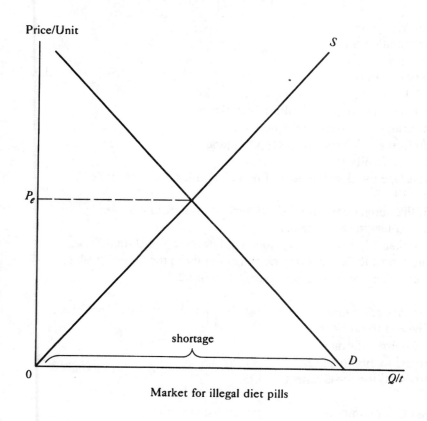

Market for illegal diet pills

CHECKING OUT

Now that you have finished studying this chapter, you should be able to:

1. Demonstrate a simple economic model by calculating the expected cost of a crime given the probability of arrest and conviction, and the penalty.

2. Describe and diagram the economic effects of rent control, the minimum wage, and price supports in agriculture.

3. Discuss how markets allocate scarce resources.

4. Use U.S. agricultural policy to investigate how intervention in markets creates incentives that further affect the market process.

ANSWERS

Trying Out the Terms

1.	I	5.	E	9.	G	13.	H	17.	K
2.	O	6.	J	10.	R	14.	P	18.	L
3.	B	7.	N	11.	A	15.	D	19.	M
4.	Q	8.	C	12.	S	16.	F		

Testing Yourself

Part I: True or False

1. false. This would not be a good deterrent, because it does not increase the expected cost of committing the crime.
2. true
3. false. They are called positive models.
4. false. It is $25 (0.5 × $50).
5. true
6. false. A price floor set above the equilibrium price will have no effect. If it is set *above* the equilibrium price, a surplus will occur.
7. false. There is likely to be a shortage, since the ceiling price is below the equilibrium price.
8. true
9. false. Shortages occur on a lasting basis only when a price ceiling is set below the equilibrium price.
10. true
11. false. It is much more likely that the level of unemployment will increase.
12. false. Most policies are designed to protect the income of farmers and to prevent a decline in the number of farmers,
13. true
14. false. Excess farm output is one cause of the farm problem.
15. true

Part II: Problems

1. a. The quantity will be 1,300 yards, and the price will be $4 per yard.
   b. The quantity sold will be 1,000 yards. This is all that suppliers are willing to supply at a price of $3. There will be a shortage of 500 yards (the difference between what demanders are willing to buy and what suppliers are willing to provide).
   c. The quantity sold will be 500 yards. This is all that demanders are willing to purchase at a price of $8.00. There will be a surplus of 2,000 yards (the difference between what demanders are willing to buy and what suppliers are willing to provide).

Chapter 4   Policy Applications of Supply and Demand   59

d.

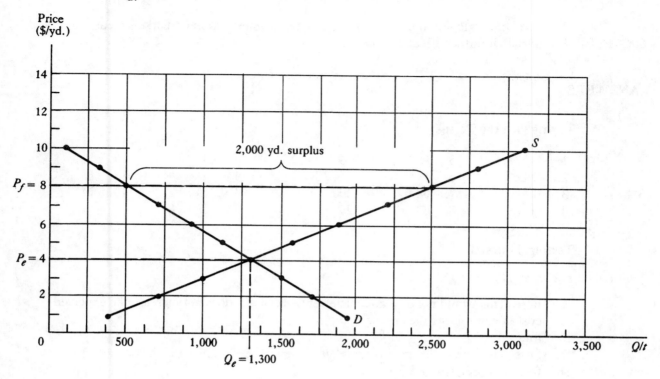

2. a. At $0.80, 50 croissants will be sold. This is all that suppliers are willing to supply at that price. There will be a shortage of 75 croissants.
   b. A price floor of $1.40 must be in place. Suppliers are willing to supply 125 croissants, but at this price demanders will buy only 50.
   c. The quantity sold will be 75 croissants, at $1.10 each.

Part III: Multiple Choice

1. d
2. a
3. b
4. c
5. b
6. c
7. c
8. c
9. d
10. d
11. c
12. b
13. a
14. a
15. c

Name _____

CHAPTER 4 EXERCISES

1. Consider the following supply and demand schedule.

Quantity Demanded	Price	Quantity Supplied
10	$7	40
15	6	35
20	5	30
25	4	25
30	3	20
35	2	15

a. If there are no price controls, what will be the equilibrium price and quantity?

b. If a price ceiling of $6 is imposed, what will be the price and the quantity? Is there a surplus or a shortage?

c. If a price floor of $6 is imposed, what will be the price and the quantity? Is there a surplus or a shortage?

d. If a price ceiling of $3 is imposed, what will be the price and the quantity? Is there a surplus or a shortage?

Chapter 4   Policy Applications of Supply and Demand   *61*

2. The graphs below show the dairy industry and the beef industry before implementation of the Dairy Termination Program. Show the effects of this program on each market.

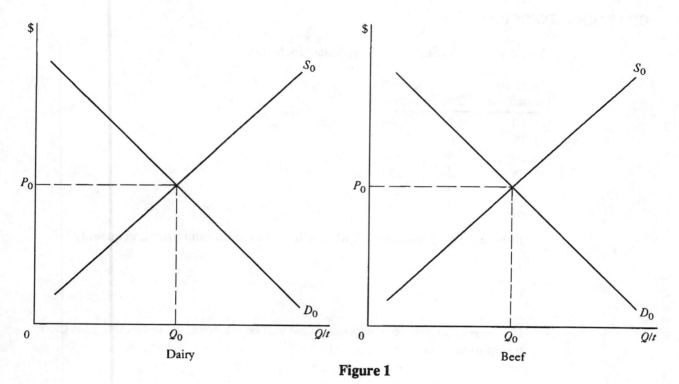

Figure 1

CHAPTER 5

ELASTICITY: THE MEASURE OF RESPONSIVENESS

CHECKING IN

The law of demand states that when price decreases, the quantity demanded increases. What it does not tell us is how much quantity responds to the change in price. Does it fall drastically or by a negligible amount? The degree of responsiveness of demand (or supply) to a change in a determinant is called *elasticity*.

Price elasticity of demand measures the responsiveness of the quantity demanded of a good to a change in its price. The coefficient of price elasticity of demand is the ratio of the percent change in quantity demanded of a good to the percent change in price. If this ratio is less than one, demand is said to be *inelastic*. If the ratio is greater than one, demand is *elastic*. Price elasticity of demand is not necessarily constant. Along a linear demand curve, elasticity will range from elastic (at higher prices) to inelastic (at lower prices), unless the curve is horizontal or vertical.

When the demand for a good is price elastic, a small change in price will cause a large change in the quantity demanded. One possible reason for this is that the good has many substitutes. If the price goes up, consumers have many other goods that they can switch to. The length of time consumers have to adjust also affects the price elasticity of a good. If they have a long time to search out new substitutes and options, their demand for the good will be elastic. If the decision to purchase must be made immediately, however, they may opt to pay the higher price; demand will be price inelastic.

Total revenue depends on price elasticity of demand. When price changes, according to the law of demand, the quantity demanded responds. If the change in quantity demanded outweighs the change in price, total revenue moves in the opposite direction from the price change, and demand is price elastic. For example, price falls and total revenue increases. If price and total revenue change in the same direction, demand is price inelastic.

We know that both supply and demand respond not only to changes in price but also to changes in other nonprice determinants (the *ceteris paribus* factors). Income elasticity of demand measures the responsiveness of demand to a change in income. If the quantity demanded of a good increases when income increases, the good is normal; if it falls when income increases, then the good is inferior. Cross elasticity of demand measures the responsiveness of demand for one good to a change in the price of another good. This measure can be used to determine whether goods are complements, substitutes, or independent.

Price elasticity of supply measures the responsiveness of changes in the quantity supplied of a good to changes in its price. The primary determinant of this measure is time. The longer the time period allowed for adjustment, the more price elastic the supply curve will be.

Adding the knowledge of elasticity to the basic concepts of supply and demand allows us to study many interesting applications of economics. One very important application is the determination of tax incidence (where the burden of any tax actually falls). The more inelastic the demand for a good or service and the more elastic the supply, the greater the amount of any excise tax on the good or service that is paid by consumers. The converse is also true. The more elastic the demand and the more inelastic the supply, the greater the amount of the tax paid by suppliers.

TRYING OUT THE TERMS

Match each of the following terms with its definition, and then check your answers. If you are having trouble, go back to the text and find the definition there.

_____ 1. coefficient of price elasticity of demand (E_d)

_____ 2. elasticity

_____ 3. arc elasticity

_____ 4. tax incidence

_____ 5. total revenue (*TR*)

_____ 6. income elasticity of demand

_____ 7. perfectly inelastic demand

_____ 8. unit elastic demand

_____ 9. cross elasticity of demand

_____ 10. price elasticity of supply

_____ 11. perfectly elastic demand

_____ 12. point elasticity

_____ 13. coefficient of price elasticity of supply (E_s)

_____ 14. excise tax

_____ 15. price elasticity of demand

A. The measure of the sensitivity or responsiveness of quantity demanded or quantity supplied to changes in price (or other factors).

B. The measure of the responsiveness of the quantity demanded to changes in price.

C. The numerical measure of price elasticity of demand, equal to the percent change in quantity demanded of a good divided by the percent change in its price.

D. Demand represented by a vertical demand curve with a coefficient of price elasticity of demand that is equal to zero. There is no response in quantity demanded to changes in price.

E. Demand represented by a horizontal demand curve with a coefficient of price elasticity of demand that is equal to infinity. The quantity demanded responds in an infinite way to a change in price.

64   *Chapter 5   Elasticity: The Measure of Responsiveness*

F. The situation where the coefficient of price elasticity of demand is unitary (equal to one).

G. The elasticity at the midpoint between two points on a demand curve.

H. The elasticity at a particular point on a demand curve.

I. The amount of money a firm takes in, equal to the quantity of the good or service sold multiplied by its price.

J. The measure of the responsiveness of demand to changes in income.

K. The measure of the responsiveness of changes in the demand for one good to changes in the price of another.

L. The measure of the responsiveness of the quantity supplied to changes in the price.

M. The numerical measure of price elasticity of supply, equal to the percent change in the quantity supplied of a good divided by the percent change in its price.

N. A tax on the purchase of a particular good, such as liquor, cigarettes, or electricity, or a broad class of goods, such as food.

O. The place where the burden of a tax actually falls after all shifting has occurred.

TESTING YOURSELF

In the next three sections, you will answer questions and work problems that are based on information in the text. Master all of the terms before you begin these sections. Work each section without referring to your notes or the text, and then check your answers.

Part I: True or False

Mark each statement as true or false. Whenever you mark a statement as false, jot down a sentence stating why it is false.

_____ 1. When the quantity demanded falls by 15 percent in response to a 10 percent increase in price, demand is perfectly elastic.

_____ 2. A local restaurant chain runs some low-price weekend specials and finds that total revenues fall. This indicates that demand is inelastic.

_____ 3. The price elasticity of a rectangular hyperbola is not constant, but varies over the range of prices.

Chapter 5   Elasticity: The Measure of Responsiveness   65

_____ 4. If Jane knows that the price elasticity of demand for the Christmas decorations she makes and sells is equal to 1.6, she can increase her total revenues by lowering her price.

_____ 5. If new substitutes for a good appear on the market, we would expect the price elasticity of demand for that product to increase.

_____ 6. You would expect the demand for food to be more inelastic than the demand for cookies.

_____ 7. When consumers are given a long time to respond to a change in price, demand becomes more price inelastic.

_____ 8. If Eleanor's income increases by 10 percent and she increases her purchases of clothing by 5 percent, then clothing is a normal good for Eleanor.

_____ 9. If the coefficient of income elasticity of demand is positive, an increase in income will shift the demand curve to the left.

_____ 10. If the coefficient of cross elasticity of demand for two goods is equal to zero, those two goods are perfect substitutes.

_____ 11. We would expect the cross elasticity of demand for canned tuna and canned salmon to be positive.

_____ 12. A vertical supply curve indicates a fixed quantity.

_____ 13. If a tax is placed on a good with an upward-sloping supply curve and a perfectly inelastic demand curve, the tax incidence will be entirely on the consumer.

_____ 14. During the period of rising gasoline prices, we might expect the demand curve for automobiles to shift to the left.

_____ 15. If braces are normal goods, then the income of orthodontists should rise during a recession.

Part II: Problems

1. For each interval along this demand schedule, find the coefficient of price elasticity of demand and state whether demand is elastic, unit elastic, or inelastic.

DEMAND FOR COFFEE MUGS

Price	Quantity Demanded	E_d (coefficient)	E_d (using total revenue)
$1.00	12	_____	_____
2.00	10	_____	_____
3.00	8	_____	_____
4.00	6	_____	_____
5.00	4	_____	_____
6.00	2	_____	_____

2. Suppose that you are a farmer who runs a roadside fruit stand. You have a bumper crop of tomatoes this year, so many that you are afraid they will rot in the field if sales don't increase. You have read that the price elasticity of demand for fresh tomatoes is 4.60. Assume that this figure is valid in your market.

   a. By what percentage must you lower your price in order to increase sales by 100 percent?

   b. If you lower your price from $2.25 a pound to $1.75 a pound, by what percentage would you expect quantity demanded to increase? Use the formula for arc elasticity.

Chapter 5   Elasticity: The Measure of Responsiveness   67

3. For each situation given, show how the changes will affect the demand curves and explain why.

   a. The price of a substitute increases; the good is normal.

   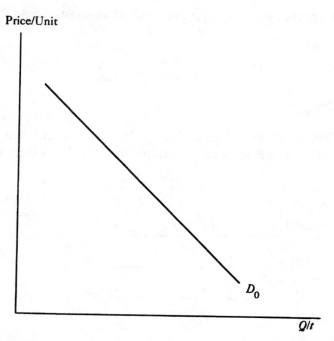

   b. The income of the consumer increases; the good is inferior.

   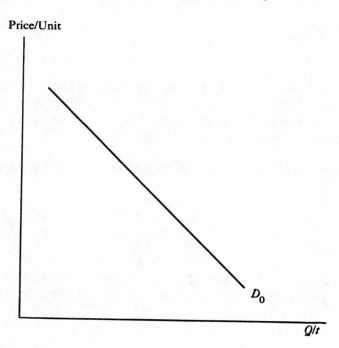

c. The price of a complement increases at the same time that income of the consumer falls; the good is normal.

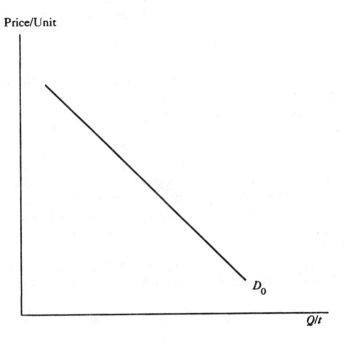

d. The price of a substitute falls at the same time that income of the consumer falls; the good is inferior.

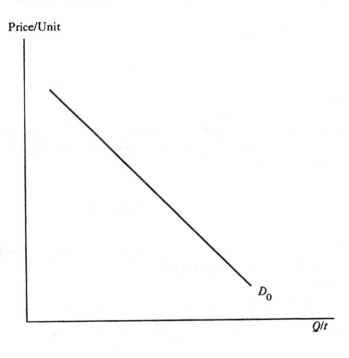

Part III: Multiple Choice

_____ 1. The formula for the coefficient of price elasticity of demand is
  a. the change in the quantity supplied of a good divided by the change in the quantity demanded.
  b. the unit change in the quantity supplied of a good divided by the unit change in price.
  c. the percent change in the quantity demanded of a good divided by the percent change in price.
  d. the percent change in price divided by the percent change in the quantity demanded.

_____ 2. If the demand for a good is elastic, then the percent change in quantity demanded is
  a. greater than the percent change in price but less than infinite.
  b. less than the percent change in price but greater than zero.
  c. the same as the percent change in price, and both are greater than zero.
  d. unchanged when prices increase.

_____ 3. The price of a product decreases by 12 percent, and the quantity demanded falls by 30 percent. What is the coefficient of price elasticity of demand (approximately)?
  a. 3.00
  b. 2.50
  c. 2.00
  d. Indeterminate

_____ 4. The price of a product increases from $10 to $14, and the quantity demanded falls from 100 to 50. According to the formula for arc elasticity, what is the coefficient of price elasticity of demand?
  a. 3.5
  b. 3.0
  c. 2.5
  d. 2.0

_____ 5. If an exclusive private kindergarten raises its price and finds that its total revenue from tuition decreases, this is an indication that demand for this school is
  a. perfectly inelastic.
  b. inelastic.
  c. unit elastic.
  d. elastic.

_____ 6. Price elasticity of demand varies over the range of prices when the demand curve
  a. is a downward-sloping straight line.
  b. has a positive slope.
  c. is a rectangular hyperbola.
  d. is a horizontal straight line.

7. If a price decrease results in a fall in total revenue, then demand is
   a. unit elastic.
   b. inelastic.
   c. elastic.
   d. indeterminate.

8. If the coefficient of price elasticity of demand is 1.35, then
   a. demand is inelastic.
   b. demand is perfectly elastic.
   c. a price increase of 1 percent will result in a decrease in quantity demanded of 135 percent.
   d. a price decrease of 10 percent will result in an increase in quantity demanded of 13.5 percent.

9. A demand curve that is perfectly inelastic is
   a. horizontal.
   b. vertical.
   c. downward sloping.
   d. upward sloping.

10. Stella receives a pay increase of 25 percent after she directs a tremendously successful ad campaign. She immediately trades her Hyundai in on a Corvette. For Stella, cars are
    a. positive goods.
    b. normal goods.
    c. price inelastic.
    d. perfect substitutes.

11. If cross elasticity of demand for two goods is negative, then those two goods are
    a. complements.
    b. substitutes.
    c. unrelated goods.
    d. inferior goods.

12. The formula for the coefficient of price elasticity of supply is
    a. the change in the quantity supplied of a good divided by the change in the quantity supplied.
    b. the unit change in the quantity supplied of a good divided by the unit change in price.
    c. the percent change in the quantity supplied of a good divided by the percent change in price.
    d. the percent change in the price of a good divided by the percent change in quantity supplied.

For Questions 13–15, use the information in Figure 1.

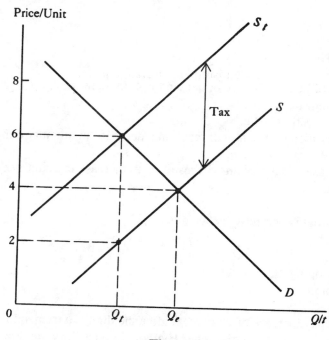

Figure 1

13. What is the amount of tax in Figure 1?
    a. $6
    b. $4
    c. $2
    d. $0

14. The amount received by the producer before the tax is imposed is _____, whereas the amount received after the tax is imposed is _____.
    a. $2, $4
    b. $6, $4
    c. $4, $2
    d. $4, $6

15. The incidence of this tax is on
    a. the government.
    b. the consumer.
    c. the supplier.
    d. the consumer and the supplier.

TAKING ANOTHER LOOK

The next time you fix frozen orange juice, look at the listing of ingredients. You will probably find that it contains some juice from Brazil, even if the word *Florida, Texas,* or *California* figures prominently in the brand name. A great deal of orange juice sold in the United States is imported from Brazil. During a recent winter, the citrus-growing regions of Brazil suffered a severe drought, and the orange crop was smaller than anticipated. How would this fall in the supply of oranges in Brazil affect the price of orange juice in the United States?

A financial analyst appearing on a television news show speculated that it would cause prices to rise less than they had after similar events in the past. This, she said, was because the demand for orange juice had become more elastic in the last few years as consumers began to realize that there were more substitutes for orange juice.

One example she cited was the presence on the market of soft drinks that contain some percentage of fresh juices. At one time, people drank orange juice only for breakfast. Now, many regard it as a good refreshment at any time of day. Of course, in this context, it has many substitutes: water, milk, other juices, and soft drinks (particularly those containing fruit juice). It is interesting that at the same time orange juice prices were rising, Coca-Cola began to market its cola drinks as good breakfast drinks.

CHECKING OUT

Now that you have finished studying this chapter, you should be able to:

1. Review the most important concepts in supply and demand analysis.

2. Define elasticity as a relationship between variables.

3. Define and calculate the coefficient of elasticity price elasticity of demand.

4. Define and calculate the income elasticity of demand and the cross elasticity of demand.

5. Define and calculate the price elasticity of supply.

6. Determine the incidence of an excise tax.

ANSWERS

Trying Out the Terms

1. C	5. I	9. K	13. M
2. A	6. J	10. L	14. N
3. G	7. D	11. E	15. B
4. O	8. F	12. H	

Testing Yourself

Part I: True or False

1. false. Demand is elastic (the coefficient is greater than one) but less than perfectly elastic (the percent change in quantity demanded is less than infinity). In this case, the coefficient of price elasticity of demand is 1.5.

2. true

3. false. The price elasticity of a rectangular hyperbola is equal to one at all points; a straight-line, downward-sloping demand curve has varying price elasticities of demand.

Chapter 5 Elasticity: The Measure of Responsiveness   73

4. true
5. true
6. true
7. false. A longer time period gives consumers more time to find substitutes. Demand becomes more elastic.
8. true
9. false. It will shift the demand curve to the right. When income increases, demand for the good also increases.
10. false. Those goods have independent demand and are completely unrelated.
11. true
12. true
13. true
14. true
15. false. Their income should fall. When income falls during a recession, people buy less of a normal good.

Part II: Problems

1.

DEMAND FOR COFFEE MUGS

Price	Quantity Demanded	E_d (coefficient)	E_d (using total revenue)
$1.00	12	—	—
2.00	10	0.273	inelastic
3.00	8	0.555	inelastic
4.00	6	1.000	unit elastic
5.00	4	1.800	elastic
6.00	2	3.667	elastic

2. a. $$4.60 = \frac{100\%}{\%\Delta P}$$

$$4.60(\%\Delta P) = 100\%$$

$$\%\Delta P = \frac{100\%}{4.60} = 21.7\%$$

   b. $$\Delta P = \frac{\dfrac{\$2.25 - \$1.75}{\$2.25 + \$1.75}}{2} \times 100\%$$

$$\$\Delta P = \left(\frac{\$0.50}{\$200}\right) \times 100\% = 25\%$$

$$4.60 = \frac{\%\Delta Q}{25\%}$$

$$\%\Delta Q = 4.60 \times 25\% = 115\%$$

74   *Chapter 5   Elasticity: The Measure of Responsiveness*

3. a. The demand curve will shift to the right as consumers substitute more of this good for its now-more-expensive substitute.

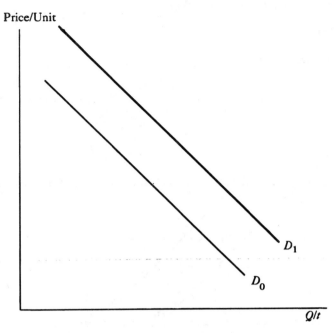

b. The demand curve will shift to the left, because the demand for an inferior good decreases when income increases.

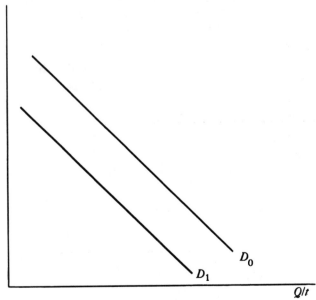

Chapter 5   Elasticity: The Measure of Responsiveness   75

c. The demand curve will shift to the left. As the price of a complement increases, less of this good is demanded; this shift is reinforced by the fall in income, which decreases demand for a normal good.

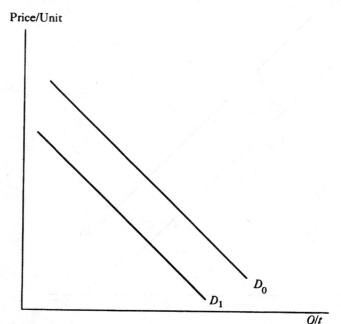

d. It is impossible to determine the outcome. The fall in the price of a substitute would cause the demand curve to shift to the left, but the falling income would cause the demand curve for an inferior good to shift to the right. The final outcome will depend on the relative sizes of the two shifts.

Part III: Multiple Choice

1. c
2. a
3. b
4. d

5. d
6. a
7. b
8. d

9. b
10. b
11. a
12. c

13. b
14. c
15. d

CHAPTER 5 EXERCISES

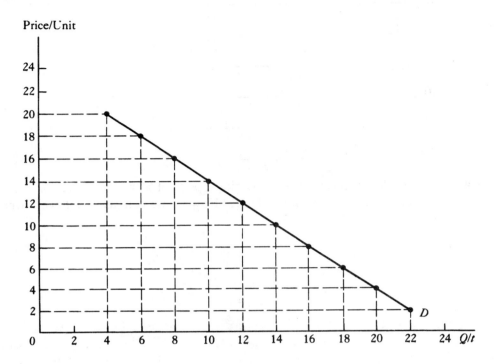

1. According to the above graph, what is the total revenue received by this firm at each of the following prices?

Price	Total Revenue	Price	Total Revenue
$2	_____	$12	_____
4	_____	14	_____
6	_____	16	_____
8	_____	18	_____
10	_____	20	_____

2. On the graph, label the area where price elasticity of demand is elastic and the area where it is inelastic.

Chapter 5   Elasticity: The Measure of Responsiveness

3. Use the formula for arc elasticity to determine the coefficient of price elasticity of demand for each interval.

Price	E_d	Price	E_d
$2	_____	$12	_____
4	_____	14	_____
6	_____	16	_____
8	_____	18	_____
10	_____	20	_____

4. Suppose this firm is presently charging a price of $6 and wishes to maximize its revenue. What price should it charge? How would you justify a lower level of sales to the management?

CHAPTER 6

DEMAND AND CONSUMER CHOICE

CHECKING IN

The law of demand tells us that price and quantity are inversely related. The market demand curves that you studied in previous chapters all obeyed this law of demand. In this chapter, you will study the individual demand curves that make up these market demand curves and discover why consumers behave according to the law of demand.

When price falls, the quantity demanded increases, *ceteris paribus*. Utility theory offers one explanation of this law of demand. People get satisfaction from the goods that they purchase and consume. This satisfaction is called *utility*. Total utility increases as a consumer acquires more and more of a good, but marginal utility (utility per additional item) decreases. Consumers decide what to buy based on the marginal utility they expect to receive for each dollar spent. Utility is maximized when the marginal utility per dollar for each good consumed is equal. If prices change, consumers will rearrange their purchases. They can get greater marginal utility per dollar by buying more of a good with a lower price. This explains the downward-sloping demand curve. There are many criticisms of utility theory, but it does a very good job of explaining how consumers behave.

Another way of understanding the law of demand is through the substitution and income effects. As one good becomes relatively cheaper, people buy more of it and less of other goods; this is the substitution effect. The income effect occurs when the price of a good falls. The same amount may now be bought for a lower price, thus increasing the consumer's real income. When income rises, consumers purchase more normal goods. When price increases, these effects work in the opposite direction.

Consumers are willing to pay a high price for the first few items they buy and a lower price for subsequent items with lower marginal utility. The difference between the benefit that a consumer derives from a purchase and the price that the consumer actually pays is called *consumer surplus*. It is a kind of bonus in utility or increase in real income.

The Appendix to this chapter develops indifference theory, an alternative approach to consumer behavior. An indifference map shows combinations of goods that yield equal amounts of satisfaction. Consumers are restrained by their budgets from consuming all they want of all goods; therefore, they find the maximum possible utility by choosing the combination of goods represented by the indifference curve that is tangent to the budget line. A price-consumption curve shows the way consumers change their behavior when prices change. The demand curve can be derived from the price-consumption curve. Consumer response to changing income can also be explained with indifference theory.

Chapter 6   Demand and Consumer Choice   79

TRYING OUT THE TERMS

Match each of the following terms with its definition, and then check your answers. If you are having trouble, go back to the text and find the definition there.

Part I

_____ 1. utility function

_____ 2. budget constraint

_____ 3. diamond-water paradox

_____ 4. consumer surplus

_____ 5. utility maximization

_____ 6. substitution effect

_____ 7. principle of diminishing marginal utility

_____ 8. interpersonal utility comparisons

_____ 9. income effect

_____ 10. marginal utility (*MU*)

_____ 11. util

_____ 12. utility

A. The fact that diamonds, although less useful than water, are more expensive than water. That is, things with the greatest value in exchange (price) often have little value in use.

B. The satisfaction that an individual expects to receive from consuming a good or service.

C. An arbitrary unit used to measure individual utility.

D. A relationship expressing a consumer's desire to consume differing amounts of a good.

E. The fact that the additional utility declines as quantity consumed increases. Less satisfaction is obtained per additional unit as more units are consumed.

F. The amount of utility that one more or less unit of consumption adds to or subtracts from total utility.

G. A given level of income that determines the maximum amount of goods that may be purchased by an individual.

H. The process by which a consumer adjusts consumption, given a budget constraint and a set of prices, in order to attain the highest total amount of satisfaction.

I. Attempts to compare the utility of one individual with that of another (or others).

J. An increase in the quantity demanded of a good (or service) because its price has fallen and it becomes a better substitute for all other goods.

K. An increase in demand for a good (or service) when its price falls, *ceteris paribus,* because the household's real income rises and the consumer buys more of all normal goods.

L. The extra utility derived from a purchase that has a value to the consumer greater than the market price.

Part II

These terms are found in the Appendix to the chapter.

_____ 1. indifference analysis

_____ 2. price-consumption curve

_____ 3. marginal rate of substitution (*MRS*)

_____ 4. indifference curve

_____ 5. income-consumption curve

_____ 6. indifference map

_____ 7. indifference set

_____ 8. principle of diminishing marginal rates of substitution

A. A curve that uses parallel budget lines to show changes in consumer equilibrium when income changes.

B. An approach to analyzing consumer behavior based on ranking the utility of choices relative to one another.

C. A plot of all combinations of goods that the consumer is indifferent among.

D. A curve that shows changes in consumer equilibrium when the price of one good on an indifference curve changes.

E. Any number of combinations of goods among which the individual consumer is indifferent (has no preference).

F. A set of indifference curves. Higher curves represent higher levels of utility.

G. The fact that as more of one good is consumed, more and more of the other must be given up to maintain indifference between the two.

H. The trade-off ratio along an indifference curve.

TESTING YOURSELF

In the next three sections, you will answer questions and work problems that are based on information in the text. Master all of the terms before you begin these sections. Work each section without referring to your notes or the text, and then check your answers.

Chapter 6   Demand and Consumer Choice   81

Part I: True or False

Mark each statement as true or false. Whenever you mark a statement as false, jot down a sentence stating why it is false. Statements 13–15 are based on material in the Appendix.

_____ 1. Choice is made necessary by the competing options offered by markets.

_____ 2. Classical economists had trouble analyzing utility because they assumed that a numerical calculation of utility was impossible.

_____ 3. Alfred Marshall held that price is determined by the interaction of supply and demand.

_____ 4. When a good or service can be obtained for some positive price in the marketplace, it has utility.

_____ 5. The diamond-water paradox was solved by Adam Smith.

_____ 6. As an individual consumes more of any one good, its marginal utility usually increases.

_____ 7. If Ralph continues to buy chocolates even after the price of chocolates goes up, his total utility of chocolates is increasing, because he is willing to pay more to get the same amount.

_____ 8. Frito, a cat, refuses to eat any more sardines, even though there are plenty in her dish. This indicates that the marginal utility of one more sardine is negative.

82   *Chapter 6   Demand and Consumer Choice*

_____ 9. If marginal utility is falling, it is an indication that total utility is falling.

_____ 10. Susan finds that the marginal utility per dollar of earrings is greater than the marginal utility per dollar of rings. Susan should buy more rings until the marginal utility per dollar for each good is equal.

_____ 11. If the price of movie tickets goes up, the substitution effect will cause people to rent more videotapes.

_____ 12. Karen had planned to buy six doughnuts. However, she bought seven, because an in-store special on doughnuts left her with extra change. This is an example of the income effect.

_____ 13. The marginal rate of substitution is measured along an indifference curve.

_____ 14. A consumer is maximizing utility when she is at a point where her indifference curve is tangent to the budget line.

_____ 15. If the price of good A increases when all other prices are unchanged, in the new equilibrium the consumer of good A will be on a new budget line and the same indifference curve.

Chapter 6   Demand and Consumer Choice   83

Part II: Problems

Problem 3 is based on the Appendix.

1. Kenny has the following utility functions for three goods, A, B, and C.

GOOD A: $P_A = \$3$

Units	Total Utility (TU)	Marginal Utility (MU)	MU/P
1	27	_____	_____
2	51	_____	_____
3	72	_____	_____
4	90	_____	_____
5	105	_____	_____
6	117	_____	_____
7	126	_____	_____
8	132	_____	_____
9	135	_____	_____
10	138	_____	_____

GOOD B: $P_B = \$7$

Units	Total Utility (TU)	Marginal Utility (MU)	MU/P
1	70	_____	_____
2	133	_____	_____
3	189	_____	_____
4	238	_____	_____
5	280	_____	_____
6	315	_____	_____
7	343	_____	_____
8	364	_____	_____
9	378	_____	_____
10	385	_____	_____

84   Chapter 6   Demand and Consumer Choice

GOOD C: $P_c = \$5$

Units	Total Utility (TU)	Marginal Utility (MU)	MU/P
1	60	_____	_____
2	110	_____	_____
3	150	_____	_____
4	185	_____	_____
5	215	_____	_____
6	240	_____	_____
7	260	_____	_____
8	275	_____	_____
9	290	_____	_____
10	295	_____	_____

a. Complete the tables.

b. If Kenny has a budget of $87, how many of each good will he purchase? What is his total utility?

c. Suppose Kenny's budget rises to $102 and he buys 3 more units of good C. Has he increased his total utility? Has he maximized his total utility?

2. Jane's demand schedule for dry cleaning each month is shown below.

Price/Garment	Number of Garments
$7.00	0
6.50	1
6.00	2
5.50	3
5.00	5
4.50	7
4.00	10
3.50	13

a. Graph Jane's demand curve below.

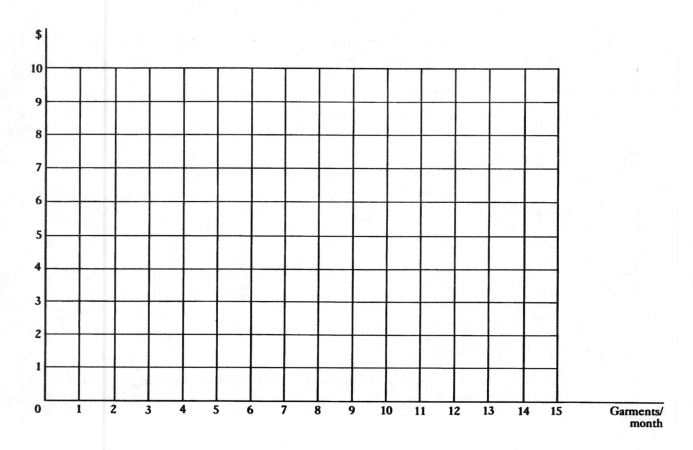

b. The current price is $5.00. Mark the area of Jane's consumer surplus on the graph.

c. Explain how the substitution effect makes Jane's demand curve downward sloping.

3. Use the figure below to answer the following questions.

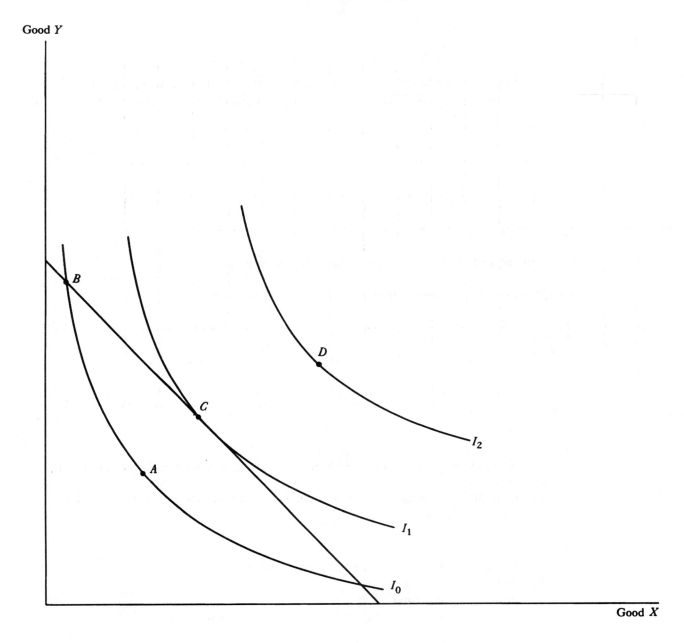

a. At what combinations of goods X and Y will the consumer have maximum utility?

b. Explain why the rational consumer would never choose point *B* or *D*.

c. Suppose the consumer has an increase in income and can now maximize consumption at point *D*. Draw the new budget line and income-consumption curve on your graph.

Part III: Multiple Choice

Questions 14 and 15 are based on material in the Appendix.

For Questions 1–3, use the following table.

Quantity	Total Utility
5	45
6	50
7	54
8	57
9	59

1. This table is an example of
   a. a budget line.
   b. an indifference curve.
   c. an indifference map.
   d. a utility function.

2. The table illustrates
   a. irrational behavior on the part of the consumer.
   b. increasing total utility.
   c. diminishing marginal utility.
   d. both increasing total utility and diminishing marginal utility.

3. What is the marginal utility associated with the eighth unit of the good described?
   a. 206
   b. 149
   c. 3
   d. 12

88   *Chapter 6   Demand and Consumer Choice*

4. If the marginal utilities associated with the first four units of consumption of good *Y* are 10, 12, 9, and 7, respectively, what is the total utility associated with the third unit?
   a. 38
   b. 31
   c. 3
   d. An amount that cannot be determined from marginal utilities

5. If the price of peanut butter decreases and Patricia buys more as a result, then
   a. total utility will likely increase.
   b. marginal utility per dollar will likely increase.
   c. the budget line will be unchanged.
   d. both total utility and marginal utility per dollar are likely to increase.

6. The sum of the marginal utilities up to one point is known as
   a. total utility.
   b. average utility.
   c. maximum utility.
   d. an indifference curve.

7. When total utility is at a maximum, marginal utility is
   a. at a maximum.
   b. falling.
   c. equal to zero.
   d. rising.

8. Suppose Steven's *MU* per dollar spent on books is 65 and his *MU* per dollar spent on movies is 80. Steven
   a. can increase his total utility by going to more movies and buying fewer books.
   b. is maximizing his total utility.
   c. can increase his total utility only if he can increase his total income.
   d. can increase his total utility by buying more books and going to fewer movies.

9. As a general rule, marginal utility will be less
   a. as less of the good is consumed.
   b. as more of the good is consumed.
   c. when average utility is at a maximum.
   d. only when the good is inferior.

10. Terry believes in the principle of diminishing marginal utility. If he wants to sell more hats in his hat shop, he will
    a. offer a wider variety of hats.
    b. advertise more.
    c. lower his prices.
    d. raise his prices.

_____ 11. Terry has done a consumer survey and believes that the demand curve for his hats is

Price	Quantity
$45	0
40	2
30	4
20	8

If Terry sets a price of $30,
a. he is not allowing his customers to maximize utility.
b. his customers have a total consumer surplus of $20.
c. his customers have a total consumer surplus of $70.
d. his price is too high.

_____ 12. The price of running shoes increases; as a result, the fall in real income causes fewer running shoes to be sold. This is an example of
a. diminishing utility.
b. the income effect.
c. the budget effect.
d. the substitution effect.

_____ 13. Sylvia's income is $800 a month. The price of chicken increases. What will happen?
a. The substitution effect will cause Sylvia to buy more tuna fish, which is cheaper.
b. The income effect will cause Sylvia to buy more chicken, since she thinks of chicken as a normal good.
c. Sylvia's consumer surplus for chicken will get bigger.
d. Sylvia's real income will rise.

_____ 14. As an individual moves from one point on an indifference curve to another point that is higher and to the left,
a. total utility decreases.
b. marginal utility decreases.
c. total utility remains the same.
d. the income effect becomes stronger.

_____ 15. If Randy's income goes down,
a. his budget line will shift to the left.
b. he can maximize utility only on a lower indifference curve.
c. he will move to a higher indifference curve.
d. his budget line will shift to the left and he will maximize utility on a lower indifference curve.

TAKING ANOTHER LOOK

The diamond-water paradox continues to puzzle many people. Apparently, some of the utility a person gets from owning a good depends on intangible attributes, such as the identity of a former owner. Following the death of the Duchess of Windsor, her jewels were auctioned off at spectacularly and unexpectedly high prices. Not long after that auction, some of Cary Grant's possessions also turned up on the auction block. An expert had estimated the value of one cigarette case when new at about $5,000. It sold for $13,200. Of course, it bore the inscription "Merci, January 18, 1942"; it had been a gift to Grant from his then-wife, Barbara Hutton.

CHECKING OUT

Now that you have finished studying this chapter, you should be able to:

1. Define utility, income effects, substitution effects, and consumer surplus and then derive an individual demand curve for a good based on the equation for maximizing total utility and the principle of diminishing marginal utility.

2. Explain the solution to the diamond-water paradox based on marginal utility and total utility.

3. Identify and describe the concept of consumer surplus.

4. Describe how advertising affects utility.

5. Describe experimental economics.

In addition, if your instructor assigned the material in the Appendix, you should be able to:

1. Define the following elements of indifference curve analysis: indifference curve, budget line, the equilibrium point in terms of the slope of the budget line, and the marginal rate of substitution.

2. Using indifference curve analysis, derive an income-consumption curve, a price-consumption curve, and a demand curve.

ANSWERS

Trying Out the Terms

Part I

1.	D	5.	H	9.	K
2.	G	6.	J	10.	F
3.	A	7.	E	11.	C
4.	L	8.	I	12.	B

Part II

1.	B	5.	A
2.	D	6.	F
3.	H	7.	E
4.	C	8.	G

Chapter 6 Demand and Consumer Choice

Testing Yourself

Part I: True or False

1. false. Choice is made necessary by scarcity.
2. false. Classical economists did not seem too concerned about the measurability of utility.
3. true
4. false. Utility is the satisfaction a consumer anticipates getting from a good or service. The good may be available, but that doesn't necessarily mean that people are willing to buy it.
5. false. It was solved by Jevons, Menger, and Walras.
6. false. Total utility usually increases, but marginal utility decreases.
7. true
8. true
9. false. If marginal utility is positive (whether rising or falling), total utility is rising. Total utility falls when marginal utility is negative.
10. false. She should buy more earrings and fewer rings until the marginal utility per dollar is equal for each item.
11. true
12. true
13. true
14. true
15. false. The consumer will be on a new budget line and a new, lower indifference curve.

Part II: Problems

1. a.   Good A: $P_A = \$3$

Units	Total Utility (*TU*)	Marginal Utility (*MU*)	*MU/P*
1	27	27	9
2	51	24	8
3	72	21	7
4	90	18	6
5	105	15	5
6	117	12	4
7	126	9	3
8	132	6	2
9	135	3	1
10	138	3	1

92   *Chapter 6   Demand and Consumer Choice*

Good B: $P_B = \$7$

Units	Total Utility (TU)	Marginal Utility (MU)	MU/P
1	70	70	10
2	133	63	9
3	189	56	8
4	238	49	7
5	280	42	6
6	315	35	5
7	343	28	4
8	364	21	3
9	378	14	2
10	385	7	1

Good C: $P_C = \$5$

Units	Total Utility (TU)	Marginal Utility (MU)	MU/P
1	60	60	12
2	110	50	10
3	150	40	8
4	185	35	7
5	215	30	6
6	240	25	5
7	260	20	4
8	275	15	3
9	290	15	3
10	295	5	1

b. Kenny will buy 5 units of good *A*, 6 units of good *B,* and 6 units of good *C*. His total utility is 660.

c. Total utility increases by 50 to 710. To maximize total utility, he should have bought one more of each good; then total utility would increase by 60 to 720.

2. a., b.

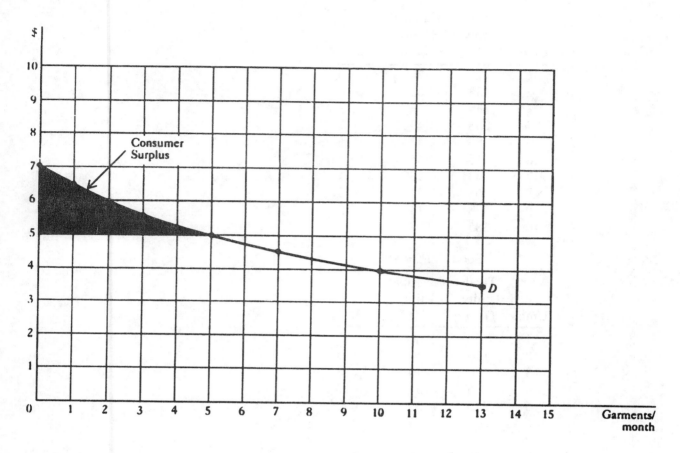

c. As the price goes down, Jane will begin to substitute dry cleaning for washing her clothes herself. She may, over time, begin to substitute "dry clean only" garments for garments that can be washed at home.

3. a. The consumer will maximize utility at point C.
   b. The consumer would not maximize utility at point B. It would exhaust the budget, but he or she could move to a higher indifference curve (I_1) by buying more of X and less of Y. Point D is unattainable, given the current budget constraints.

c.

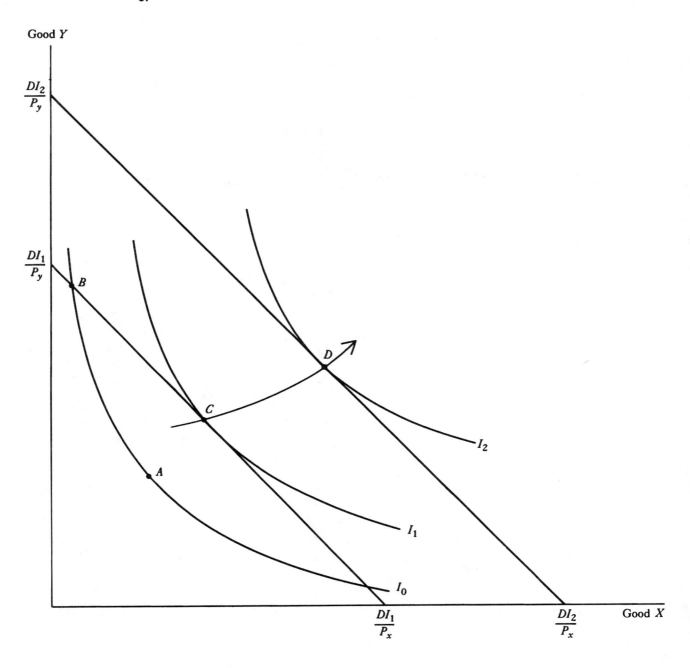

Part III: Multiple Choice

1. d
2. d
3. c
4. b
5. d
6. a
7. c
8. a
9. b
10. c
11. b
12. b
13. a
14. c
15. d

Name _____

CHAPTER 6 EXERCISES

1. a. Complete the following table.

Units of Good	Total Utility (TU)	Marginal Utility (MU)
1	20	_____
2	23	_____
3	25	_____
4	23	_____
5	20	_____
6	16	_____
7	11	_____
8	5	_____
9	0	_____
10	−2	_____

b. Where does diminishing marginal utility set in?

c. Where is total utility at a maximum?

d. If this good were free, how much would this consumer use?

Chapter 6   Demand and Consumer Choice   97

2.

Unit/Fun	Marginal Utility (*MU*)	Unit/Games	Marginal Utility (*MU*)
1	10	1	32
2	8	2	24
3	5	3	20
4	3	4	12
5	1	5	8

a. Suppose that Fred has $15 to spend. Fun is free, but games cost $4 per unit. How much fun will Fred have? How many games will he buy? He can't buy part of a game.

b. Now suppose that fun costs $1 per unit and games still cost $4 per unit. How will Fred divide up his budget?

c. What is Fred's total utility at this point?

d. If Fred's income goes up to $20, how will he spend his income?

CHAPTER 7

FIRMS AND PRODUCTION

CHECKING IN

Goods and services are supplied to the market by firms. In this chapter and the next, you will learn how firms obtain and pay for the inputs used in production.

Entrepreneurs seeking to make a profit combine inputs to produce goods and services. Nonprofit firms, both private and governmental, also produce goods and services; however, they have different incentives and do not attempt to maximize profits.

The greatest number of firms in the United States are organized as sole proprietorships. Many former sole proprietorships and partnerships are now registering as S corporations because this type of firm enjoys some of the advantages of corporate organization while avoiding double taxation on income. Corporations account for about 85 percent of annual U.S. business sales.

One way firms attempt to maximize profits is by producing in an economically efficient manner. This is done by combining inputs so that a certain level of output can be produced for the least possible cost. A firm's production opportunities can be illustrated by a production function, which gives the technical relationship between inputs and output. In the short-run production function, some inputs are fixed and others are variable. In the long-run production function, all inputs are variable. As more and more variable inputs are added to the fixed inputs in the short run, the total output increases in smaller and smaller quantities. This is known as the principle of diminishing returns. This principle does not hold for the long run. In the long run, firms can increase production by varying all inputs. The combination of inputs is based on relative prices and cost constraints.

The Appendix to this chapter analyzes production and cost decisions using isoquant curves and isocost lines. These are very similar to indifference curves and budget lines.

TRYING OUT THE TERMS

Match each of the following terms with its definition, and then check your answers. If you are having trouble, go back to the text and find the definition there.

Chapter 7   Firms and Production   99

Part I

_____ 1. industry

_____ 2. production

_____ 3. stock

_____ 4. horizontally integrated firms

_____ 5. stockholders

_____ 6. shirk

_____ 7. partnership

_____ 8. vertically integrated firms

_____ 9. board of directors

_____ 10. corporation

_____ 11. conglomerates

_____ 12. sole proprietorship

_____ 13. S corporation

_____ 14. transaction costs

_____ 15. business firm

_____ 16. teams

_____ 17. bond

_____ 18. limited liability

_____ 19. residual claimant

A. The process of transforming inputs into marketable outputs.

B. Firms that perform many sequential steps in a production process.

C. Firms that perform many similar production operations in the same industry.

D. Firms that perform many unrelated operations or produce in many different industries.

E. Costs associated with gathering information about markets (prices and quantities supplied) for consuming or producing.

F. Groups of employees that work together to produce something.

G. To put forth less effort than agreed on.

H. An organization formed by an entrepreneur to combine inputs in order to produce marketable outputs.

I. A group of firms producing similar or related products.

J. A form of enterprise in which no legal distinction is made between the firm and its owner.

K. A form of enterprise in which there is more than one owner, and the firm does not have a legal existence separate from the owners.

L.   A form of enterprise in which stockholders are the owners of the firm but have limited liability.

M.   The owners of a corporation.

N.   Individual or group of individuals who shares in the profits of an enterprise.

O.   The individuals elected by the stockholders of a corporation to select the managers and oversee the management of the corporation.

P.   Interest-earning certificate issued by governments or corporations in exchange for borrowed funds and has a fixed face value, annual interest payment, and maturity date.

Q.   A certificate of ownership in a corporation.

R.   A hybrid type of corporation that passes income directly to the owners, avoiding the double taxation of corporate profits.

S.   The fact that the stockholders of a corporation cannot be sued for failure of the corporation to meet its obligations.

Part II

(Terms 12 and 13 are found in the Appendix.)

_____   1.   economic efficiency   _____   8.   marginal product

_____   2.   fixed inputs   _____   9.   production function

_____   3.   long run   _____   10. principle of diminishing returns

_____   4.   short run   _____   11. total product (*TP*)

_____   5.   technical efficiency   _____   12. isocost line

_____   6.   average product (*AP*)   _____   13. isoquant

_____   7.   variable inputs

A.   A curve that shows all combinations of quantities of two inputs that can be used to produce a given quantity of output.

B.   A line that shows the amounts of inputs that can be purchased with a fixed sum of money (a firm's budget line).

C.   The basis for minimizing the inputs to a production method according to some specific rule (an engineering concept).

D.   The least-cost method of production.

Chapter 7   Firms and Production   *101*

E. A description of the amounts of output expected from various combinations of inputs.

F. The productive resources that cannot be varied in the short run.

G. The productive resources that can be increased or decreased in the short run.

H. The period of time that is too short to vary all the inputs.

I. The period of time in which all inputs, including plant and equipment, can be varied.

J. The fact that as more and more units of a variable input are added to a set of fixed inputs, the resulting additions to output eventually become smaller.

K. The change in total output that is produced by a unit change in an input.

L. The total product (output) divided by the number of units of input used.

M. The amount of output that a firm produces.

TESTING YOURSELF

In the next three sections, you will answer questions and work problems that are based on information in the text. Master all of the terms before you begin these sections. Work each section without referring to your notes or the text, and then check your answers.

Part I: True or False

Mark each statement as true or false. Whenever you mark a statement as false, jot down a sentence stating why it is false. (Questions 14 and 15 are based on material in the Appendix.)

_____ 1. If it is more efficient for them to produce than to purchase, households will not buy certain goods from firms.

_____ 2. A firm that owns three grocery stores in one state and three farms and a bakery in another state is vertically integrated.

_____ 3. Ronald Coase contends that there are different sizes and forms of firms because firms can't get enough information to operate efficiently.

102   *Chapter 7   Firms and Production*

_____ 4. Firms exist so that they can combine inputs to produce marketable outputs.

_____ 5. Shirking would most likely be observed in a sole proprietorship.

_____ 6. The residual claimant gets what is paid after the stockholders' claims are met.

_____ 7. Production changes inputs into outputs.

_____ 8. In the short run, some inputs are variable and some are fixed.

_____ 9. According to the principle of diminishing returns, adding more and more units of a variable input to a set of fixed inputs will eventually result in increasingly smaller additions to output.

_____ 10. If the marginal product (_MP_) is greater than the average product (_AP_), we know that _AP_ is at a maximum.

_____ 11. The change in total output per unit change in an input is the average product.

_____ 12. When the total product is at a maximum, the marginal product is equal to zero.

_____ 13. Firms maximize profits by choosing a mix of inputs so that the marginal product of a dollar's worth of each input is equal to the marginal product of a dollar's worth of every other input.

_____ 14. An isoquant is a line that shows the amounts of two inputs that can be purchased with equal total cost.

_____ 15. When a firm changes its choice of inputs because the price of one of them has changed, the firm is moving along an expansion path.

Part II: Problems

1. Consider the following production function.

Capital	Number of Workers	Total Product	Marginal Product	Average Product
10	0	0	_____	_____
10	1	90	_____	_____
10	2	200	_____	_____
10	3	330	_____	_____
10	4	440	_____	_____
10	5	540	_____	_____
10	6	630	_____	_____
10	7	700	_____	_____
10	8	720	_____	_____

a. Complete the table.

b. Is this firm operating in the short run or the long run? How can you tell?

c. In terms of number of workers, where do diminishing marginal returns begin?

2. You are given the following information about factor inputs and their marginal products. Also, $P_L = \$2$ and $P_K = \$4$.

Labor Units	MP_L	Capital Units	MP_K
1	12	1	20
2	10	2	16
3	8	3	12
4	6	4	8
5	4	5	4

a. What combinations of inputs fulfill the requirement that $MP_L/P_L = MP_K/P_k$?

b. If the budget is $20, what combination of inputs will be used? Why is this combination preferable to any of the others that fulfill the requirement?

Chapter 7   Firms and Production   105

3. (Problem 3 is based on the Appendix.) Consider the isoquant map below.

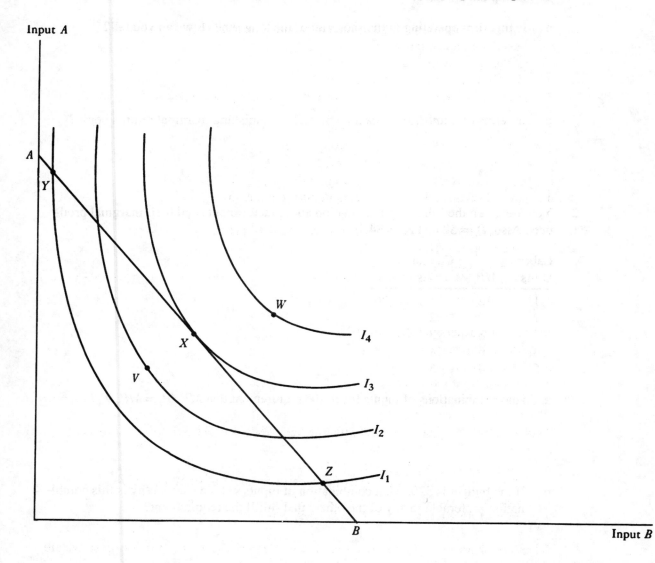

a. If the firm's total cost is given by isocost line *AB*, where will the firm operate? Explain why this point is preferable to any of the other marked points.

b. Suppose the price of input *B* falls while the price of input *A* remains unchanged. Draw the new isocost line on the graph, and trace the firm's expansion path. You do not need to know amounts; just show the direction of change.

Part III: Multiple Choice

1. When Steve Eliot bakes a cake instead of buying one at the bakery, he is
    a. misallocating his resources.
    b. acting like a firm.
    c. involved in household production.
    d. both acting like a firm and involved in household production.

2. A vertically integrated firm might own
    a. a ski factory, an Alpine resort hotel, and a hospital.
    b. several plants that manufacture skis of different qualities.
    c. a ski factory, a cigar manufacturer, and a carpet factory.
    d. several ski-manufacturing plants in different countries.

3. Which of the following is *not* a basic legal form for a firm?
    a. Sole proprietorship
    b. Chartered organization
    c. Partnership
    d. Corporation

4. How can a partnership raise funds?
    a. Borrowing from a bank
    b. Issuing bonds
    c. Selling common stock
    d. Selling restricted stock

5. S corporations became popular during the late 1980s because this form of business organization
    a. facilitates the merger of large firms.
    b. offers some of the advantages of corporate structure to small businesses.
    c. provided a way to avoid capital gains tax.
    d. allows foreigners to invest in U.S. securities.

6. When inputs are combined so that total production has the lowest possible cost, we are observing
    a. technical efficiency.
    b. optimal engineering.
    c. economic efficiency.
    d. average-cost production.

7. If Anne Morris buys wood and ivory (synthetic, of course) every month to manufacture pianos in the plant she has leased for four years, Anne is operating
    a. in the long run.
    b. without a production function.
    c. in the short run.
    d. a vertically integrated firm.

Chapter 7   Firms and Production   107

8. A production function
   a. is the technical relationship between inputs and outputs.
   b. indicates whether a plant is operating at technical efficiency.
   c. indicates the various costs of different levels of production.
   d. indicates both the various costs of different levels of production and whether a plant is operating at technical efficiency.

9. In the short run
   a. all inputs are variable.
   b. some inputs are variable and some are fixed.
   c. all inputs are fixed.
   d. the time period cannot exceed one year.

10. When Adam hires Nancy to work in the box factory, output goes from 1,000 boxes to 1,200 boxes; when Adam then hires Rachel, output increases to 1,350 boxes. This example demonstrates that
    a. the factory is operating in the short run.
    b. Rachel is not as good a boxmaker as Nancy.
    c. the factory is operating inefficiently.
    d. the factory is not on its production function.

11. When the box factory has 12 workers, total output is 1,200. When the factory has 13 workers, total output is 1,350. Which of the following is true?
    a. The factory is operating in the long run.
    b. The average product of 12 workers is 100 boxes.
    c. The marginal product of 12 workers is 1,000 boxes.
    d. The plant should reduce production.

12. Joanna runs a shoe repair shop. When she has 4 employees, total output is 80 pairs of shoes a day. After she hires a fifth worker, total output rises to 95 pairs a day. Which of the following is true?
    a. Total product has increased.
    b. Average product has decreased.
    c. Marginal product is greater than average product.
    d. Total product has increased while average product has decreased.

(Questions 13-15 are based on material in the Appendix.)

13. Output can be increased without increasing cost if a firm is operating at a point
    a. on an isoquant curve that is beyond the isocost curve.
    b. on an isoquant curve that intersects the isocost curve.
    c. on an isoquant curve that is tangent to the isocost curve.
    d. anywhere along the isocost curve.

14. When the slope of the isocost curve changes, the
    a. slope of the isoquant curve will also change.
    b. firm is operating on a new production function.
    c. price of at least one of the inputs has changed.
    d. firm will find it necessary to change the level of production.

108   Chapter 7   Firms and Production

_____ 15. If isoquant *B* lies below and to the left of isoquant *A*,
   a. costs will be higher along isoquant *B*.
   b. isoquant *B* is preferable to isoquant *A*.
   c. isoquant *A* and isoquant *B* have the same level of output with different levels of inputs.
   d. output will be lower along isoquant *B*.

TAKING ANOTHER LOOK

Shareholders don't have to wait for the annual meeting to communicate displeasure with the managers of their firm; they do so through the movement of share prices in the stock market. Although many forces affect prices, stock prices remain the fundamental evaluation of what buyers and sellers think the firm is worth. If earnings (profits) fall, stock prices usually respond quickly. This is the shareholders' way of telling management, "We are not receiving the profits we expect from this firm, so we are going to reallocate our resources elsewhere."

CHECKING OUT

Now that you have finished studying this chapter, you should be able to:

1. Explain why firms come into existence.

2. Define the various types of firms and list the advantages and disadvantages of each business organization.

3. Describe the difference between a for-profit firm and a nonprofit firm.

4. Calculate the least-cost method of production to determine economic efficiency.

5. Use a production function to explain increasing and diminishing marginal returns.

6. Show how a firm chooses its mix of inputs to maximize output.

In addition, if your instructor assigned the material in the Appendix, you should be able to:

1. Define isoquant, isocost, and the highest level of production along an isocost line.

2. Derive an expansion path using isoquant-isocost analysis.

ANSWERS

Trying Out the Terms

Part I

1. I	5. M	9. O	13. R	17. P
2. A	6. G	10. L	14. E	18. S
3. Q	7. K	11. D	15. H	19. N
4. C	8. B	12. J	16. F	

Part II

1.	D	5.	C	9.	E	13.	A
2.	F	6.	L	10.	J		
3.	I	7.	G	11.	M		
4.	H	8.	K	12.	B		

Testing Yourself

Part I: True or False

1. true
2. true
3. false. Coase contends that different sizes and forms of firms more efficiently reduce transaction costs for different kinds of production activities.
4. true
5. false. It is most likely to be observed in nonprofit organizations.
6. false. A residual claimant is one who shares in the profits of the firm; therefore, stockholders are residual claimants.
7. true
8. true
9. true
10. false. If MP is greater than AP, then AP is increasing.
11. false. The change in total output per unit change of resource use is the marginal product.
12. true
13. true
14. false. This is the definition of the isocost line. An isoquant curve shows all combinations of two inputs that can be used to produce a given output.
15. true

Part II: Problems

1. a.

Capital	Number of Workers	Total Product	Marginal Product	Average Product
10	0	0	—	—
10	1	90	90	90
10	2	200	110	100
10	3	330	130	110
10	4	440	110	110
10	5	540	100	108
10	6	630	90	105
10	7	700	70	100
10	8	720	20	90

    b. The firm is operating in the short run because capital is fixed and the MP is decreasing (beyond three workers).

    c. Beginning with the fourth worker, marginal product is diminishing.

110   *Chapter 7   Firms and Production*

2. a. 2 labor units and 1 capital unit; 3 labor units and 2 capital units; 4 labor units and 3 capital units; and 5 labor units and 4 capital units.
   b. The firm will use 4 units of labor (costing $8) and 3 units of capital (costing $12). None of the other combinations have a cost equal to the budget.
3. a. The firm will operate at point X. Points Y and Z will exhaust the budget, but the firm can produce more for the same cost at point X. Point V will not exhaust the budget. Point W is unattainable with the current budget.
   b.

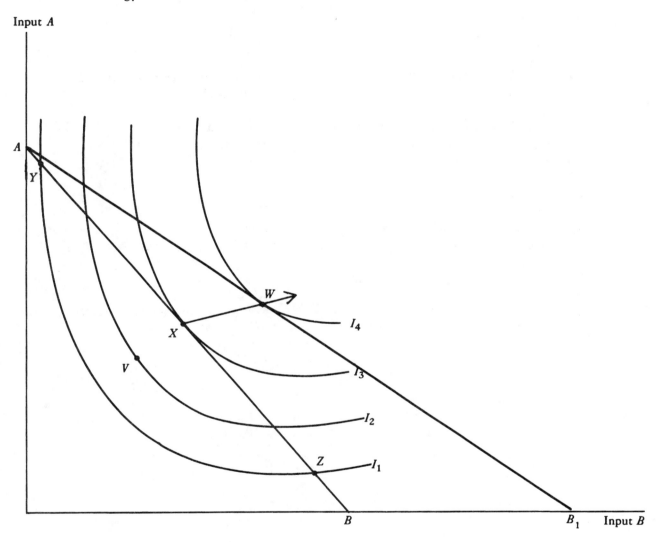

Part III: Multiple Choice

1. d
2. a
3. b
4. a
5. b
6. c
7. c
8. a
9. b
10. a
11. b
12. d
13. b
14. c
15. d

Chapter 7 Firms and Production   111

Name _____

CHAPTER 7 EXERCISES

1. Complete the following short-run production function.

Units of Labor	AP_L	TP_L	MP_L
1	150	_____	_____
2	170	_____	_____
3	180	_____	_____
4	190	_____	_____
5	180	_____	_____
6	170	_____	_____
7	160	_____	_____
8	150	_____	_____
9	140	_____	_____
10	130	_____	_____
11	120	_____	_____
12	110	_____	_____

2. Graph this production function on the graph on the next page. Mark the area of increasing returns and diminishing returns on your graph.

Chapter 7   Firms and Production   *113*

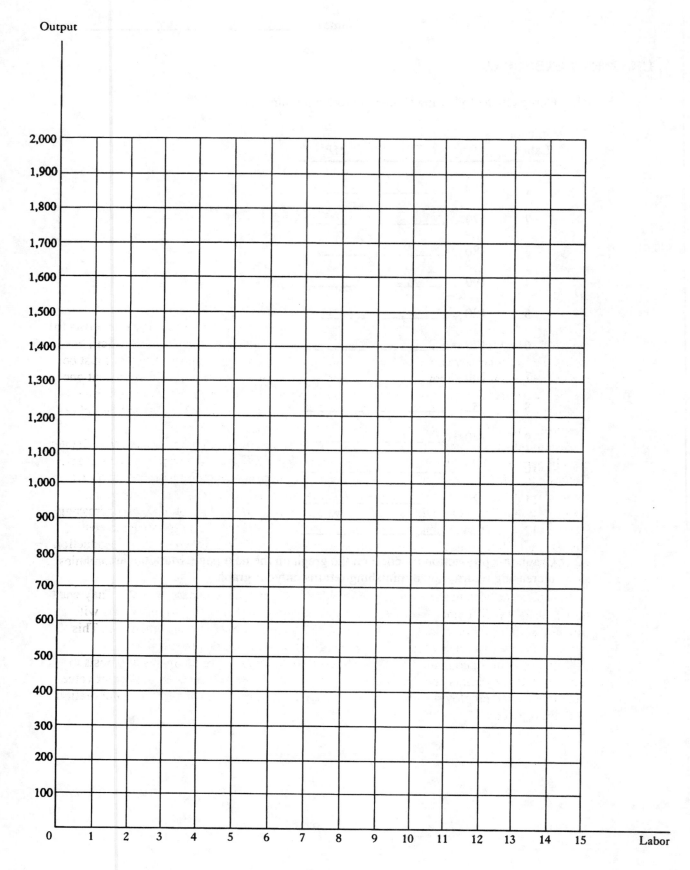

CHAPTER 8

COSTS AND PROFITS

CHECKING IN

Firms have to pay for the inputs that they use as in production. These payments are costs to the firms. Sometimes it is difficult to find all the costs, since not all costs are explicit, or expressed in dollar terms. Some costs are implicit; they are opportunity costs that must be recognized, even when they do not represent a dollar outlay. Normal profits represent one implicit cost. If the owners of capital and the entrepreneur do not receive some minimum return, they will leave the industry for another. In economics, normal profits are thought of as a cost; only profits greater than normal are considered economic profits.

Because decisions about production and costs are interrelated, the analysis in this chapter closely parallels the previous chapter's analysis of production. In the short run, as variable factors are added to fixed factors, firms may experience increasing returns, but marginal returns eventually begin to diminish. As a result, marginal costs may fall at low output levels, but marginal costs will increase as returns diminish. Increasing and then decreasing returns account for the U shape of the short-run average cost and average variable cost curves. In the long run, all factors can be varied. As a result, the average cost of production may either increase or decrease, depending on whether the firm or industry has economies of scale or diseconomies of scale.

Firms do not wish to merely make a profit or have revenue in excess of costs. They want to *maximize* the difference between total revenues and total costs. To do this, firms will produce at the level of output where marginal cost and marginal revenue are equal. This choice ensures that every possible profit-contributing unit will be produced.

Two problems encountered by entrepreneurs are valuing future payments and costs in terms of today's dollars and incorporating risk into decision making. Using present value calculations and employing insurance, diversity, and information can provide amelioration of these problems.

TRYING OUT THE TERMS

Match each of the following terms with its definition, and then check your answers. If you are having trouble, go back to the text and find the definition there.

_____   1.   diseconomies of scale

_____   2.   total cost (*TC*)

_____   3.   long-run average cost (*LRAC*) curve

_____   4.   planning curve

_____   5.   risk loving

_____   6.   discounting

_____   7.   implicit costs

_____   8.   average total cost (*AC*)

_____   9.   marginal revenue (*MR*)

_____   10.   total fixed costs (*TFC*)

_____   11.   economic profit

_____   12.   natural monopoly

_____   13.   marginal cost (*MC*)

_____   14.   normal profit

_____   15.   optimal-size plant

_____   16.   average fixed cost (*AFC*)

_____   17.   economies of scale

_____   18.   average variable cost (*AVC*)

_____   19.   risk averse

_____   20.   total variable cost (*TVC*)

_____   21.   accounting profit

_____   22.   total revenue (*TR*)

_____   23.   explicit costs

_____   24.   risks neutral

_____   25.   present value (*PV*)

A.   Accounting costs or money outlays.

B.   Costs measured by the value of alternatives given up.

C.   The difference between total sales and explicit costs.

D.   The difference between total sales and the total of explicit and implicit costs of production.

E.   The opportunity cost of capital and enterprise, or the rate of return that is necessary for a firm to remain in a competitive industry.

F.   The sum of all the costs of production for a given level of output.

G.   The costs of the fixed inputs of production, which can't be avoided in the short run.

H.   The total of costs that vary directly with output, increasing as more output is produced.

I.   Total costs of producing a level of output divided by the number of units of output.

J. Total fixed costs of production divided by number of units of output.

K. Total variable costs of production divided by the number of units of output.

L. The change in total cost from producing one more (or one less) unit of output.

M. The long-run average cost curve used in the planning stage.

N. A curve tangent to all the possible short-run cost curves and representing the lowest attainable average cost of producing any given output.

O. The plant represented by the short-run average cost curve with the lowest attainable per-unit costs.

P. Declines in long-run average cost that are due to increased plant size.

Q. Increases in long-run average cost that are due to increased plant size.

R. A monopoly that emerges because economies of scale mean that there is room for only one firm in the market.

S. The change in total revenue from selling one more (or one less) unit.

T. The value of a future payment or series of future payments discounted to the present.

U. The technique of calculating present values by adjusting for interest that would be earned between now and some specified future time.

V. The price an item sells for multiplied by the number of units sold.

W. The preference for a certain outcome to a risky outcome with the same expected value.

X. Indifference between outcomes with the same expected values.

Y. The preference for an expected value that is lower, but has a higher variance.

TESTING YOURSELF

In the next three sections, you will answer questions and work problems that are based on information in the text. Master all of the terms before you begin these sections. Work each section without referring to your notes or the text, and then check your answers.

Part I: True or False

Mark each statement as true or false. Whenever you mark a statement as false, jot down a sentence stating why it is false.

Chapter 8 Costs and Profits 117

_____ 1. When a firm earns a return that is greater than both explicit and implicit costs, it is earning excessive profits.

_____ 2. Jennifer owns a launderette. She doesn't pay herself, since she gets to keep all the profits. This means she has only explicit costs.

_____ 3. Jim's video shop has accounting profits of $25,000, but Jim figures his economic profits are $3,000. This means that Jim's implicit costs are $22,000.

_____ 4. Normal profit is the required return to capital and enterprise.

_____ 5. An explicit cost is the same as an accounting cost.

_____ 6. When fixed costs are subtracted from total costs, the remainder is marginal cost.

_____ 7. AVC equals TVC divided by Q.

_____ 8. In the short run, all costs are fixed.

_____ 9. When marginal costs are added up, they are equal to total costs.

_____ 10. Average fixed costs are constant.

_____ 11. An upward-sloping planning curve indicates that an industry has economies of scale.

_____ 12. If *LRAC* is tangent to the minimum point on *AC*, then plant size is optimal.

_____ 13. A wise professional athlete will insist on being paid the present value of a contract up front, in a lump sum, instead of being paid a larger amount over time.

_____ 14. Jermaine can work in one of two businesses. If he joins his mother's insurance agency, he can expect a certain income of $25,000 a year; if he sells real estate, the expected value of his earnings is only $20,000 but it may range between $5,000 and $100,000. Jermaine goes with the real estate company. He is risk loving.

_____ 15. Japan followed the infant industry argument in the period after World War II.

Part II: Problems

1.

Output (Q)	Total Cost (TC)	Average Cost (AC)	Marginal Cost (MC)
0	$25	—	—
1	30	_____	_____
2	36	_____	_____
3	45	_____	_____
4	60	_____	_____
5	80	_____	_____
6	108	_____	_____
7	147	_____	_____

Chapter 8   Costs and Profits   *119*

a. Complete the cost schedule on the previous page.

b. What are the total fixed costs?

c. When output is 5, what are the average variable costs?

d. When output is 6, what are the averaged fixed costs?

2. Label the graph below correctly.

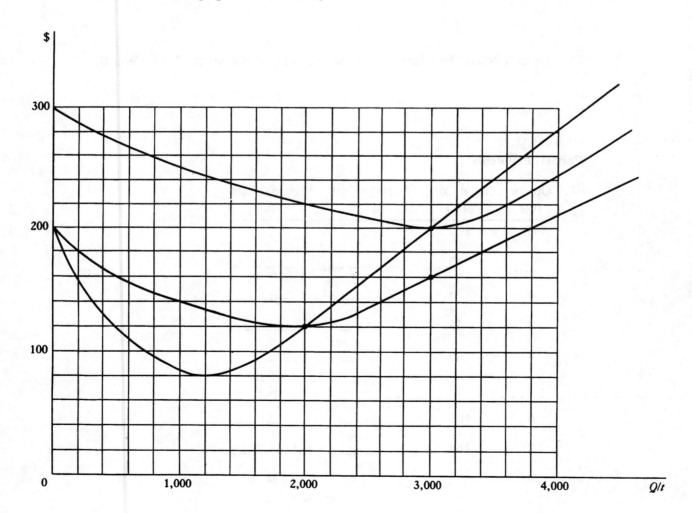

120   Chapter 8   Costs and Profits

b. What are the total fixed costs at an output of 3,000?

c. At what output is marginal cost equal to average variable cost? to average cost?

d. Explain why the output at which $MC = AVC$ is lower than the output at which $MC = AC$.

Part III: Multiple Choice

1. Ralph's Travel Agency had accounting profits of $50,000 and implicit costs of $30,000. What were economic profits?
   a. $50,000
   b. $30,000
   c. $20,000
   d. An amount that cannot be determined from the given information

2. The Southern Tree Trimming Corporation reported accounting profits of $35,000 and a normal rate of return of 15 percent on capital and enterprise valued at $30,000. The opportunity cost of labor is $15,500. What is the economic profit?
   a. $110,500
   b. $19,500
   c. $15,000
   d. $5,000

3. The costs of alternatives given up that do not carry dollar cost are
   a. not of interest to a business enterprise.
   b. assigned dollar values and recorded as explicit costs.
   c. considered implicit costs.
   d. part of economic profits.

4. Martha has opened a temporary employment service and is earning twice as much as she did when she ran a successful newspaper delivery service. She is
   a. earning an economic profit.
   b. earning normal profits only.
   c. suffering an economic loss.
   d. charging too much.

Chapter 8   Costs and Profits   121

5. Total costs are the sum of
   a. marginal costs and average costs.
   b. average fixed costs and average variable costs.
   c. variable costs and fixed costs.
   d. implicit costs and marginal costs.

6. If marginal costs are rising,
   a. total costs are falling.
   b. fixed costs are at a minimum.
   c. average variable costs are at a maximum.
   d. average variable costs may be falling or rising.

7. The short-run marginal cost curve falls and then rises because of
   a. fixed costs.
   b. diseconomies of scale.
   c. diseconomies and economies of scale.
   d. the principle of diminishing returns.

8. Ajax Better-Bilt Furniture shows average cost as $540, and the marginal cost of the last increase in production was $560. Ajax is anticipating further expansion; management should expect
   a. marginal cost to fall.
   b. average cost to be constant.
   c. average cost to rise.
   d. total fixed cost to fall.

9. Last spring, Coil Spring Co. reported that average fixed costs had increased, but average variable costs were unchanged. This indicates that
   a. marginal costs are less than AVC but greater than AC.
   b. fixed costs have increased.
   c. output is declining.
   d. marginal costs have increased.

122   Chapter 8   Costs and Profits

For Questions 10 and 11, use Figure 1.

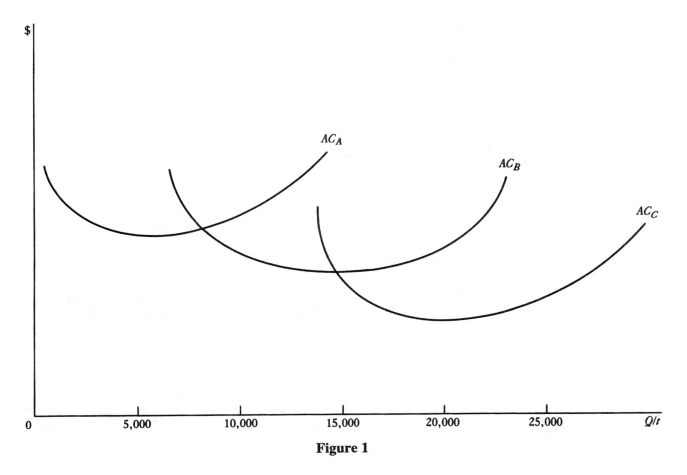

Figure 1

_____ 10. Which average cost curve shows that production of 10,000 units is possible in the plant?
   a. AC_A
   b. AC_B
   c. AC_C
   d. Both AC_A and AC_B

_____ 11. According to the graph, this firm has
   a. economies of scale.
   b. diseconomies of scale.
   c. long-run diminishing returns.
   d. increasing average cost.

_____ 12. If a firm is operating at the point where marginal cost is equal to marginal revenue, it should
   a. leave the level of production unchanged.
   b. increase production.
   c. decrease production but remain in operation.
   d. decrease production to zero.

_____ 13. The _____ the interest rate, the _____ the present value of future payments.
  a. higher; higher
  b. lower; lower
  c. lower; higher
  d. None of the alternatives is true.

_____ 14. What is the approximate present value of a payment of $150 to be made in two years if the interest rate is 10 percent?
  a. $182
  b. $150
  c. $124
  d. $115

_____ 15. The argument in favor of trade protection for infant industries is that
  a. some industries must operate on a smaller scale than others, and they deserve to be protected.
  b. some industries will eventually enjoy economies of scale, but only if they are protected from competition while they are growing.
  c. new industries are less likely to suffer from diminishing marginal productivity.
  d. research and development won't occur unless the government forces trading partners to pay for it.

TAKING ANOTHER LOOK

In the long run, all costs are variable. The firm may change all factors as it attempts to maximize profits by lowering costs. Usually, we think of the decisions as being between larger and smaller plants or between higher and lower technology. Sometimes, however, the long-run changes may be drastic, involving entirely new methods and techniques.

Several years ago, for example, the government of Singapore commissioned a study to find new ways of producing food at lower costs to the densely populated city. One plan suggested a sea-going, self-contained dairy farm. About 600 cows would live aboard a ship. The cows would eat grass grown on deck and drink converted sea water. The power for the ship would come from manure-generated methane gas.

CHECKING OUT

Now that you have finished studying this chapter, you should be able to:

1. Define and explain the difference between accounting profit and economic profit.

2. Calculate the various short-run cost curves and illustrate their relationships graphically.

3. List the reasons for economies and diseconomies of scale.

4. Determine the profit-maximizing level of production.

5. Calculate the present value of a future stream of income.

6. Discuss how risk and uncertainty affect decision making and determine what can be done to reduce this risk and uncertainty.

ANSWERS

Trying Out the Terms

1. Q	6. U	11. D	16. J	21. C
2. F	7. B	12. R	17. P	22. V
3. N	8. I	13. L	18. K	23. A
4. M	9. S	14. E	19. W	24. X
5. Y	10. G	15. O	20. H	25. T

Testing Yourself

Part I: True or False

1. false. It is earning economic profits.
2. false. The wages she could earn somewhere else are an implicit (opportunity) cost.
3. true
4. true
5. true
6. false. The remainder is variable costs.
7. true
8. false. In the short run, there are both fixed and variable costs.
9. false. They are equal to total variable costs.
10. false. They decline as production increases.
11. false. It has diseconomies of scale; average cost increases as the size of the operation increases on an upward-sloping curve.
12. true
13. false. Either will have the same value.
14. true
15. true

Part II: Problems

1. a.

Output (Q)	Total Cost (TC)	Average Cost (AC)	Marginal Cost (MC)
0	$25	—	—
1	30	$30	$5
2	36	18	6
3	45	15	9
4	60	15	15
5	80	16	20
6	108	18	28
7	147	21	39

   b. Total fixed costs are $25.
   c. When output is 5, total variable costs are $80 – $25, or $55. Average variable costs are $55/5, or $11.
   d. When output is 6, average fixed costs are $25/6, or $4.17.

Chapter 8   Costs and Profits   125

2. a.

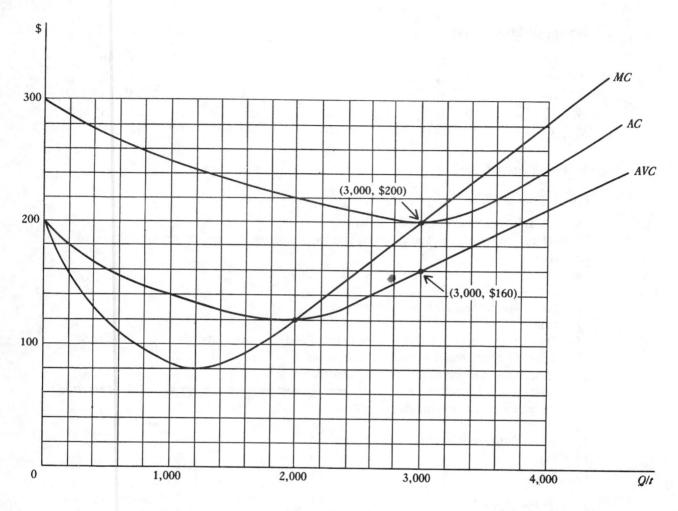

b. $120,000. At an output of 3,000, AC is $200 and AVC is $160. The $40 is AFC. Remember, AFC × output = TFC, so TFC is $40 × 3,000, or $120,000.
c. AVC = MC at 2,000; AC = MC at 3,000.
d. Average costs include fixed costs; variable costs do not. Therefore, the minimum of AC is greater than the minimum of AVC.

Part III: Multiple Choice

1. c
2. c
3. c
4. a
5. c
6. d
7. d
8. c
9. b
10. d
11. a
12. a
13. c
14. c
15. b

Name _____

CHAPTER 8 EXERCISES

1. Fixed costs are $130. Fill in the table.

Q	MC	TVC	TC
0	—	—	—
1	30	_____	_____
2	25	_____	_____
3	18	_____	_____
4	23	_____	_____
5	29	_____	_____
6	36	_____	_____
7	44	_____	_____
8	53	_____	_____
9	63	_____	_____
10	74	_____	_____

2. Randy is going to tape some TV shows this weekend. He decides that he will need two blank tapes and stops to buy them on his way home. While he is in the store, the manager announces a 15-minute special. One blank tape is free with the purchase of another for $6. Randy gets two tapes for $6 and goes home. Later that evening, his neighbor calls and asks if he has a blank videotape she can buy from him right now. She needs to tape a show for her sociology class. Randy tells her, "Sure, you can have it for my cost." Should Randy charge her $6, $3, or give it to her for free?

Chapter 8   Costs and Profits   127

CHAPTER 9

PERFECT COMPETITION

CHECKING IN

Firms maximize profits (or minimize losses) by considering both the costs of production and forecasted revenues. Although all firms face similar cost curves, forecasted revenues depend on the industry. This chapter and the two chapters that follow consider the various forms of market structure and explain how firms make their production decisions.

The basic market model is that of perfect competition. This model provides the standard by which we can evaluate other models. Perfect competition has six basic characteristics: a large number of sellers, a large number of buyers, a homogeneous product, free entry into and exit from the industry, perfect knowledge, and perfect mobility of resources. A firm in an industry with these characteristics will have a perfectly elastic demand curve. This type of firm is known as a price taker. It can sell all it wants at the price set in the market, but it has no influence on price.

Such firms will maximize profits or minimize losses by choosing the output level where $MC = MR = P$, as long as the firm is covering its fixed costs. This means that above the minimum point of the AVC curve, the MC curve is the short-run supply curve for a perfectly competitive firm. In the short run, a firm may earn economic profits or normal profits, or it may sustain losses. In long-run equilibrium, each firm in the industry will be earning a normal profit. If there are short-run economic profits, more firms will enter the industry (easy entry is a characteristic of perfect competition). Losses, on the other hand, will cause firms to leave the industry.

Perfectly competitive industries may have long-run supply curves that are upward sloping, downward sloping, or horizontal, depending on how the factor market responds to changes in demand. If the entry of new firms into an industry drives factor prices up, the industry has increasing costs, which will be reflected in an upward-sloping supply curve. As the industry expands, costs may remain constant (a horizontal supply curve) or decline (a downward-sloping supply curve). In a perfectly competitive industry, the long-run equilibrium will have $P = AC = LRAC = LRMC$. This gives both allocative efficiency and least-cost production. All other industry equilibria are compared to this ideal standard. Sometimes it appears that some firms in perfect competition earn persistent economic profits. This case is not a violation of the model. These returns are economic rent (payments in excess of opportunity cost) to specific factors of production.

Chapter 9   Perfect Competition   129

TRYING OUT THE TERMS

Match each of the following terms with its definition, and then check your answers. If you are having trouble, go back to the text and find the definition there.

_____ 1. short-run supply curve

_____ 2. perfect competition

_____ 3. decreasing cost industry

_____ 4. shutdown point

_____ 5. market power

_____ 6. economic rent

_____ 7. price taker

_____ 8. constant cost industry

_____ 9. average revenue (AR)

_____ 10. representative firm

_____ 11. increasing cost industry

A. The market structure in which there are many sellers and buyers, firms produce a homogeneous product, and there is free entry into and exit out of the industry.

B. The ability of buyers or sellers to affect price.

C. A seller (or buyer) in perfect competition that has no influence on price and can sell any amount at the market-clearing price.

D. Total revenue divided by the quantity sold, or the revenue per unit sold (the price).

E. A typical firm in perfect competition, one of the many identical firms in the market.

F. The supply curve for the period in which the size of the plant cannot be varied (in perfect competition, the same as the short-run marginal cost curve).

G. The minimum point on the average variable costs (AVC) curve, or the level of output at which a firm minimizes its losses by ceasing operation.

H. An industry in which expansion of output does not cause average costs to rise in the long run.

I. An industry in which expansion of output causes average cost to rise in the long run.

J. An industry in which expansion of output causes average cost to fall in the long run.

K. A payment to a productive resource in excess of its opportunity cost.

130   Chapter 9   Perfect Competition

TESTING YOURSELF

In the next three sections, you will answer questions and work problems that are based on information in the text. Master all of the terms before you begin these sections. Work each section without referring to your notes or the text, and then check your answers.

Part I: True or False

Mark each statement as true or false. Whenever you mark a statement as false, jot down a sentence stating why it is false.

_____ 1. A homogeneous product is characteristic of perfect competition.

_____ 2. The basic assumptions of perfect competition were developed by David Ricardo.

_____ 3. If a perfectly competitive firm increases output, it will have marginal revenue that is less than price.

_____ 4. A typical firm in the industry can be called a representative firm.

_____ 5. If a new, low-cost technique for harvesting tomatoes is developed, the short-run effect in a perfectly competitive market will be a lower price and a higher output of tomatoes.

_____ 6. John Evans sells his products in a perfectly competitive market. If he can maximize profits by producing at a level where marginal cost is $45, he will also have a selling price of $45.

_____ 7. Because the demand curve for a firm in perfect competition is perfectly elastic, the firm can increase revenue and sales by lowering price.

Chapter 9   Perfect Competition   *131*

_____ 8. In the short run, a firm can avoid paying fixed costs by closing down.

_____ 9. Sloan is operating her vegetable farm at a level where $MC = MR = \$55$ and $AC = \$30$. She is making an economic profit.

_____ 10. If a firm is making zero economic profits, it will operate in the short run and close down in the long run.

_____ 11. An increasing cost industry has a long-run supply curve that is positively sloped.

_____ 12. In perfect competition, if P is greater than MC, not enough of the product is being produced.

_____ 13. The theory of differential rents was developed by Adam Smith.

_____ 14. Differential rent is an economic profit and should not be viewed as a cost.

_____ 15. Some cultures view risk-taking as unacceptable; therefore, it is difficult for an entrepreneurial class to develop in those cultures.

Part II: Problems

1. a. Complete the table. (Round your answer to the nearest dollar.)

Output (Q)	Average Revenue (AR)	Average Fixed Cost (AFC)	Average Variable Costs (AVC)	Total Cost (TC)	Marginal Cost (MC)
1	$35	$120.00	$35.00	_____	_____
2	35	60.00	27.50	_____	_____
3	35	40.00	23.33	_____	_____
4	35	30.00	21.25	_____	_____
5	35	24.00	22.00	_____	_____
6	35	20.00	23.33	_____	_____
7	35	17.14	25.00	_____	_____
8	35	15.00	26.88	_____	_____
9	35	13.33	28.89	_____	_____
10	35	12.00	31.00	_____	_____

b. Where will this firm operate in order to maximize profits or minimize losses?

c. At this point, will the firm have an economic profit, a normal profit, or an economic loss? What is the amount?

d. What is the level of output at the firm's shutdown point?

e. What will this firm do if the market price rises to $45? What will be the economic profit or loss?

Chapter 9   Perfect Competition   *133*

2. Use the figure below to answer the following questions.

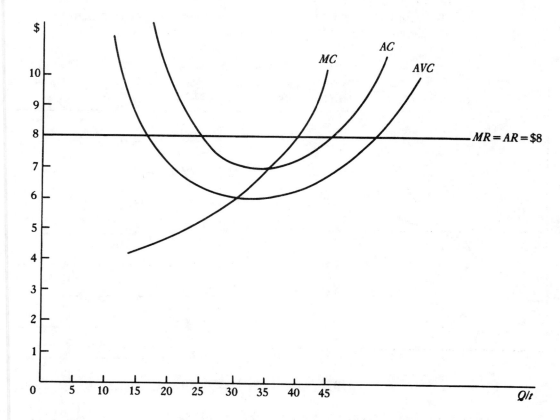

a. If $P = \$8$ and this firm is maximizing profits or minimizing losses, how many units will it produce?

b. What is the shutdown point for this firm?

c. Suppose that the market price falls to $7. Draw the new demand curve for the firm on the graph. How many units will it produce now? Will it make a profit?

3. The firm shown in the figure below is initially in equilibrium at (P_1, x_1), but then market demand increases.

   a. On the graph, mark the short-run adjustment for the representative firm.

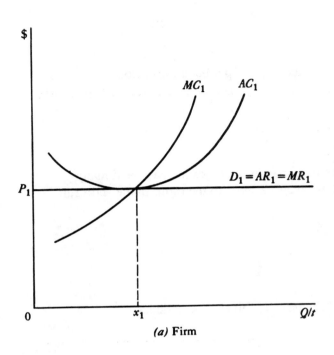
(a) Firm

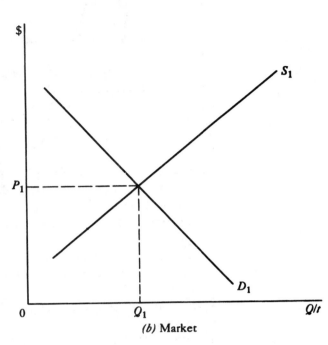
(b) Market

   b. This is an increasing cost industry. Draw the firm's new AC and MC. What will happen to the market supply curve and the equilibrium price? Show this on your graph.

   c. Show the long-run market supply curve on your graph.

Chapter 9 Perfect Competition   135

Part III: Multiple Choice

_____ 1. For a perfectly competitive firm, the demand curve is
   a. the marginal revenue curve.
   b. perfectly inelastic.
   c. always equal to marginal cost.
   d. the same as the market demand curve.

_____ 2. Which of the following is _not_ a basic characteristic of perfect competition?
   a. A homogeneous product
   b. Large number of sellers
   c. Resource immobility
   d. Absence of market power

_____ 3. Anna sells timber in a perfectly competitive market. Incomes increase, and many people buy new homes; the market demand curve shifts to the right. In the short run, she should expect
   a. the price of timber to be unchanged.
   b. profits to fall.
   c. the price of timber to rise.
   d. firms to leave the timber business.

_____ 4. A firm that must sell at market price if it wishes to sell at all is called a
   a. price taker.
   b. price seeker.
   c. marginal firm.
   d. loss taker.

_____ 5. Average revenue (AR)
   a. occurs when $MC = MR$.
   b. equals TR/Q.
   c. is greater than price when economic profits are present.
   d. does not appear in the model of perfect competition.

_____ 6. The marginal cost curve above the minimum AVC
   a. indicates points where the firm will realize an economic profit.
   b. covers the area where a firm should shut down.
   c. is equal to the firm's marginal revenue curve.
   d. is the firm's short-run supply curve.

_____ 7. Economic profits equal zero when
   a. $P = AVC = TC$.
   b. $P = AR = MR = AC$.
   c. normal profits are absent.
   d. market demand increases in the short run.

136   Chapter 9   Perfect Competition

8. If $P = \$25$, $MR = \$25$, $MC = \$25$, $AVC = \$35$, and $AC = \$50$, the firm should
   a. increase output.
   b. decrease output but continue to produce.
   c. increase price.
   d. shut down.

9. An equilibrium price of $9.50 in a perfectly competitive industry means that the MR for a firm in that industry will be
   a. equal to $9.50.
   b. greater than $9.50.
   c. equal to AVC and equal to $9.50.
   d. greater than its average revenue of $9.50.

10. A profit-maximizing (or loss-minimizing) firm in perfect competition will set its output where
    a. it is operating at capacity.
    b. its total cost is equal to its total revenue.
    c. its average variable cost is equal to its average revenue.
    d. its marginal cost is equal to its marginal revenue.

11. If a firm has $P > AC$, it
    a. should reduce output.
    b. is losing money.
    c. is earning an economic profit.
    d. should shut down.

12. At its profit-maximizing output, a perfectly competitive firm has an AVC of $3.19 and an AC of $4.23. What is its total fixed cost?
    a. $1.04
    b. $(\$4.23 - \$3.19) \times Q$
    c. The same as its total revenue
    d. $7.42

13. A perfectly competitive industry experienced a decrease in demand. In response, some firms left the industry. The original equilibrium price was $3.90; the new equilibrium price is $4.05. This industry has
    a. increasing costs.
    b. decreasing costs.
    c. inefficiencies.
    d. a vertical long-run supply curve.

14. A firm is using the least-cost method of production when
    a. $MC = AR$.
    b. $P = AC = MC$.
    c. $TR = (AR)Q$.
    d. $MC = MR$.

Chapter 9   Perfect Competition   137

15. Economic rent occurs
   a. when some factors of production are used more intensely than others.
   b. when land is the only input.
   c. when the payment to a factor of production is greater than its opportunity cost.
   d. only in the short run; in the long run, there can be only normal rent.

TAKING ANOTHER LOOK

All firms, large or small, have to face the necessity of closing down when variable costs cannot be covered. In 1980, with high hopes and an optimistic marketing forecast, RCA launched its version of the videodisc player. RCA was able to sell its player to distributors for about $250 (retail price was around $500). The variable costs of production were estimated to be about $150. In 1984, RCA withdrew from the market. It had seriously overestimated demand by not taking competition from VCRs into account. In 1984, RCA was receiving about $100 for each unit it sold to a distributor. RCA couldn't cover its variable costs, so it left the business with a loss of more than $500 million. A decade later, videodiscs became popular and were marketed successfully.

CHECKING OUT

Now that you have finished studying this chapter, you should be able to:

1. List the assumptions of perfect competition.

2. Diagram the relationship between a firm and the total market. Calculate profits, given quantity, marginal revenue, marginal cost, average cost, and price. Identify the profit-maximizing level of output.

3. Define the shutdown point in terms of price and average variable costs or total fixed costs and losses.

4. Describe the long-run supply curve for a constant cost industry, an increasing cost industry, and a decreasing cost industry.

5. Identify the long-run equilibrium for the firm and the industry under perfect competition.

6. Explain how economic rent might exist in perfect competition, even in long-run equilibrium.

ANSWERS

Trying Out the Terms

1. F	5. B	9. D
2. A	6. K	10. E
3. J	7. C	11. I
4. G	8. H	

138   Chapter 9   *Perfect Competition*

Testing Yourself

Part I: True or False

1.   true
2.   false. They were developed by Adam Smith.
3.   false. For perfectly competitive firms, price and marginal revenue are always equal.
4.   true
5.   true
6.   true
7.   false. A perfectly competitive firm can sell all it wants at the prevailing price. $P = MR$, so lower prices would mean lower revenue.
8.   false. Fixed costs must be paid, even if output equals zero. A firm can avoid paying variable costs by closing down.
9.   true
10. false. The firm is at a long-run equilibrium and is making normal profits. A firm will not close down until it is actually losing money.
11. true
12. true
13. false. It was developed by David Ricardo.
14. false. Differential rent is a payment to better factors of production and should be considered a cost.
15. true

Part II: Problems

1.   a.

Output (Q)	Average Revenue (AR)	Average Fixed Cost (AFC)	Average Variable Costs (AVC)	Total Cost (TC)	Marginal Cost (MC)
1	$35	$120.00	$35.00	$155	$35
2	35	60.00	27.50	175	20
3	35	40.00	23.33	190	15
4	35	30.00	21.25	205	15
5	35	24.00	22.00	230	25
6	35	20.00	23.33	260	30
7	35	17.14	25.00	295	35
8	35	15.00	26.88	335	40
9	35	13.33	28.89	380	45
10	35	12.00	31.00	430	50

(To find total cost, find TVC and TFC; then add them together.)

   b.   To maximize profits or minimize losses, this firm will produce 7 units at a price of $35. This is the output where $MC = MR$. (Remember, in perfect competition $MC = AR$.)
   c.   The firm will have an economic loss of $50 (TR – TC = $245 – $295).
   d.   The level of output at the shutdown point is 4 units, where AVC is at its minimum ($21.25).
   e.   The firm will sell 9 units and make an economic profit of $25.

2.

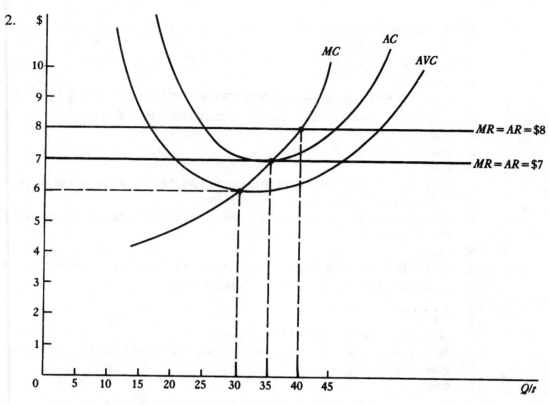

a. The firm will produce 40 units. This is where $MR = MC$.
b. The shutdown point is at 30 units, where $AVC = \$6$.
c. The firm will produce 35 units and make a normal profit.

3.

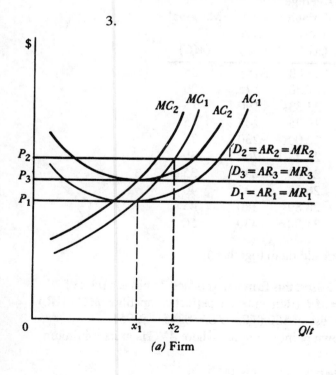
(a) Firm

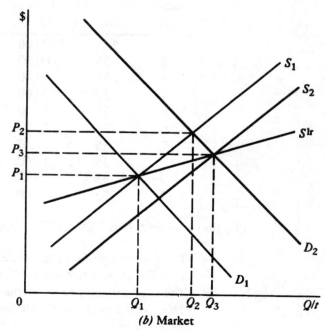
(b) Market

140   Chapter 9   Perfect Competition

a. In the short run, firms will move along the *MC* curve to $MC = P2$. They will earn an economic profit.
b. The economic profit will attract new firms into the industry. The market supply curve shifts to the right, and market price falls. However, it does not fall to its original level, because the new firms bid up the factor prices, and all firms now face new, higher cost curves. Firms will earn normal profits only with a higher market price.
c. The long-run supply curve intersects the old and new equilibrium points on graph (b).

Part III: Multiple Choice

1.	a	5.	b	9.	a	13.	b
2.	c	6.	d	10.	d	14.	b
3.	c	7.	b	11.	c	15.	c
4.	a	8.	d	12.	b		

Name _____

CHAPTER 9 EXERCISES

1. Fill in the tables. Mark the profit-maximizing (loss-minimizing) output using the $MR = MC$ approach. Is it at the same level as the $TR - TC$ approach?

Total Output (Q)	Total Revenue (TR)	Cost (TC)	Profit (Loss)
0	$0	$24	_____
1	15	32	_____
2	30	36	_____
3	45	42	_____
4	60	52	_____
5	75	70	_____
6	90	96	_____
7	105	133	_____

Output (Q)	Marginal Cost (MC)	Marginal Revenue (MR)	Average Variable Costs (AVC)	Average Cost (AC)
1	_____	_____	_____	_____
2	_____	_____	_____	_____
3	_____	_____	_____	_____
4	_____	_____	_____	_____
5	_____	_____	_____	_____
6	_____	_____	_____	_____
7	_____	_____	_____	_____

Chapter 9   Perfect Competition   143

2. Graph *AC*, *AVC*, *MC*, and *MR* on the following figure. Mark the profit-maximizing output level and the shutdown point.

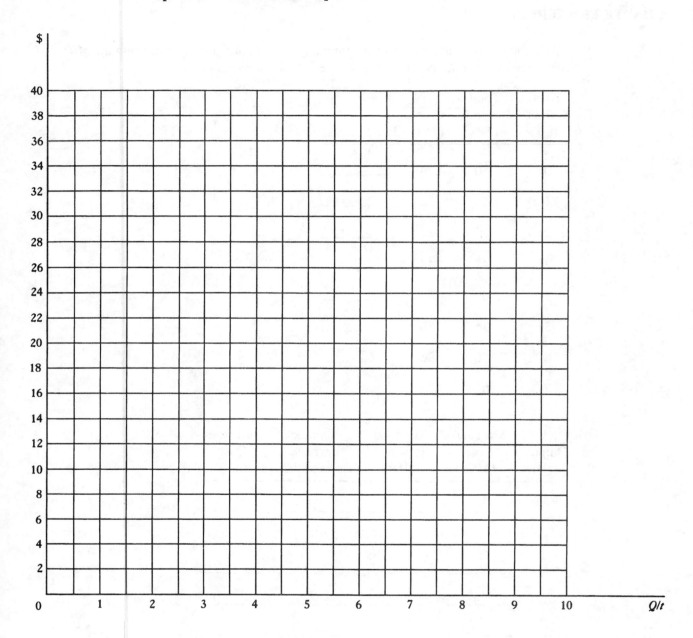

144　　Chapter 9　Perfect Competition

CHAPTER 10

MONOPOLY

CHECKING IN

Monopoly is at the other end of the market continuum from perfect competition. Monopoly exists when there is but one seller in a market for a product with no close substitutes. Such a firm faces a downward-sloping demand curve with a marginal revenue curve that lies beneath it.

Like a firm in perfect competition, a monopoly firm maximizes profit by operating where $MC = MR$, but because $MR < P$, price is greater than marginal cost. This is a different result from that of perfect competition. In the short run, monopolists may make economic profits or normal profits, or they may sustain losses. A monopolist making economic profits attempts to keep them by erecting barriers to entry that will prevent other firms from entering the industry and taking a share of the profits. Some barriers to entry are natural, such as economies of scale; other barriers are artificial. It is hard for a firm to maintain artificial barriers to entry; the government may help by passing legislation favorable to the monopolist.

Monopolies may try to increase their revenues, and hence their profits, by practicing price discrimination. To do this, the firm must be able to divide its customers into groups with different price elasticities of demand. The firm then raises the price for the customers with inelastic demand and lowers the price for those customers with more elastic demand. This practice works only when the group paying a lower price can be prevented from reselling the product to the other group.

There are costs associated with monopoly that are not present in the model of perfect competition. Monopoly misallocates resources, causes a loss of a portion of consumer surplus (deadweight loss), wastes resources in monopoly rent seeking, and often suffers from x-inefficiency, or slack management due to monopoly power and the lack of market discipline.

There are few examples of a true monopoly in the real world. In the United States, monopoly is prohibited, except for a few regulated cases of natural monopoly. Most of the firms that approach the monopoly model are publicly held corporations. In these firms, there is a separation of ownership and management. Often, the managers of these firms will not attempt to maximize profits. Rather, they may satisfy the shareholders by seeking some acceptable profit target. They may also attempt to maximize sales rather than profits.

Chapter 10   Monopoly   145

TRYING OUT THE TERMS

Match each of the following terms with its definition, and then check your answers. If you are having trouble, go back to the text and find the definition there.

_____ 1. dumping

_____ 2. long-run profit maximization

_____ 3. monopoly

_____ 4. monopoly rent seeking

_____ 5. constrained sales maximization

_____ 6. barriers to entry

_____ 7. contestable markets

_____ 8. *x*-inefficiency

_____ 9. monopoly power

_____ 10. price searcher

_____ 11. deadweight loss

_____ 12. separation of ownership and control

_____ 13. satisficing hypothesis

_____ 14. price discrimination

_____ 15. local monopoly

A. The market structure in which there is a single seller of a product that has no close substitutes.

B. The ability to exercise some of the economic effects predicted in the model of monopoly by restricting output.

C. A firm that sets price in order to maximize profits and thus has monopoly power.

D. Natural or artificial obstacles that keep new firms from entering an industry.

E. A firm that has monopoly power in a geographic region because of the large distance from other suppliers of its product (or substitutes).

F. The practice of charging different prices to different consumers or to a single consumer for different quantities purchased.

G. The practice of selling in foreign markets at lower prices than in domestic markets (a form of price discrimination).

H. The lost consumer surplus due to monopolistic restriction to output.

I. The efforts and resources expended by those attempting to establish monopolies to earn monopoly profits.

J. The inefficiency associated with the "slack" management of monopoly firms because of the lack of market discipline.

146   *Chapter 10   Monopoly*

K. The idea that large firms are controlled by hired managers, not the owners, and the managers might have different goals from those of the owners.

L. The argument that managers do not seek to maximize profits but rather seek target levels of output and profits that are satisfactory to the ownership interests.

M. The hypothesis that managers' primary goal is to increase the sales of the firm because they will be rewarded by stockholders for increasing the firm's relative share of the market.

N. The argument that even if managers seem to behave in accord with satisficing or constrained sales maximization, they only do so because it leads to higher profits in the long run.

O. Markets composed of large firms that are nevertheless efficient because easily reversible entry into the market is possible.

TESTING YOURSELF

In the next three sections, you will answer questions and work problems that are based on information in the text. Master all of the terms before you begin these sections. Work each section without referring to your notes or the text, and then check your answers.

Part I: True or False

Mark each statement as true or false. Whenever you mark a statement as false, jot down a sentence stating why it is false.

_____ 1. Monopoly is on one end of the market continuum, and perfect competition is on the other.

_____ 2. A monopolist is a price taker with a perfectly elastic demand curve.

_____ 3. A monopolist selling the eighth unit of a product for $150 should expect a marginal revenue greater than $150.

_____ 4. A monopolistic firm with costs identical to those of a firm in perfect competition will charge a higher price than the perfectly competitive firm.

_____ 5. A monopolist can increase revenue by lowering prices when operating in the elastic range of the demand curve.

_____ 6. Monopolists always earn high profits.

_____ 7. The monopolist's supply curve is the short-run marginal cost curve.

_____ 8. If the value placed on an item by the consumer exceeds the opportunity cost of producing that item, then $P > MC$.

_____ 9. If a monopoly firm is earning more than its opportunity costs, it is earning a normal profit.

_____ 10. Economies of scale are a natural barrier to entry.

_____ 11. A monopolist is charging a price of $34.89. If the firm is in equilibrium, this is a point where $MC = MR$ will be less than $34.89.

_____ 12. Because a monopoly industry is so big, it is usually more efficient than a perfectly competitive industry.

_____ 13. Consumer surplus cannot exist in the presence of monopoly.

_____ 14. A price-discriminating monopolist can increase profits by lowering prices for consumers with elastic demand and raising prices for consumers with inelastic demand.

_____ 15. The separation of ownership and management may lead to satisficing behavior by firm managers.

Part II: Problems

1. a. Fill in the table.

Output (Q)	Price (P)	Total Revenue (TR)	Marginal Revenue (MR)
0	$24	$ 0	—
1	22	_____	_____
2	20	_____	_____
3	18	_____	_____
4	16	_____	_____
5	14	_____	_____
6	12	_____	_____
7	10	_____	_____
8	8	_____	_____

b. Name the region where demand is price elastic.

Chapter 10   Monopoly   149

c. The following table gives the marginal costs for the output levels in the table in a. If the marginal cost for this firm is given by MC_1, what is the profit-maximizing price and quantity?

Output (Q)	MC_1	MC_2
0	—	—
1	$8	$7
2	11	8
3	14	9
4	17	10
5	20	11
6	23	12
7	26	13
8	29	14

d. Suppose the firm finds a new, lower cost producer and now faces MC_2. What is the new profit-maximizing price and quantity?

2. On each of the following graphs, draw the appropriate demand and marginal revenue curves for a profit-maximizing or loss-minimizing monopoly firm.

   a. A monopoly firm earning an economic profit.

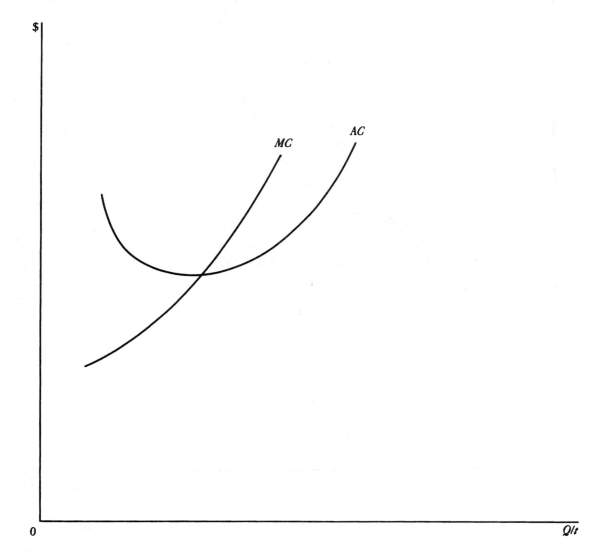

Chapter 10 Monopoly   151

b. A monopoly firm earning normal profits.

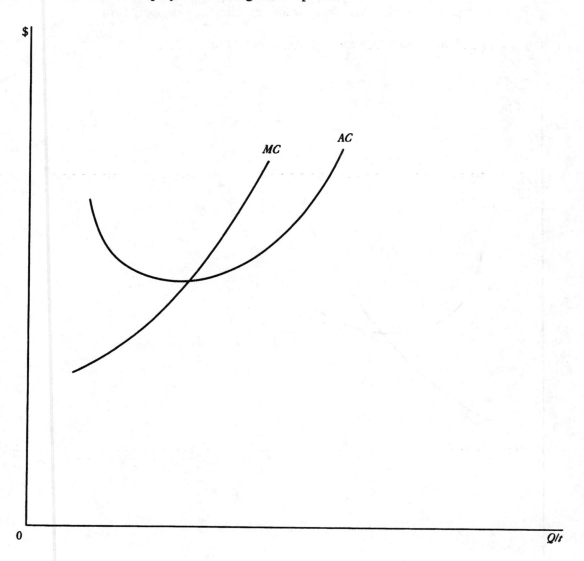

c. A monopoly firm sustaining short-run losses.

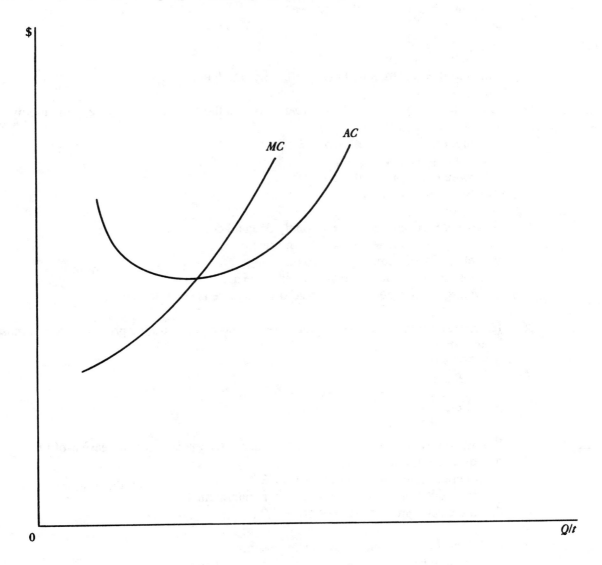

Part III: Multiple Choice

_____ 1. A monopolist will have a marginal revenue curve that is
   a. identical to the demand curve.
   b. identical to the marginal cost curve.
   c. below the demand curve.
   d. above the marginal cost curve.

_____ 2. A monopolist will try to operate
   a. where marginal cost equals marginal revenue.
   b. in the inelastic range of the demand curve.
   c. where average revenue equals marginal revenue.
   d. at the highest price on the demand curve.

3. A monopoly firm is selling eight units of output for a price of $95. In order to sell a ninth unit, it must expect to receive a price
   a. equal to $95.
   b. less than $95.
   c. greater than $95.
   d. less than the marginal revenue on the eighth unit.

4. Compared to a perfectly competitive firm with the same cost structure, a monopoly firm will charge a
   a. higher price and sell more.
   b. lower price and sell more.
   c. higher price and sell less.
   d. lower price and sell less.

5. Along a downward-sloping monopoly demand curve,
   a. marginal revenue is greater than price.
   b. elasticity of demand is constant.
   c. marginal revenue decreases when price decreases.
   d. marginal revenue is equal to zero when price is equal to zero.

6. If a monopoly firm observes an increase in total revenue after a price increase, it must be true that
   a. $MR > 0$.
   b. $MR < 0$.
   c. $MR = 0$.
   d. $MR = TR$.

7. If a monopoly firm produces an output where $MC < MR$, it can increase profit by
   a. decreasing fixed costs.
   b. decreasing production until $AC = AR$.
   c. increasing production until TR is at a maximum.
   d. increasing production until $MC = MR$.

8. In the short run, a monopolist may experience
   a. economic profits.
   b. normal profits.
   c. losses.
   d. economic profits, normal profits, or losses.

9. Which of the following is *not* a barrier to entry?
   a. Economies of scale
   b. Patents and controls over material
   c. Easy entry into the industry
   d. Government regulations

154   Chapter 10   Monopoly

_____ 10. If a profit-maximizing monopoly firm experiences an increase in marginal costs, it will
    a. increase price and reduce output.
    b. increase price and maintain output.
    c. decrease price and decrease output.
    d. remain at the same point.

_____ 11. When a firm charges different people different prices for the same good, it is engaging in
    a. price fixing.
    b. price discrimination.
    c. market manipulation.
    d. vertical monopoly.

_____ 12. A profit-maximizing monopoly firm will operate with $P > MC$. This is indicative of
    a. economies of scale.
    b. long-run normal profits.
    c. misallocation of resources.
    d. price discrimination.

_____ 13. The cost of monopoly in terms of management problems stemming from the lack of competition is called
    a. allocative inefficiency.
    b. x-inefficiency.
    c. satisficing.
    d. disadvantage of scale.

_____ 14. It takes time, effort, and resources to establish a monopoly. Such activity is called
    a. imperialism.
    b. price searching.
    c. monopoly market allocation.
    d. monopoly rent seeking.

_____ 15. The theory of contestable markets holds that
    a. monopoly profits will not persist if monopolists are subject to pro-competitive legislation.
    b. monopoly profits will be present in small firms as well as large firms.
    c. economic efficiency can exist in a monopoly market if there is easy entry.
    d. monopolies cannot exist in a market economy.

TAKING ANOTHER LOOK

While no true monopoly exists in this country, we observe many instances of monopoly-like behavior. The next time you take an automobile trip, notice the price of gasoline in towns of various sizes. In most instances, you will observe higher prices in smaller towns. This is because people have few alternatives to buying locally. Prices will be particularly high in small towns with only one or two station owners. If you live in a town 70 miles from Atlanta where all three gas stations are named "The Jones Boys'," you ought to fill up in Atlanta before you head home.

Chapter 10 Monopoly   155

CHECKING OUT

Now that you have finished studying this chapter, you should be able to:

1. Define monopoly and calculate average revenue and marginal revenue, given data on price and output. Diagram average revenue, marginal revenue, marginal cost, and average cost curves for a monopolistic firm making an economic profit, a loss, and finally, a normal profit.

2. Explain the economic role of natural and artificial barriers to entry into an industry.

3. Describe price discrimination.

4. Discuss how a monopolist misallocates resources in terms of price and costs.

5. Describe the costs associated with monopoly.

6. Discuss why managers may pursue goals other than profit maximization.

7. Explain facts and fallacies of monopoly organization.

8. Evaluate the concept of contestable markets.

ANSWERS

Trying Out the Terms

1. G	5. M	9. B	13. L
2. N	6. D	10. C	14. F
3. A	7. O	11. H	15. E
4. I	8. J	12. K	

Testing Yourself

Part I: True or False

1. true
2. false. A monopolist is a price searcher with a demand curve that is also the downward-sloping demand curve for the industry.
3. false. For the monopolist, marginal revenue is less than price.
4. true
5. true
6. false. Monopolists may earn economic profits or normal profits, or they may sustain losses, depending on demand.
7. false. The monopolist's supply curve cannot be determined.
8. true
9. false. It is earning an economic profit.
10. true
11. true

156   Chapter 10   Monopoly

12. false. The higher monopoly price indicates an inefficient allocation of resources, and there is no competition to drive the monopolist into least-cost production.

13. false. Some consumer surplus exists, some is transferred to the monopolist as economic profit, and some (but not all) is lost. The part that is lost is the deadweight loss.

14. true

15. true

Part II: Problems

1. a.

Output (Q)	Price (P)	Total Revenue (TR)	Marginal Revenue (MR)
0	$24	$ 0	—
1	22	22	$22
2	20	40	18
3	18	54	14
4	16	64	10
5	14	70	6
6	12	72	2
7	10	70	−2
8	8	64	−6

b. The elastic range is the region where marginal revenue is positive, from ($P = \$24$, $Q = 0$) to ($P = \$12$, $Q = 6$).

c. With MC_1, the firm will produce 3 units and charge $18.

d. With MC_2, the firm will produce 4 units and charge $16.

Chapter 10   Monopoly   157

2. a. Average revenue (price) is greater than average cost, and the monopoly firm is earning an economic profit.

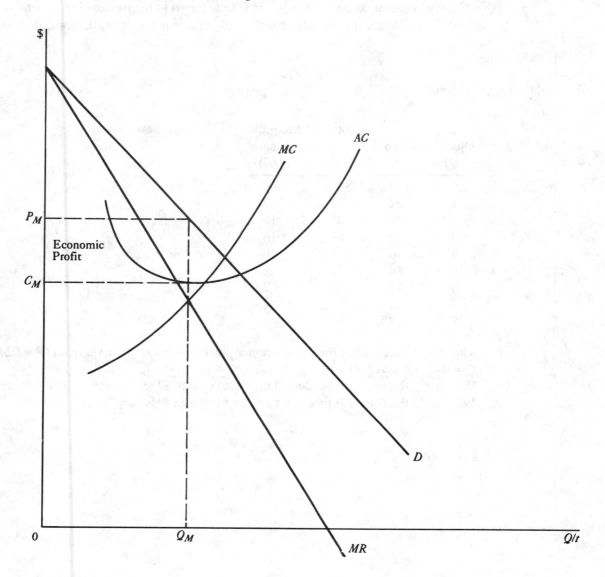

158   Chapter 10   Monopoly

b. Average revenue (price) is equal to average cost, and the monopoly firm is earning normal profits.

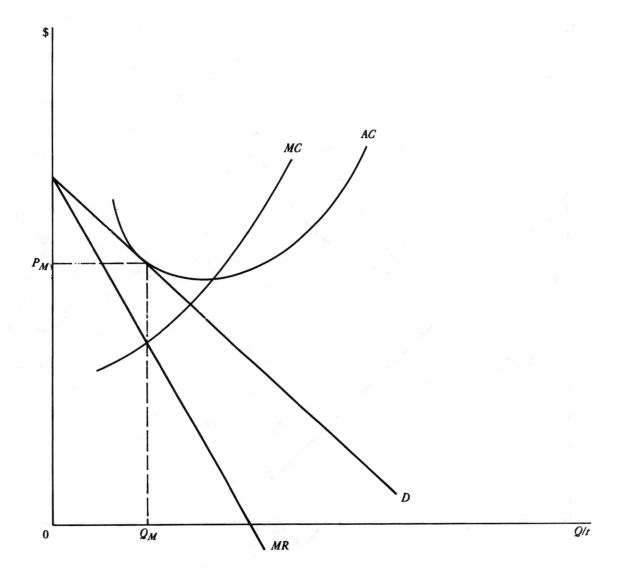

c. Average revenue (price) is less than average cost, and the monopoly firm is sustaining short-run losses.

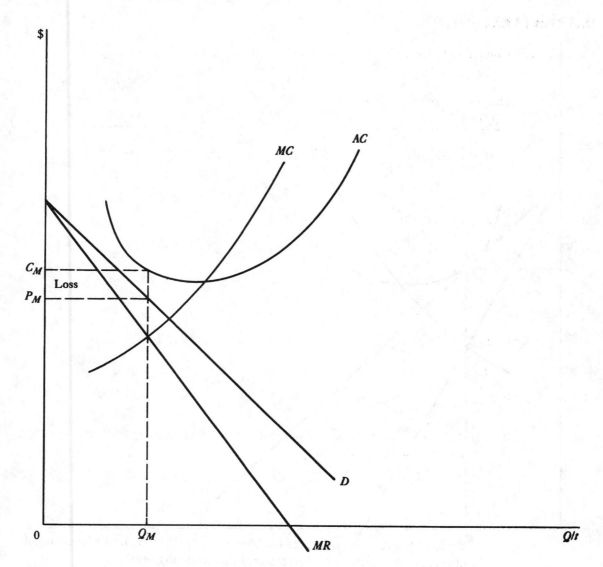

Part III: Multiple Choice

1. c
2. a
3. b
4. c
5. c
6. b
7. d
8. d
9. c
10. a
11. b
12. c
13. b
14. d
15. c

160   Chapter 10   Monopoly

Name _____

CHAPTER 10 EXERCISES

1. Consider the following revenue and cost data for a monopoly firm.

Output (Q)	Price (P)	Total Revenue (TR)	Marginal Revenue (MR)	Total Cost (TC)	Marginal Cost (MC)
0	$22,500	_____	—	$10,000	—
1	22,000	_____	_____	20,000	_____
2	21,500	_____	_____	32,000	_____
3	21,000	_____	_____	46,000	_____
4	20,500	_____	_____	62,000	_____
5	20,000	_____	_____	80,000	_____
6	19,500	_____	_____	100,000	_____
7	19,000	_____	_____	122,000	_____

a. Complete the table.

b. If this is a profit-maximizing monopoly firm, what quantity will be produced? What will the price be?

c. Demonstrate that your answer to b is correct by finding the profit levels at one unit more and one unit less than the profit-maximizing level.

d. On the following page, graph the demand, marginal cost, and marginal revenue curves from the table. Label the profit-maximizing price and quantity.

Chapter 10   Monopoly   161

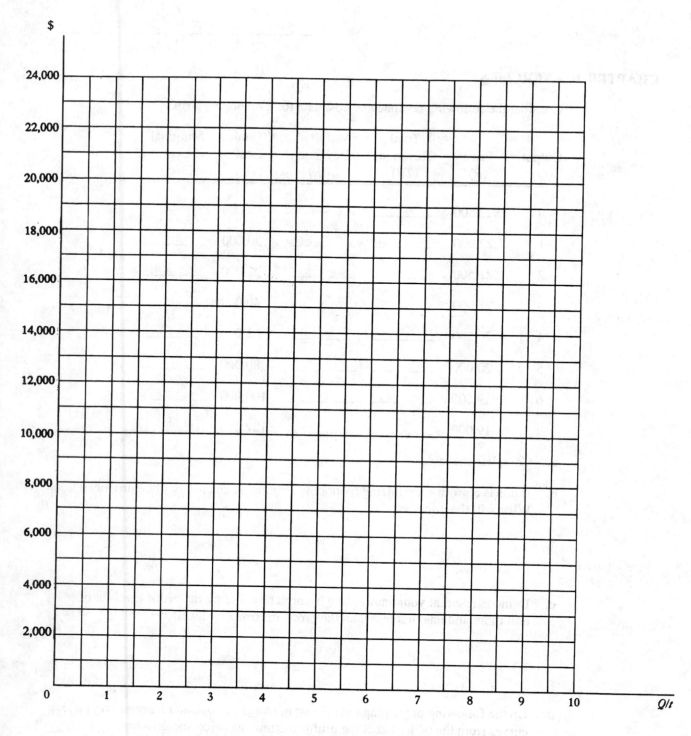

2. Explain why a monopoly firm does not have a supply curve.

CHAPTER 11

MONOPOLISTIC COMPETITION AND OLIGOPOLY

CHECKING IN

Most real-world firms can be classified as either monopolistic competitors or oligopolists. These two models lie between the two extremes of perfect competition and monopoly, and they are referred to as imperfect competition.

Monopolistic competition has many of the characteristics of perfect competition: a large number of producers, easy entry into the industry, and, in the long run, zero economic profits for the firm. However, there are important differences between perfect competition and monopolistic competition. In monopolistic competition, the product is differentiated. Firms compete in many ways as they attempt to stress the differences between their products. Because of differentiation, firms do not have the perfectly elastic demand curves of perfect competitors. Instead, they have downward-sloping demand curves resembling those of monopolists. Like monopolists, monopolistic competitors seek the output where marginal revenue is equal to marginal cost. Price, then, is greater than marginal cost in both the short run and the long run. In the long run, each firm earns only a normal profit, and price is equal to average cost. A least-cost method of production is not used; therefore, there is excess capacity in the industry.

Industries with only a few firms are called oligopolies. They may produce either homogeneous or differentiated goods. When there are only a few firms in an industry, those firms are interdependent. Each firm must consider the other firms' behavior when making decisions about prices and output. An oligopoly may act as a cartel (this is illegal in the United States); it may pursue some imperfect methods of joint action; or the firms in the oligopoly may behave independently and only be able to guess at what other firms are doing. Oligopolies are much like monopolies: there are strong barriers to entry, and there may be long-run economic profits.

Successful cartels are able to act as if they were monopolists; however, cartels tend to fall apart because of strong incentives for members to chisel. Cartels are threatened if new firms enter the industry. The more firms there are in a cartel, the more likely it is to fall apart.

Chapter 11   Monopolistic Competition and Oligopoly   *163*

TRYING OUT THE TERMS

Match each of the following terms with its definition, and then check your answers. If you are having trouble, go back to the text and find the definition there.

_____ 1. monopolistic competition	_____ 12. nonprice competition
_____ 2. pure oligopoly	_____ 13. competitive fringe
_____ 3. excess capacity	_____ 14. coordination
_____ 4. game theory	_____ 15. product group
_____ 5. price leadership	_____ 16. shared monopoly
_____ 6. cartel	_____ 17. dominant firm
_____ 7. differentiated product	_____ 18. differentiated oligopoly
_____ 8. oligopoly	_____ 19. price clusters
_____ 9. kinked demand curve	_____ 20. collusion
_____ 10. tacit collusion	_____ 21. chiseling
_____ 11. communication	_____ 22. name brand capital

A. A good or service that has real or imagined characteristics that are different from those of other goods or services.

B. A market for a set of goods that are differentiated but have a large number of close substitutes.

C. The unutilized part of existing production facilities by a monopolistically competitive firm.

D. Competing with rival firms through advertising, style changes, color changes, and techniques other than lowering price.

E. The market structure in which a few firms compete imperfectly and recognize their interdependence.

F. The model of oligopoly that says that oligopolists coordinate and share markets to act as a monopoly.

G. An oligopoly that produces heterogeneous products that are very close substitutes.

H. An oligopolistic industry that produces a homogeneous product.

I. Groupings of prices for similar, but not homogeneous, products.

164   Chapter 11   Monopolistic Competition and Oligopoly

J. Firms' ability to signal their intentions to each other.

K. Firms' ability to relate their production decisions to those made by other firms in an industry.

L. Agreements between firms in an industry to set a certain price or to share a market in certain ways.

M. A group of independent firms that agree not to compete but rather to determine prices and output jointly.

N. Cheating on a cartel agreement by lowering prices in an attempt to capture more of the market.

O. Unorganized and unstated attempts by informally coordinated oligopolies to practice joint actions.

P. The form of tacit collusion in an oligopolistic industry in which one firm, the price leader, sets the price or initiates price changes and the other firms follow that lead.

Q. The most influential firm in an industry, usually the largest firm.

R. The smaller competitors in informally coordinated markets with one large, dominant firm.

S. A mathematical theory about rational decision making under conditions of uncertainty that can provide insight into oligopolistic behavior.

T. A demand curve with a bend in it at the price settled on in an oligopolistic industry because other firms' price cuts, but not price increases, are matched.

U. The value that consumers place on a product because of experience, reputation, or image.

V. The market structure in which a large number of firms sell differentiated products.

TESTING YOURSELF

In the next three sections, you will answer questions and work problems that are based on information in the text. Master all of the terms before you begin these sections. Work each section without referring to your notes or the text, and then check your answers.

Part I: True or False

Mark each statement as true or false. Whenever you mark a statement as false, jot down a sentence stating why it is false.

_____ 1. Monopolistic competition and oligopoly are examples of imperfect competition.

Chapter 11 Monopolistic Competition and Oligopoly 165

_____ 2. When the representative firm in a monopolistically competitive industry is sustaining losses, some firms will leave the industry. This will shift the demand curve of the remaining firms to the left.

_____ 3. Industries in both perfect competition and monopolistic competition produce homogeneous products.

_____ 4. A highly differentiated product will have a more elastic demand curve than a less differentiated product.

_____ 5. In monopolistic competition, the long-run equilibrium is $P = AC$.

_____ 6. A firm with an output that does not fully utilize its plant size has excess capacity.

_____ 7. Trademarks are used as a means of product differentiation.

_____ 8. The grocery stores in a city are an example of an oligopolistic industry.

_____ 9. Joan Robinson developed a theory of monopolistic competition.

_____ 10. A pure oligopoly is one composed of three or fewer firms.

_____ 11. Organized collusive activity in private industry is prohibited in the United States.

_____ 12. Barriers to entry are low in oligopolistic industries.

_____ 13. Cartels often break up because of chiseling by member firms.

_____ 14. Oligopolies are marked by mutual independence.

_____ 15. Price clusters may appear just above and just below the kink in a kinked demand curve.

Part II: Problems

1. Use the table below to answer the following questions.

Output (Q)	Average Revenue (AR)	Average Cost (AC)	Average Variable Cost (AVC)
1	$5	$6.00	$5.00
2	4	4.25	3.75
3	3	3.00	2.67
4	2	2.50	2.25
5	1	3.50	3.30

a. What is the TFC of producing 2 units of output?

b. What is the profit or loss from producing 5 units of output?

c. What would be the long-run equilibrium for a monopolistically competitive firm?

d. What would be the long-run equilibrium for a perfectly competitive firm?

e. What would be the excess capacity in this representative monopolistically competitive firm?

2. Use the figure below to answer the following questions.

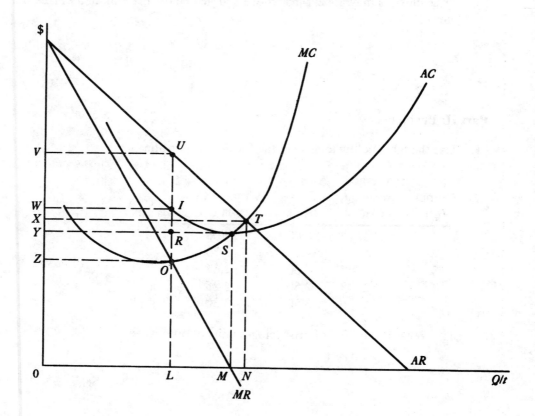

a. What is the profit-maximizing price and quantity for this monopolistically competitive firm?

168   Chapter 11   Monopolistic Competition and Oligopoly

b. At this price and quantity, is this firm operating in the short run or the long run?

c. Does the firm have profits or losses? How much?

d. What would the long-term equilibrium price and quantity be if the industry were perfectly competitive?

Part III: Multiple Choice

1. A firm in a monopolistically competitive industry faces a downward-sloping demand curve because
    a. the product is homogeneous.
    b. the product is differentiated.
    c. nonprice competition is missing.
    d. barriers to entry are high.

2. A firm in a(n) _____ industry will have the most elastic demand curve.
    a. monopolistic
    b. oligopolistic
    c. monopolistically competitive
    d. perfectly competitive

3. Jane's Malt Shop is in short-run equilibrium, with $P = \$1.50$, $AC = \$0.90$, and $MC = MR$ at $0.75. Jane should
    a. expect other, similar shops to open in the area.
    b. lower her price to increase profits.
    c. increase prices until $AC = P$.
    d. close down.

4. Sydney's Super Toys is operating at an output where $MC = \$4.50$ and $MR = \$3.76$. Sydney should
    a. be happy with a profit of $0.74.
    b. increase output.
    c. decrease output.
    d. decrease output and lower prices.

5. Monopoly and monopolistically competitive industries share the characteristic of
   a. making long-run economic profits.
   b. being able to sustain long-run losses without closing down.
   c. facing downward-sloping demand curves.
   d. having $MR = AR$.

6. One way a monopolistically competitive firm can cause its demand curve to shift to the right is by
   a. lowering price.
   b. advertising.
   c. encouraging entry of new firms.
   d. making the product more homogeneous.

7. The long-run equilibrium of a monopolistically competitive firm will differ from that of a firm in perfect competition because, in a monopolistically competitive long-run equilibrium,
   a. $MC < MR$.
   b. $AC > P$.
   c. $P = MR$.
   d. $P > MR$.

8. Monopolistic competition is less efficient that perfect competition because of the long-run presence of
   a. homogeneous products.
   b. excess capacity.
   c. profit-maximizing behavior.
   d. strong barriers to entry and exit.

9. If an oligopoly produces a homogeneous product, it is called a
   a. pure oligopoly.
   b. monopolistic oligopoly.
   c. cartel.
   d. differentiated oligopoly.

10. A small group of firms trying to maximize joint profits is called
    a. monopolistic competition.
    b. a cartel.
    c. a price searcher group.
    d. a pure oligopoly.

11. There is an oligopoly with three firms all charging a price of $400. If firm A raises its price to $450, the kinked demand curve theory would predict that firms B and C would
    a. follow firm A's price leadership and raise their prices to $450.
    b. lower prices to some level below $400.
    c. do nothing.
    d. endure economic losses equal to $50 a unit.

_____ 12. Cartels are destroyed by
   a. chiseling.
   b. inelastic demand.
   c. new entry.
   d. either chiseling or new entry.

_____ 13. In an oligopoly with a dominant firm,
   a. price is set by the dominant firm at its profit-maximizing price, and firms on the competitive fringe accept this price as the market price.
   b. the dominant firm makes a normal profit, and the firms on the competitive fringe make a profit that is less than normal.
   c. the presence of the competitive fringe causes an excess supply in the market.
   d. the output level is the same as if the industry were a monopoly.

_____ 14. Which of the following is likely to prolong the life of a cartel?
   a. Fluctuating demand
   b. Many firms
   c. A homogeneous product
   d. Weak entry barriers

_____ 15. George Stigler disagrees with the kinked demand curve models because he feels that
   a. oligopolists will always cheat.
   b. long-run prices in oligopoly are not necessarily more stable than prices in other industries.
   c. there are too many firms in an oligopoly.
   d. it is impossible to prevent collusion.

TAKING ANOTHER LOOK

I. Fast-food restaurants are in a monopolistically competitive industry. There is lots of nonprice competition and a seemingly endless variety of food choice. In their advertising, these firms stress speed and convenience. In the 1990s, people stay at home more cocooning. Two reasons for this may be the growing number of VCRs and better frozen meals. In response, an increasing number of fast-food restaurants offer delivery service, a practice formerly limited to very large cities. One enterprising firm offers to not only deliver dinner but also bring along a videotape. It says it can do everything but the dishes—and you can throw those away.

II. Everyone knows Mr. Peanut. He's been the symbol of Planters' Peanuts since 1916, and he's a good example of name brand capital. As such, he's worth a lot to Nabisco, which owns Planters'. In 1993, Nabisco's market researchers decided the old boy wasn't appealing to younger consumers, and management made a marketing policy decision: Mr. Peanut underwent a makeover emerging as "a '90s kind of guy" lying on the beach and kicking around in cowboy boots. He got to keep the top hat, though.

Chapter 11   Monopolistic Competition and Oligopoly   _171_

CHECKING OUT

Now that you have finished studying this chapter, you should be able to:

1. Describe the characteristics of monopolistic competition.

2. Explain why interdependence is unique to oligopoly.

3. Understand why government policy is often necessary to assure the success of a cartel.

4. Use game theory to understand oligopolistic behavior.

5. Describe how and why equilibrium price and output under monopolistic competition and oligopoly differ from that of perfect competition.

ANSWERS

Trying Out the Terms

1.	V	6.	M	11.	J	16.	F	21.	N
2.	H	7.	A	12.	D	17.	Q	22.	U
3.	C	8.	E	13.	R	18.	G		
4.	S	9.	T	14.	K	19.	I		
5.	P	10.	O	15.	B	20.	L		

Testing Yourself

Part I: True or False

1. true
2. false. The market will be divided among a smaller number of firms; therefore, the demand curve of each remaining firm will shift to the right.
3. false. In monopolistic competition, the product is differentiated.
4. false. A highly differentiated product has fewer substitutes; hence, a less elastic demand curve.
5. true
6. true
7. true
8. false. They are closer to the model of monopolistic competition.
9. true
10. false. A pure oligopoly is one that produces a homogeneous product.
11. true
12. false. There are usually strong barriers to entry in these industries.
13. true
14. false. Oligopolies are marked by mutual interdependence.
15. false. Price clusters are groups of prices for similar, but not homogeneous, products.

172   *Chapter 11   Monopolistic Competition and Oligopoly*

Part II: Problems

1. a. $1
   b. loss of $12.50
   c. $P = \$3, Q = 3$
   d. $P = \$2.50$ and Q is between 3 and 4 (where AC is at its minimum).
   e. The excess capacity is between 0 and 1 unit of output.

2. a. price = V; quantity = L
   b. The firm is operating in the short run, because it is making economic profits.
   c. The firm is making an economic profit equal to the area $WIUV$.
   d. price = Y; quantity = M

Part III: Multiple Choice

1. b	5. c	9. a	13. a
2. d	6. b	10. b	14. c
3. a	7. d	11. c	15. b
4. c	8. b	12. d	

Name _____

CHAPTER 11 EXERCISES

_____ 1. In which market structure do firms face the flattest (most elastic) demand curve?
   a. Perfect competition
   b. Monopolistic competition
   c. Oligopoly
   d. Monopoly

_____ 2. A highly elastic, downward-sloping demand curve is most representative of
   a. monopoly.
   b. industry.
   c. oligopoly.
   d. perfect competition.
   e. monopolistic competition.

_____ 3. A wide variety of styles, colors, qualities, and brands is provided by
   a. monopoly.
   b. monopsony.
   c. monopolistic competition.
   d. perfect competition.
   e. All of the above

_____ 4. Which of the following is *not* implied by the excess capacity of monopolistically competitive industries?
   a. Many firms will be operating at a loss.
   b. The consumer pays for the greater differentiation between goods.
   c. The same total output could have been produced by fewer firms at a lower cost.
   d. Price will be higher than it would be for the same industry operating in perfect competition.
   e. In long-run equilibrium, average cost will be higher for monopolistically competitive firms than for perfectly competitive firms producing the same output.

_____ 5. In striving for joint profit maximization, it is necessary for a cartel to
   a. set prices, outputs, and market areas.
   b. reduce the profits of each of its members.
   c. force each member to produce more.
   d. force each member to set $P < AC$.

_____ 6. An oligopoly that produces resources that will be used by other firms would probably be
   a. a differentiated oligopoly.
   b. a pure oligopoly.
   c. a genuine oligopoly.
   d. not an oligopoly at all.
   e. the dominant firm.

Chapter 11   Monopolistic Competition and Oligopoly   175

_____ 7. Which model assumes that competitors will not follow price increases but will follow price cuts?
   a. Price leadership
   b. Dominant firm
   c. Kinked demand curve
   d. Competitive fringe
   e. Price discrimination

_____ 8. The presence of name brand capital
   a. allows consumers to participate in the ownership of the firm.
   b. encourages the entry of new firms.
   c. is most prevalent in perfect competition.
   d. is prohibited by law in the United States.
   e. can act as a barrier to entry in oligopolistic industries.

CHAPTER 12

REGULATION, DEREGULATION AND ANTITRUST POLICY

CHECKING IN

You have studied the four theoretical models of market structure. Now it is time to discuss the ways firms actually behave. As you have learned, groups of firms operate in an industry. But what is an industry? The Commerce Department classifies firms by means of the Standard Industrial Classification (SIC) system. The firms within one four-digit code group are considered an industry.

The degree of concentration in an industry can be measured to estimate the degree of monopoly power. A four-firm concentration ratio measures the concentration in a particular industry by comparing the sales of the top four firms with total industry sales. A Herfindahl Index accounts for all of the firms in an industry by totaling the squares of the market shares of all the firms in that industry. Many consider the Herfindahl Index a better measure of monopoly power than a simple concentration ratio.

Although concern exists about the degree of monopoly power in the United States, there is no conclusive evidence that the degree of concentration is increasing. In fact, it appears to be relatively stable. Because of a wave of merger and acquisition activities, there was serious concern about increasing concentration in the 1980s. Mergers in the 1990s appear to be based on the desire of firms to become more internationally oriented.

There is considerable debate about the performance of highly concentrated industries, including such issues as whether these industries engage in monopoly pricing and whether pricing in these industries is as flexible as in the economy as a whole. Some people argue that a highly concentrated structure results in the antisocial behavior and unsatisfactory performance expected of a monopoly (the market concentration doctrine). Others argue that the presence of monopoly on both sides of the market (countervailing power) controls monopoly excesses and that concentrated industries are conducive to innovation.

Sometimes natural monopolies are permitted to exist with regulation. Usually, regulators allow such monopolies to engage in cost-plus pricing. However, this type of pricing is inefficient, because it provides little incentive for firms to minimize costs. Another alternative for regulators is to tax the monopoly profits; this practice, however, does not affect price or output.

Chapter 12   Regulation, Deregulation, and Antitrust Policy   **177**

U.S. law prohibits most monopolies and highly concentrated industries. Congress passed the first antitrust law, the Sherman Act, in 1890. In the succeeding years, there have been many other antitrust laws, usually in response to prevailing business practices. These laws are enforced by the Justice Department and the Federal Trade Commission. Presidential administrations since 1890 have enforced these laws with varying degrees of enthusiasm and success. Lawsuits can take a long time and do not often result in a more competitive situation. Politics play an important role in antitrust prosecution.

TRYING OUT THE TERMS

Match each of the following terms with its definition, and then check your answers. If you are having trouble, go back to the text and find the definition there.

Part I

_____ 1. number equivalent

_____ 2. Lerner Index of monopoly power (LMP)

_____ 3. Standard Industrial Classification (SIC) system

_____ 4. trusts

_____ 5. countervailing power

_____ 6. cost-plus pricing

_____ 7. concentration ratio

_____ 8. industry studies

_____ 9. fair rate of return

_____ 10. market concentration doctrine

_____ 11. marginal cost pricing

_____ 12. Herfindahl Index

_____ 13. administered prices

_____ 14. holding companies

_____ 15. industry

A. A group of firms producing similar or related products.

B. Investigations of specific industries to determine the degree of competitive behavior.

C. A code devised by the U.S. Census Bureau for classifying industries using about 400 four-digit numbers.

D. A measure of the distribution of economic power among firms in an oligopolistic market.

E. A summed index of concentration that takes into account all the firms in an industry.

F. A measure of the theoretical number of equal-sized firms that should be found in an industry (the reciprocal of the Herfindahl Index).

178   _Chapter 12   Regulation, Deregulation, and Antitrust Policy_

G. The hypothesis that the degree of concentration in an industry is a reliable index of monopoly power and that a high concentration ratio is likely to be associated with undesirable monopoly behavior.

H. Prices that are relatively rigid, or changed only infrequently.

I. The offsetting power possessed by both sides of the market in a monopoly.

J. A policy tool for forcing a monopoly to behave more like a competitive firm by regulating the monopoly price so that it is equal to marginal cost.

K. An index that evaluates the gap between price and marginal cost as a measure of monopoly power.

L. The form of price regulation that allows firms a markup that is a percentage of average costs of production.

M. The normal profit that a regulated industry must earn in order to stay in business.

N. Organizations set up to control the stock of other companies through boards of trustees.

O. Firms set up for the sole purpose of owning and thus controlling other firms.

Part II

_____ 1. National Recovery Administration (NRA)

_____ 2. tying contracts

_____ 3. Hart-Scott-Rodino Antitrust Improvement Act

_____ 4. Federal Trade Commission Act

_____ 5. Clayton Act

_____ 6. Sherman Antitrust Act

_____ 7. Robinson-Patman Pact

_____ 8. predatory pricing

_____ 9. Celler-Kefauver Antimerger Act

_____ 10. Wheeler-Lea Act

A. The first federal antitrust law in the United States, passed in 1890. Section 1 of the act declared every contract, combination, or conspiracy in restraint of trade to be illegal. Section 2 made it illegal to monopolize or attempt to monopolize.

B. Federal law, passed in 1914, prohibiting the acquisition of the stock of a competing company if such an acquisition would "substantially lessen competition." It also prohibits tying contracts.

C. Agreements between producers and retailers that call for the retailer to stock certain items in return for being allowed to stock other items.

Chapter 12   Regulation, Deregulation, and Antitrust Policy   179

D. A federal law that amended the Clayton Act in 1936, making predatory pricing illegal.

E. The act of selling below cost to destroy competitors.

F. A federal law that strengthened the Clayton Act in 1950 by making it illegal in certain circumstances for a firm to merge with another by purchasing its assets.

G. A federal law passed in 1914 that set up the Federal Trade Commission (FTC) to police unfair and deceptive business practices.

H. A 1938 federal law amending the FTC Act to make unfair or deceptive acts or practices in commerce illegal.

I. A 1970 federal law amending the FTC Act to require firms to report mergers or acquisitions to the FTC and Department of Justice before the fact.

J. A major New Deal program that was aimed at business recovery but was anticompetitive since it allowed and encouraged agreements between firms. It was eventually declared unconstitutional.

TESTING YOURSELF

In the next three sections, you will answer questions and work problems that are based on information in the text. Master all of the terms before you begin these sections. Work each section without referring to your notes or the text, and then check your answers.

Part I: True or False

Mark each statement as true or false. Whenever you mark a statement as false, jot down a sentence stating why it is false.

_____ 1. An industry is composed of firms producing the same or highly similar products.

_____ 2. In the United States, industries are designated by the Commerce Department according to the system established by the Federal Trade Commission.

_____ 3. We would expect to find a negative coefficient of cross elasticity of demand between products made by firms in the same industry.

180   *Chapter 12   Regulation, Deregulation, and Antitrust Policy*

_____ 4. Suppose the efficient firm size is estimated to be approximately 15 percent of industry sales. If the four-firm concentration ratio is 70 percent, there are probably too many firms in this industry.

_____ 5. Antitrust activity may introduce inefficiencies into industries that have large economies of scale.

_____ 6. If a high level of concentration in an industry is illegal, *per se*, the court can restructure an industry solely on the grounds of concentration.

_____ 7. Countervailing power theory holds that the best way of measuring monopoly is by measuring the concentration of the industry.

_____ 8. Natural monopolies have constantly declining average cost curves.

_____ 9. A government can capture monopoly profits by taxing the monopoly.

_____ 10. The rule of reason was established in 1914 by the Clayton Act.

_____ 11. If one firm purchases a customer, it is a vertical merger.

_____ 12. If the government supported a policy of easing entry into concentrated industries, competitive pressure would increase in those industries.

Chapter 12   Regulation, Deregulation, and Antitrust Policy   181

_____ 13. The primary casuality in a price war is usually the customer.

_____ 14. Japan's trading conglomerates can be compared to U.S. holding companies.

Part II: Problems

1. Consider the following industry data.

Industry I		Industry II	
Firm	Sales (in millions)	Firm	Sales (in millions)
A	$200	A	$300
B	150	B	50
C	50	C	25
D	50	D	25
E	50	E	25
		F	25
Total	$500	G	25
		H	25
		Total	$500

a. What is the four-firm concentration ratio in each industry? Which is more concentrated?

b. What is the Herfindahl Index for each industry? Which is more concentrated? Why does the Herfindahl Index give a different result than the four-firm concentration ratio?

c. What is the number equivalent in each industry?

182   _Chapter 12   Regulation, Deregulation, and Antitrust Policy_

2. Use the figure below to answer the following questions.

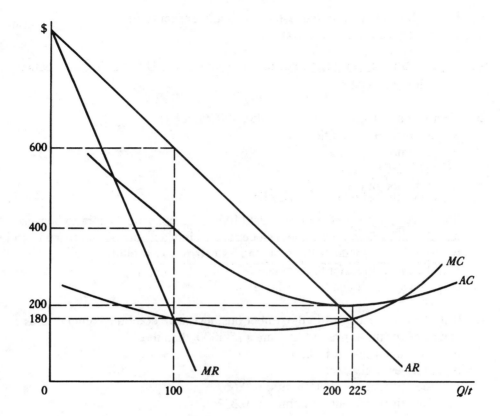

a. If the monopoly shown in the graph is not regulated, what price and quantity combination will it choose?

b. What price and quantity combination will a regulatory authority using marginal cost pricing choose? Why is this an unlikely outcome?

c. What price and quantity combination will allow the monopoly firm to earn a fair rate of return?

Part III: Multiple Choice

_____ 1. In a highly concentrated industry, we would expect to find
   a. purely competitive firms.
   b. many barriers to entry.
   c. a low Herfindahl Index.
   d. a low SIC code.

_____ 2. If an industry has a Herfindahl Index of 0.25, it has
   a. a concentration ratio of 1.
   b. a number equivalent of 4.
   c. too many firms.
   d. not enough firms.

_____ 3. Some economists prefer a Herfindahl Index to a concentration ratio because
   a. the index is more accurate, since it takes into account all the firms in an industry.
   b. the index concentrates on the top four firms in the industry.
   c. the index is easier to calculate.
   d. data are more readily available.

_____ 4. If the four largest firms in the timber business have combined annual sales of $250,000 and sales for the entire industry are $750,000, then the
   a. Herfindahl Index is 0.250.
   b. number equivalent is 5.
   c. four-firm concentration ratio is 0.667.
   d. four-firm concentration ratio is 0.333.

_____ 5. If the ideal number of firms in an industry is seven, what is the Herfindahl Index?
   a. 0.143
   b. 0.700
   c. 1.7
   d. A number that cannot be calculated with the information given

_____ 6. An industry is less differentiated when
   a. the product is more income elastic.
   b. cross elasticity between firms is negative.
   c. there are fewer digits in the SIC code.
   d. its number equivalent is high.

_____ 7. In the 1980s, U.S. corporations
   a. engaged in very little merger activity because of the Reagan administration's attitude toward mergers.
   b. were severely damaged by unorthodox merger activity by a few large firms.
   c. engaged in a huge reshuffling of corporate assets.
   d. tended to become more regional and less national.

184   Chapter 12   Regulation, Deregulation, and Antitrust Policy

8. The market concentration doctrine
   a. holds that only structure should be a criterion for antitrust action.
   b. is an innovative and unproven approach to evaluating monopoly power.
   c. is used more in Europe than in the United States.
   d. is the basis of the theory of countervailing power.

9. Gardiner Means found that prices in highly concentrated industries
   a. are virtually the same as in unconcentrated industries.
   b. tend to be rigid and change infrequently.
   c. fluctuate more than competitive prices.
   d. are lower than those in unconcentrated industries.

10. If a highly concentrated industry must negotiate with a strong union, the countervailing power theory would predict that
    a. consumers will benefit.
    b. consumers will be worse off than if only one monopoly were present.
    c. the monopoly profits will be shared by the industry and the union.
    d. the union will absorb all of the industry's monopoly profits, leaving it with only normal profits.

11. Suppose that a monopoly is charging a price of $25. An economist estimates that the purely competitive price for this industry would be $10. What is the Lerner Index?
    a. 2.5
    b. 1.67
    c. 0.6
    d. 0.4

12. Studies conducted by Choi and Philippatos found that
    a. the filing of antitrust cases causes restraint in pricing, but with diminishing returns.
    b. collusive firms are more profitable than noncollusive firms.
    c. stock prices are very sensitive to the filing of antitrust cases.
    d. markets in the 1980s are less concentrated than those in the 1930s.

13. The text suggests that, as an alternative to monopoly regulation, the federal government could
    a. subsidize small firms wishing to enter heavily concentrated industries.
    b. base the corporate tax structure on the degree of industry concentration.
    c. give antitrust authority to the states.
    d. dismantle artificial barriers to entry.

14. Following World War II, in dealing with Germany and Japan, the U.S. government
    a. imposed antitrust regulations intended to decrease economic efficiency.
    b. imposed antitrust regulations intended to foster pure competition and growth of the industrial base.
    c. assumed a *laissez-faire* attitude.
    d. nationalized all vital industries.

Chapter 12   Regulation, Deregulation, and Antitrust Policy   185

CHECKING OUT

Now that you have finished studying this chapter, you should be able to:

1. Define an industry and use the SIC system, a Herfindahl Index, and a Lerner Index to characterize the structure of an industry, interpret concentration ratios in U.S. industry, and discuss U.S. merger movements.

2. Describe the results of studies of the relationship between concentration and prices, and concentration and profits.

3. Diagram the regulation of monopoly power through price regulation and through taxation.

4. Identify and discuss the major events in the history of antitrust legislation and the economic consequences of this antitrust activity.

5. Describe the public policy debate concerning competitiveness.

6. Evaluate the alternatives in public policy toward monopoly power.

ANSWERS

Trying Out the Terms

Part I

1. F	5. I	9. M	13. H
2. K	6. L	10. G	14. O
3. C	7. D	11. J	15. A
4. N	8. B	12. E	

Part II

1. J	5. B	9. F
2. C	6. A	10. H
3. I	7. D	
4. G	8. E	

Testing Yourself

Part I: True or False

1. true
2. false. They are designated by the Standard Industrial Classification (SIC) system, which was established by the Commerce Department.
3. false. The coefficient of cross elasticity of demand would be positive, indicating that the goods are substitutes.
4. false. The concentration ratio does not indicate an appropriate number of firms; it is simply a measure.

186   *Chapter 12   Regulation, Deregulation, and Antitrust Policy*

5. true
6. true
7. false. This is the market concentration doctrine. Countervailing power theory holds that monopolies on both sides of the market offset each other's power.
8. true
9. true
10. false. It was established by the Supreme Court in 1911.
11. true
12. true
13. false. The customer stands to gain from the lower price. The firms, particularly high-cost combatants, lose as revenues drop.
14. false. These informal associations of financial, industrial, and commerical companies could not exist under U.S. law.

Part II: Problems

1. a. Industry I = 90 percent; industry II = 80 percent. Industry I is more concentrated.
    b. Industry I = 0.280, or 2800; industry II = 0.385, or 3850. Industry II is more concentrated. The results differ because the Herfindahl Index (which sums the square of each firm's percentage of sales) gives more weight to the heavy concentration in the larger firm. The four-firm concentration ratio gives the first four firms equal weight.
    c. Industry I = 3.57, or approximately 4; industry II = 2.60, or approximately 3.
2. a. $P = \$600, Q = 100$
    b. $P = \$180, Q = 225$. It is an unlikely outcome because the firm is not earning a normal profit ($P < AC$).
    c. $P = \$200, Q = 200$

Part III: Multiple Choice

1. b	5. a	9. b	13. d
2. b	6. c	10. c	14. a
3. a	7. c	11. c	
4. d	8. a	12. a	

Chapter 12   Regulation, Deregulation, and Antitrust Policy

Name _____

CHAPTER 12 EXERCISES

1. Name each of the laws described below, and give the year of its adoption.

	Act	Year	Major Provision(s)
a.	_____	_____	Made it illegal to monopolize or attempt to monopolize. Made contracts, combinations, or conspiracies in restraint of trade illegal.
b.	_____	_____	Prohibited the acquisition of the stock of another company if such an acquisition would substantially lessen competition. Prohibited tying contracts and price discrimination.
c.	_____	_____	Amendment to Clayton Act that made predatory pricing illegal.
d.	_____	_____	Amendment to the Clayton Act that made it illegal in certain circumstances for one firm to merge with another by purchasing its assets.
e.	_____	_____	Established the FTC to police unfair and deceptive business practices.
f.	_____	_____	Amendment to the FTC Act that made unfair or deceptive trade practices illegal.
g.	_____	_____	Required firms to notify the FTC and Justice Department prior to mergers or acquisitions.

2. Mark each of the following statements as true or false. Whenever you mark a statement as false, jot down a sentence stating why it is false.

_____ a. Industry studies concentrate on comparing the results given by the model of pure competition to those of monopoly industries.

_____ b. A Standard Industrial Code of 30 would represent a major industry group.

Chapter 12   Regulation, Deregulation, and Antitrust Policy   189

_____ c. Yale Brozen found that the rate of profit is uniformly higher in concentrated industries than in unconcentrated industries.

_____ d. One argument in favor of industry concentration is that it leads to innovation and technological advances.

_____ e. John Galbraith feels that the presence of highly concentrated industries impedes technological advances.

_____ f. If a regulated monopoly is operating at a level of output where $P < MC$, there is economic efficiency.

_____ g. From the point of view of economic efficiency, it is better to regulate the price of a natural monopoly than to tax it.

_____ h. The Lerner Index of monopoly power is the ratio of the difference in price to marginal cost.

_____ i. A state government attempting to increase competitiveness might offer tax relief to an out-of-state firm considering relocation.

CHAPTER 13

MARGINAL PRODUCTIVITY THEORY
AND LABOR MARKETS

CHECKING IN

This chapter shifts the focus from product markets to resource markets. Firms are the demanders in these markets, and households are the suppliers. Income is earned in resource markets by all of the inputs. Here we discuss the labor market.

The demand for labor is derived from the demand for the final product that the labor produces. The amount of other inputs used and the level of technology also affect the demand for labor. A firm bases its demand for labor on that labor's productivity. A firm will pay a wage up to the amount that the increase in production adds to the firm's revenue; the marginal revenue product curve is a firm's demand curve for labor. A firm in a perfectly competitive product market will use more labor than a firm in an imperfectly competitive market because that firm will restrict output.

If the labor market is competitive, a firm will face a perfectly elastic supply curve of labor. It can hire as many workers as it wishes at the prevailing wage, and the marginal resource cost curve is equal to the supply curve. If the labor market is not competitive and there is a monopsonistic employer (a single purchaser of labor), the marginal resource cost curve will lie above the labor supply curve, because the firm must pay a higher wage rate as it hires more labor. This means that a monopsonistic firm will restrict employment, compared to one in a competitive labor market.

A change in the wage rate will cause a change in the quantity of labor that is employed. That change can be measured by the elasticity of demand for labor. The price elasticity of demand for the final product, the importance of labor in the production process, and the degree of input substitutability all directly affect the elasticity of demand for labor. A change in demand for the final product or a change in the use of other inputs can cause a shift in the demand curve for labor.

Individuals may attempt to become more productive by investing in human capital. One reason frequently given for the lower wages received by blacks and women is that, historically, they have invested less in human capital than have white males.

Chapter 13   Marginal Productivity Theory and Labor Markets   191

TRYING OUT THE TERMS

Match each of the following terms with its definition, and then check your answers. If you are having trouble, go back to the text and find the definition there.

_____ 1. value of the marginal product of labor (VMP_L)

_____ 7. monopsonistic exploitation

_____ 2. marginal resource cost of labor (MRC_L)

_____ 8. marginal revenue product of labor (MRP_L)

_____ 3. derived demand

_____ 9. interdependent demand

_____ 4. comparable worth

_____ 10. marginal productivity theory

_____ 5. monopsony

_____ 11. backward-bending supply curve

_____ 6. technologically determined demand

A. Demand for a productive resource that results from demand for a final good or service.

B. Demand that depends on another type of demand.

C. Demand that depends on the techniques of production and technological progress.

D. An explanation of how the distribution of income is determined in a market system. Each input is paid according to its contribution or its marginal productivity.

E. A measure of the value of the additional output that each unit of additional labor adds to a firm's total, found by multiplying the marginal product by the price at which the firm can sell the product.

F. The amount that an additional unit of labor adds to a firm's total revenue.

G. A labor supply that slopes back to the left at the point where the income effect dominates the substitution effect.

H. The cost of each additional unit of labor.

I. A market structure in which there is a single purchase of a productive resource.

J. The difference in wages paid by a firm that has monopsony power, compared to what would be paid in a competitive market.

K. A standard for determining wages that calls for equal pay for jobs that require similar levels of training, responsibility, and skills.

192   _Chapter 13   Marginal Productivity Theory and Labor Markets_

TESTING YOURSELF

In the next three sections, you will answer questions and work problems that are based on information in the text. Master all of the terms before you begin these sections. Work each section without referring to your notes or the text, and then check your answers.

Part I: True or False

Mark each statement as true or false. Whenever you mark a statement as false, jot down a sentence stating why it is false.

_____ 1. XYZ Steel increases employment of steelworkers because sales of domestically produced automobiles have increased. This is an example of derived demand.

_____ 2. In the circular flow model, businesses are suppliers in both the product and the resource markets.

_____ 3. Consumer demand determines the techniques of production.

_____ 4. A profit-maximizing firm will employ or purchase a resource until $MRP = MRC$.

_____ 5. A firm that takes the prices of both its inputs and its product as given is operating in perfect competition in both product and resource markets.

_____ 6. A large university in a small town would be in a perfectly competitive labor market.

_____ 7. A firm's demand curve for labor is labor's marginal revenue product curve.

Chapter 13   Marginal Productivity Theory and Labor Markets   *193*

_____ 8. The marginal resource cost curve is the supply curve for labor in imperfectly competitive resource markets.

_____ 9. The fact that a worker receives a lower wage in a monopsonistic market than a similar worker receives in a purely competitive market is evidence of an unfair labor practice.

_____ 10. An increase in the wage rate will cause the demand curve for labor to shift.

_____ 11. If $VMP > MRP$, there is imperfect competition in the product market.

_____ 12. If more labor is hired in a monopsonistic market, the wage rate will fall.

_____ 13. If salt is a very small component in the production of Max's Mighty Snack Morsels, we would expect Max's demand for salt to be very elastic.

_____ 14. The presence of reserve clauses in professional sports contracts keeps the level of payments to players lower than it otherwise would be.

_____ 15. Patty and Bob are employed as Level II electricians by the city. Since they earn the same wage, we can assume that the city is following a comparable worth policy.

Part II: Problems

1. a. Complete the table.

Units of Labor	Total Product	Product Price (P)	Marginal Product (MP)	Marginal Revenue Product (MRP)
1	8	$7	_____	_____
2	15	7	_____	_____
3	21	7	_____	_____
4	26	7	_____	_____
5	30	7	_____	_____
6	33	7	_____	_____

b. In what kind of product market is this firm operating?

c. If the firm is operating in a perfectly competitive resource market with an equilibrium wage of $30, how many units of labor will be hired?

d. If the prevailing wage rises to $40, how many units of labor will be hired?

Chapter 13   Marginal Productivity Theory and Labor Markets

2. Use the figure below to answer the following questions.

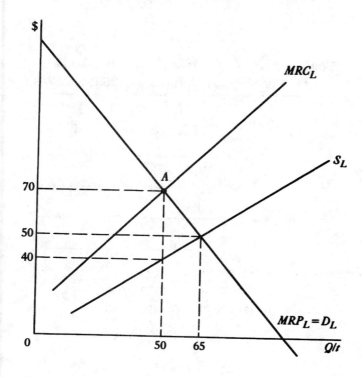

a. If this firm is operating in a perfectly competitive resource market, how many units of labor will be hired? What will the wage rate be?

b. Suppose a monopsonist enters this market. What will happen to the level of employment and the wage rate? Is there any monopsonistic exploitation?

Part III: Multiple Choice

1. Which one of the following is *not* a characteristic of the demand for labor?
   a. It is technologically determined.
   b. It is derived.
   c. It is perfectly inelastic.
   d. It is interdependent with the demand for other resources.

2. Derived demand is demand that is derived from the
   a. supply of the input.
   b. demand for the final product or service.
   c. demand for other inputs.
   d. production function.

3. When John hires the 35th worker in his box plant, he determines that the *MRC* of that worker is $5.50 and the worker's *MRP* is $7. Assuming that the market for boxes is perfectly competitive, John should
   a. lay off the new employee.
   b. hire more workers.
   c. maintain the current level of employment.
   d. obtain more capital.

4. The labor supply curve is typically upward sloping because
   a. it indicates that the firm is operating in an imperfectly competitive labor market.
   b. most people are willing to work more hours for higher wages.
   c. more people are willing to work for higher wages.
   d. higher wages induce both longer hours and more workers.

5. If a firm has a perfectly elastic labor supply curve, it is
   a. operating in a perfectly competitive resource market.
   b. operating in a perfectly competitive product market.
   c. acting as if it were an oligopsonist.
   d. making only a normal profit.

6. The value of the physical product sold
   a. is total revenue.
   b. equals price times quantity sold.
   c. equals average revenue times quantity sold.
   d. All of the above

7. A worker in John's box factory can add 100 boxes a week to total production. John can sell the boxes for $2.50 each in a perfectly competitive product market. At which marginal resource cost of labor will John maximize profits?
   a. $1.00
   b. $2.50
   c. 100/$2.50
   d. $250

8. When there is only one firm in a labor market, it is called
   a. a monopolist.
   b. a monopsonist.
   c. an oligopsonist.
   d. illegal.

Chapter 13   Marginal Productivity Theory and Labor Markets   *197*

9. The cost of adding a unit of labor is shown in the
   a. marginal resource cost curve.
   b. total resource cost curve.
   c. marginal revenue curve.
   d. marginal revenue product curve.

10. If a firm is operating in perfect competition in both the resource and the product market, it will have
    a. wage > MRP > MRC.
    b. wage = MRC > MRP.
    c. wage = MRP > MRC.
    d. wage = MRP = MRC.

11. If there is a monopsonistic employer, the imposition of a minimum wage may
    a. further depress the wage rate and leave employment unchanged.
    b. result in a higher wage but lower employment.
    c. result in increases in both wages and employment.
    d. increase employment while decreasing the wage rate.

12. If the demand for the final product is highly inelastic, we would expect resource demand to be
    a. relatively elastic.
    b. relatively inelastic.
    c. perfectly inelastic.
    d. unrelated to product demand.

13. Andy is tired of being a clerk in a convenience store, so he enrolls in an introductory management class at the community college. Andy is
    a. acting, in some ways, like an entrepreneur.
    b. investing in human capital.
    c. attempting to increase his lifetime earnings.
    d. All of the above

14. James P. Smith's research indicates that income differences between blacks and whites exist because
    a. of discrimination.
    b. blacks invest less in human capital.
    c. the returns to human capital investment have long lags.
    d. of the geographical concentrations of blacks in urban centers.

15. Many women should expect to earn more in the future because
    a. equal wages will be required by comparable worth legislation.
    b. human capital investments by women are reaching the same level as those by men.
    c. more men are entering low-paying occupations, such as nursing, and driving up wages in those occupations.
    d. women are investing in human capital at the same time that men are entering the low-paying occupations.

CHECKING OUT

Now that you have finished studying this chapter, you should be able to:

1. Explain what makes the demand for labor different from the demand for final goods.

2. Describe how a profit-maximizing firm in pure competition decides how much labor to employ in terms of its marginal revenue product and marginal resource cost.

3. Use a resource market diagram to illustrate and explain the difference between the use of labor under pure competition versus monopoly in the product market.

4. Define monopsony and discuss why monopsonistic exploitation may occur.

5. Determine the factors that affect the elasticity of demand for labor and describe possible causes for a shift in the demand for labor.

6. Explain how human capital relates to racial and gender differences between income levels.

ANSWERS

Trying Out the Terms

1. E	5. I	9. B
2. H	6. C	10. D
3. A	7. J	11. G
4. K	8. F	

Testing Yourself

Part I: True or False

1. true
2. false. Businesses are suppliers in the product market and demanders in the resourse market.
3. false. The techniques of production are determined by engineers in a production function. Consumer preference determines what is produced.
4. true
5. true
6. false. It would be a monopsonistic employer.
7. true
8. false. The marginal resource cost curve is the supply curve of labor in perfectly competitive factor markets.
9. false. It is monopsonistic exploitation.
10. false. A change in the wage rate will cause a movement along the demand curve for labor.
11. true

Chapter 13   Marginal Productivity Theory and Labor Markets   199

12. false. It will rise. In order to hire another worker, the monopsonist must offer a higher wage to all workers.
13. false. Demand for a factor is more inelastic when the factor represents an insignificant cost of production.
14. true
15. false. Patty and Bob have the same job. Comparable worth refers to equal pay for jobs that require similar levels of training, responsibility, and skill but do not carry the same job description.

Part II: Problems

1. a.

Units of Labor	Total Product	Product Price (P)	Marginal Product (MP)	Marginal Revenue Product (MRP)
1	8	$7	8	$56
2	15	7	7	49
3	21	7	6	42
4	26	7	5	35
5	30	7	4	28
6	33	7	3	21

   b. The firm is in a perfectly competitive product market; it has a perfectly elastic demand curve.
   c. 4 units of labor, which is the last level of output where $MRP > MRC$
   d. 3 units of labor, which is the last level of output where $MRP > MRC$
2. a. quantity of labor = 65; wage = $50
   b. Employment will fall to 50, and the wage rate will fall to $40. There is $10 of monopsonistic exploitation.

Part III: Multiple Choice

1.	c	5.	a	9.	a	13.	d
2.	b	6.	d	10.	d	14.	c
3.	b	7.	d	11.	c	15.	b
4.	d	8.	b	12.	b		

200   *Chapter 13   Marginal Productivity Theory and Labor Markets*

Name _____

CHAPTER 13 EXERCISES

1. Complete the table.

Units of Labor	Total Product	Marginal Product (MP_L)	Product Price (P)	Total Revenue	Value of the Marginal Product (VMP_L)	Marginal Revenue Product (MRP_L)
1	20	_____	_____	$16	_____	_____
2	36	_____	_____	14	_____	_____
3	48	_____	_____	12	_____	_____
4	56	_____	_____	10	_____	_____
5	60	_____	_____	8	_____	_____

Chapter 13   Marginal Productivity Theory and Labor Markets

2. Graph and label the marginal revenue product curve and the value of the marginal product curve.

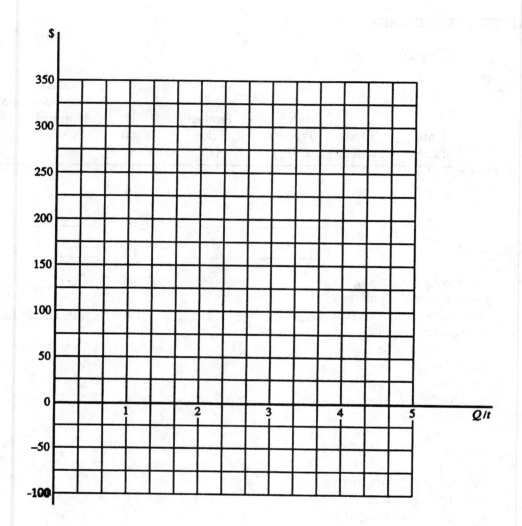

3. How do you know that the product market is not competitive? Why is MRP < VMP?

CHAPTER 14

ORGANIZED LABOR IN THE UNITED STATES

CHECKING IN

You have surveyed the theory of resource markets in the preceding chapters. In this chapter, you will examine one specific part of the labor market: labor unions. Although unions may have many objectives, such as political power and social reform, this chapter concentrates on the economic goals of unions.

Unions may be exclusive or inclusive. An exclusive union restricts membership and raises the wages of members by shifting the supply curve of labor to the left. Inclusive unions attempt to enroll all the workers in an industry and gain higher wages through negotiation and the threat of strikes. Exclusive unions are usually more successful in securing higher wages than inclusive unions.

Unions have generally been successful in gaining higher wages for their members. These increases come mainly from higher consumer prices and lower nonunion wages. Only a small portion of higher union wages come from business profits. Unions are often criticized for causing inflation and hampering the growth of productivity. There is evidence to counter both of these arguments. Unions may increase productivity by reducing employee turnover and increasing employee well-being. Long-term union contracts can actually cause union wages to rise more slowly than nonunion wages during an inflationary period.

The first unions sought political and social reform in addition to economic gain. These unions were mostly unsuccessful. The American Federation of Labor was the first business union (a union with exclusively economic goals). Unions faced hostility from businesses and the public until the election of Franklin D. Roosevelt in 1932. Since then, Congress has passed several important labor laws. The Norris-La Guardia Act and the Wagner Act encouraged the formation of unions. The Taft-Hartley Act established the rights of employers, and the Landrum-Griffin Act established rules of conduct for unions.

In recent years, the role of unions in the U.S. economy has diminished. Union membership appears to be shifting away from its original base in heavy manufacturing industries and toward service industries and the government. The Reagan administration did not provide an extremely friendly environment for unions.

Conditions in factor markets and the market for the final product can increase or decrease union power. Unions are stronger in industries with monopoly market power and an inelastic demand for labor. Unions are weakened by increased competition, right-to-work laws, increased international trade, and deregulation.

Chapter 14   Organized Labor in the United States   203

TRYING OUT THE TERMS

Match each of the following terms with its definition, and then check your answers. If you are having trouble, go back to the text and find the definition there.

Part I

_____ 1. United Mine Workers (UMW)

_____ 2. AFL-CIO

_____ 3. featherbedding

_____ 4. bilateral monopoly

_____ 5. Industrial Workers of the World (IWW)

_____ 6. injunctions

_____ 7. Knights of Labor

_____ 8. Congress of Industrial Organizations (CIO)

_____ 9. inclusive union

_____ 10. American Federation of State, County, and Municipal employees (AFSCME)

_____ 11. yellow-dog contracts

_____ 12. business union

_____ 13. exclusive union

_____ 14. wildcat strikes

_____ 15. industrial union

_____ 16. National Labor Union

_____ 17. craft union

_____ 18. American Federation of Labor (AFL)

A. The maintenance of jobs that management claims are unnecessary or redundant.

B. A union that restricts the supply of labor and maintains a higher-than-competitive wage for its members by excluding workers from a trade or occupation. Craft unions are examples of these.

C. A union composed of specific kinds of skilled workers, such as plumbers or carpenters.

D. A union that attempts to organize all the workers in an industry and to maintain a strong bargaining position with respect to management.

E. An inclusive union that gains power by organizing all (or a large share) of the workers in an industry.

F. A market structure in which monopolies deal with each other as buyers and sellers, such as when an inclusive union sells labor to a monopsonistic firm.

G. The first successful national union in the United States, founded in 1867 by William Sylvis.

204   *Chapter 14   Organized Labor in the United States*

H. Organized as a secret organization by Uriah Stevens in 1869, it won the first major strike in the United States against the railroad industry but had political reformist goals that led to its demise.

I. An exclusive union for skilled workers founded by Samuel Gompers in 1886 as the first business union.

J. According to Samuel Gompers, a union that works for economic goals without wanting to change or destroy the business organization or the political environment in which it functions.

K. The industrial union for mine workers.

L. Local strikes that are unauthorized by the national union.

M. An international union that organized U.S. steelworkers after World War I and was viewed as a socialistic organization, which contributed to its demise.

N. Contracts that require employees to agree to refrain from union activity as a precondition for employment and that allow firms to discharge workers who violate that agreement.

O. Court orders to cease some activity, such as ordering labor to stop a strike or walkout.

P. An affiliation of industrial unions that was organized when the AFL decided not to move into the mass-production industries.

Q. An organization formed by the merger of the American Federation of Labor and the Congress of Industrial Organizations in 1955, which gave labor a more unified political front.

R. A union of public employees that was one of the few unions that grew in the 1970s.

Part II

_____ 1. right-to-work laws

_____ 2. secondary boycotts

_____ 3. Landrum-Griffin Act

_____ 4. arbitration

_____ 5. Humphrey-Hawkins Act

_____ 6. union shops

_____ 7. Workplace Fairness Act

_____ 8. Taft-Hartley Act

_____ 9. National Labor Relations Board (NLRB)

_____ 10. Mediation

_____ 11. Wagner Act

_____ 12. closed shops

_____ 13. Norris-La Guardia Act

A. A law passed in 1932 that vastly strengthened the power of labor unions by limiting the court's use of injunctions in labor-management disputes.

B. A law passed in 1935 that gave employees the right to organize and bargain collectively and outlawed certain unfair labor practices by employers.

C. A board established by the Wagner Act in 1935 and empowered to investigate employer unfair labor practices and to determine the legitimate bargaining agent for labor when there are competing unions.

D. Act passed in 1947 to reverse some of the Wagner Act's favoring of labor by shifting some legal rights back to employers.

E. Firms where contract provisions require that workers must be union members before being employed.

F. Firms where union membership is necessary for a worker to remain employed.

G. State laws that allow people to hold jobs without belonging to unions.

H. Union actions to stop an employer from doing business with other firms.

I. Third-party intervention in a dispute consisting of attempts to keep the parties together and talking by offering suggestions and clarifying issues.

J. Third-party intervention in a dispute consisting of hearing the arguments of both sides, studying their positions, and rendering a decision. When this is binding, both sides must abide by the decision.

K. An act passed in 1959 and aimed at curbing union power by making unions more democratic, restricting Communist Party members and convicted felons from union leadership, and making picketing illegal under certain circumstances.

L. A 1978 amendment to the Employment Act of 1946 that set specific targets for output, employment, and prices.

M. An act that prohibits firms from permanently replacing striking workers.

TESTING YOURSELF

In the next three sections, you will answer questions and work problems that are based on information in the text. Master all of the terms before you begin these sections. Work each section without referring to your notes or the text, and then check your answers.

Part I: True or False

Mark each statement as true or false. Whenever you mark a statement as false, jot down a sentence stating why it is false.

_____ 1. The main goal of labor unions is to raise wages for all workers.

_____ 2. Unions may attempt to increase the demand for union labor by working with the firm and the government to increase the demand for the product the union firm produces.

_____ 3. If a union persuades a firm to employ an elevator operator to run a self-service elevator, the union is featherbedding.

_____ 4. A union that lobbies Congress for strict immigration controls is probably a craft union.

_____ 5. A union that has a minimum age and requires a long apprenticeship is an industrial union.

_____ 6. If workers in a monopsonistic industry organize into a union, they create a bilateral monopoly.

_____ 7. The only cost of unions' getting higher wages is lower profits to business.

_____ 8. If unions allow workers a voice in the firm and encourage workers to stay longer in one job, then unions may cause workers to be more productive.

_____ 9. When unions have long-term contracts, they exert an inflationary influence on the economy.

_____ 10. If productivity rises, wages can rise without a price increase.

_____ 11. The first successful union in the United States was the American Federation of Labor.

_____ 12. During the 1920s, firms frequently attempted to slow the growth of unions by obtaining injunctions.

_____ 13. Union growth has slowed in the last 20 years.

_____ 14. A monopoly firm is more likely to fight union organization than is a firm in perfect competition or monopolistic competition.

_____ 15. If the share of labor cost in total cost is small, demand for labor will be inelastic and a union will be stronger.

Part II: Problems

1. Each of the following graphs depicts a competitive labor market. Illustrate the given events on the appropriate graph. Label the new levels of wage and labor. Use arrows to mark the direction of change.

208   *Chapter 14   Organized Labor in the United States*

a. A union raises the passing grade on the examination required for full membership from 70 percent to 85 percent.

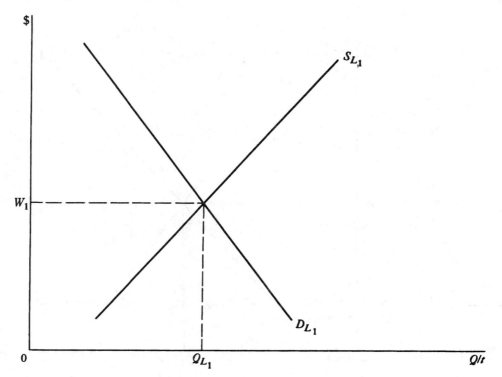

b. A firm is operating without a union in a monopsony market.

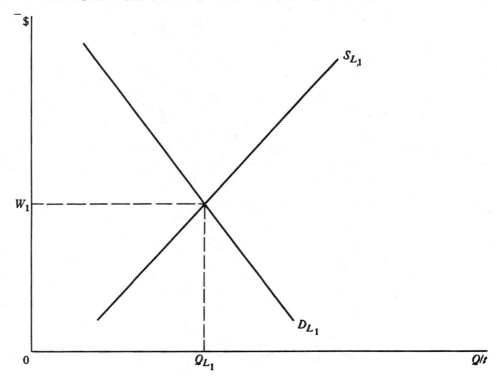

Chapter 14   Organized Labor in the United States   209

c. A union organizes all workers in an industry and threatens a strike unless wages are raised above the competitive level.

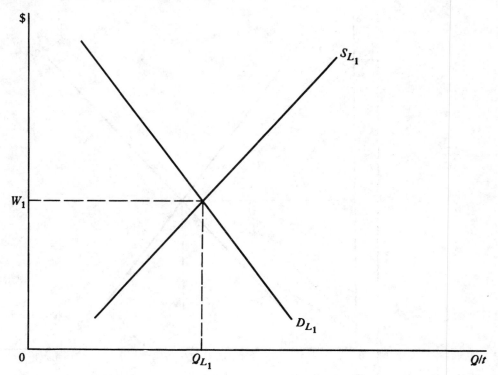

d. A union extensively advertises its product on television.

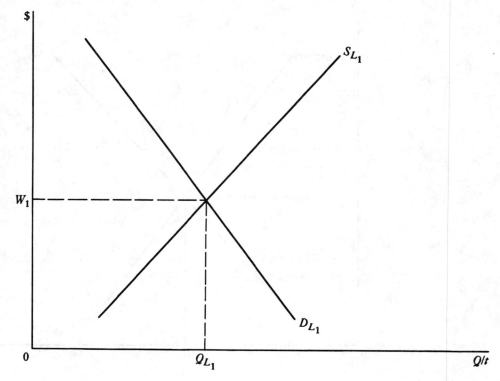

2. The graph below shows a bilateral monopoly.

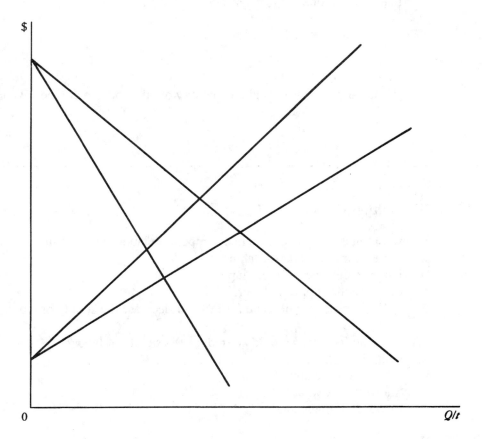

a. Label the graph correctly.

b. What is the highest wage a union would demand? Why wouldn't it ask for the highest possible wage?

c. Why is the union more likely to ask for a wage that is at or below the level associated with a monopsonist employer?

d. Over what range of wages will the level of employment be greater with a union than without one?

e. What would the wage and the quantity of labor be in a competitive labor market?

Part III: Multiple Choice

_____ 1. In order to increase wage rates in a competitive labor market, a union must
a. increase the demand for labor.
b. increase the price of other inputs.
c. decrease the supply of labor.
d. either increase the demand for labor or decrease the supply of labor.

_____ 2. Which of the following would *not* reduce the supply of labor?
a. Child labor laws
b. More overtime hours
c. Shorter work weeks
d. Lower retirement age

_____ 3. When unions raise wages, employment among union members
a. always falls.
b. is unaffected.
c. falls when supply decreases.
d. falls when demand increases.

_____ 4. A craft union
a. is ineffective unless it has the power to strike.
b. raises wages through negotiation.
c. raises wages by restricting the labor supply.
d. attempts to organize all of the workers in an industry.

_____ 5. Historically, union members have earned
a. about the same as nonunion workers.
b. more than nonunion workers.
c. less than nonunion workers.
d. twice as much as nonunion workers.

212   *Chapter 14   Organized Labor in the United States*

6. A union negotiated a new contract. The wage had been $7.50 an hour; the new wage per 40-hour week is $360. If nothing else changes, we would expect a
   a. decrease in the quantity of labor demanded.
   b. decrease in the quantity of labor supplied.
   c. decrease in the supply of labor.
   d. wage lower than $8 an hour.

7. If a union negotiates a 7 percent wage increase when productivity in that industry has risen by 10 percent, we would most likely observe
   a. that the increase in wages was passed on to the consumer in the form of higher prices.
   b. inflation.
   c. that the price remained the same or fell.
   d. an increase in the supply of labor.

8. The National Labor Union was
   a. a welfare union.
   b. the first successful national union in the United States.
   c. the first union to successfully strike a U.S. railroad.
   d. both politically active and the first successful national union in the United States.

9. The American Federation of Labor was
   a. the first business union.
   b. the first successful inclusive union.
   c. founded by Uriah Stevens.
   d. founded by Uriah Stevens and the first successful inclusive union.

10. Samuel Gompers thought that
    a. unions should have both economic and social goals.
    b. economic gain for union members was impossible unless the government became socialist.
    c. economic gains should be the only goal of a union.
    d. economic gains could be obtained through negotiation, and strikes were unnecessary.

11. Firms were prohibited from firing a worker who engaged in union activity by the
    a. Taft-Hartley Act.
    b. Norris-La Guardia Act.
    c. Humphrey-Hawkins Act.
    d. Landrum-Griffin Act.

12. A company must recognize and bargain with a union if
    a. a majority of the workers vote to have a union.
    b. 30 percent of the workers vote to have a union.
    c. union workers obtain an injunction ordering the firm to negotiate.
    d. the company has more than 20 employees and is engaged in interstate commerce.

Chapter 14   Organized Labor in the United States   213

13. We would expect to find strong unions in industries where
    a. the demand for the final product is highly elastic.
    b. there are very few substitutes for labor.
    c. the share of labor in total cost is large.
    d. the supply of labor is elastic.

14. The movement of U.S. industry from the North and Midwest to the South and West may be because of
    a. the right-to-work laws in many southern and western states.
    b. the right-to-work laws in many northern and midwestern states.
    c. many nonunion workers in southern and western states.
    d. the presence of many nonunion workers in the area as a result of the right-to-work laws.

15. The deregulation of a unionized industry may
    a. strengthen the unions in that industry.
    b. present the unions with a good opportunity to strike.
    c. weaken the unions in that industry.
    d. invite new unions to compete with the existing union.

CHECKING OUT

Now that you have finished studying this chapter, you should be able to:

1. List the economic goals of unions and the ways they can be achieved.

2. Diagram and analyze the economic effects of an exclusive union and an inclusive union.

3. Discuss the effects of unions on wages and productivity.

4. Trace the history of the U.S. labor movement.

5. Analyze the economic factors that strengthen unions and weaken unions.

ANSWERS

Trying Out the Terms

Part I

1. K	5. M	9. D	13. B	17. C
2. Q	6. O	10. R	14. L	18. I
3. A	7. H	11. N	15. E	
4. F	8. P	12. J	16. G	

214   *Chapter 14   Organized Labor in the United States*

Part II

1.	G	5.	L	9.	C	13.	A
2.	H	6.	F	10.	I		
3.	K	7.	M	11.	B		
4.	J	8.	D	12.	E		

Testing Yourself

Part I: True or False

1. false. The main goal of unions is to raise wages for *their members*.
2. true
3. true
4. false. It is more likely to be an industrial union. This type of union has a great deal to fear from an influx of new, nonunion workers.
5. false. This would be a craft union.
6. true
7. false. Most likely, higher wages will be at the expense of consumers (higher prices) and nonunion workers (lower wages), as well as profits.
8. true
9. false. Long-term contracts with set wage rates cause union wages to rise more slowly than nonunion wages.
10. true
11. false. The first successful union was the National Labor Union.
12. true
13. true
14. false. A monopolist has control over prices and can pass wage increases on to the consumer in the form of higher prices. A firm with competition cannot do this.
15. true

Chapter 14   Organized Labor in the United States   215

Part II: Problems

1. a. This is an attempt to decrease the supply of labor, which will shift supply to the left and result in a higher wage.

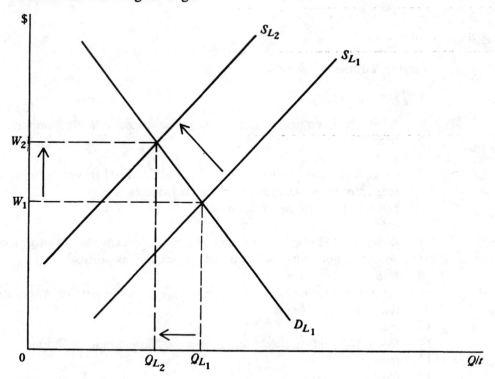

b. In a monopsony market, wages and employment will be below competitive levels.

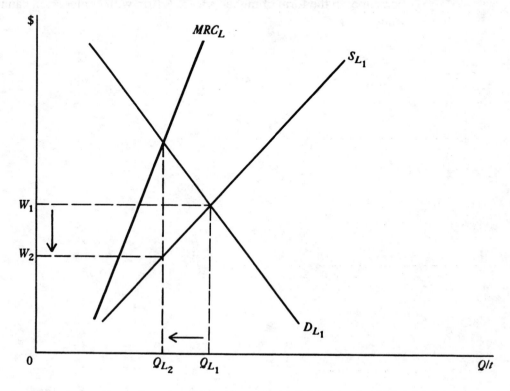

216 Chapter 14 Organized Labor in the United States

c. This situation is caused by an industrial (inclusive) union.

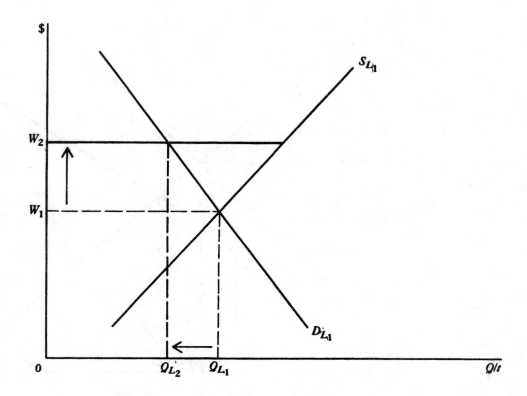

d. This is an attempt to raise wages by increasing demand for a union-made product.

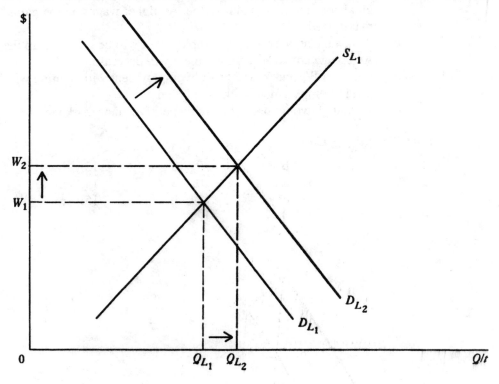

2. a.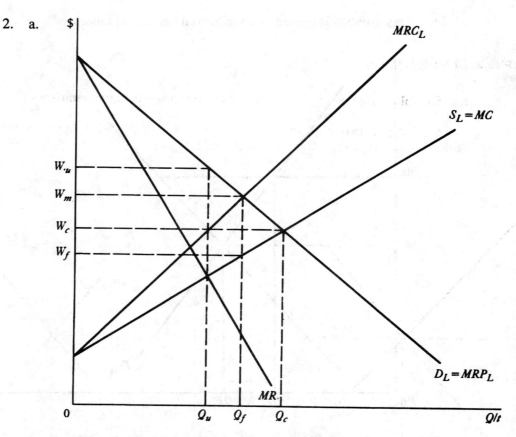

b. The highest wage a union would demand is W_u, which equates the union's marginal cost and marginal revenue. At higher wages, union gains would not be maximized.

c. At a wage at or below W_m, employment will be greater than the monopsony level. At a wage above W_m, employment will decrease.

d. Between W_m and W_f the level of employment with a union will be greater than the level of employment without a union.

e. W_c and Q_c would prevail in a competitive labor market.

Part III: Multiple Choice

1. d
2. b
3. c
4. c
5. b
6. a
7. c
8. d
9. a
10. c
11. b
12. a
13. b
14. d
15. c

CHAPTER 14 EXERCISES

1. The following two graphs illustrate the labor markets in two industries.

   a. Suppose that the workers in industry A form an inclusive union and successfully negotiate a wage higher than W_1. Illustrate this effect on the graph for industry A.

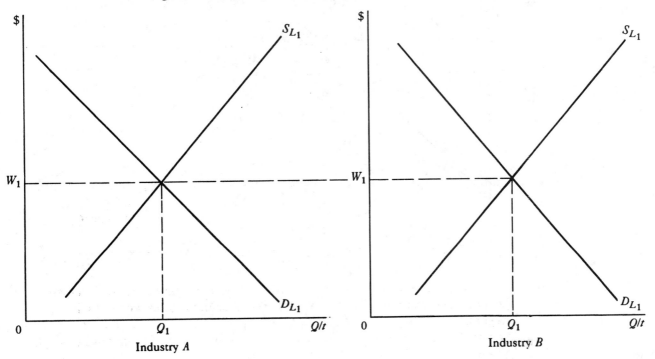

   b. What effect will this unionization have on industry B?

   c. Illustrate this change on the graph for industry B. Mark the new levels of wage and employment.

2. Trace the history of the U.S. labor movement by noting the important event(s) that occurred in each of the following years:

1867:

1869:

1886:

1932:

1935:

1947:

1959:

1977:

1978:

CHAPTER 15

RENT, INTEREST, AND PROFIT

CHECKING IN

Until now, our study of factor markets has focused on the labor market. In this chapter, we discuss the markets for land and capital and, in addition, give some consideration to the role of profits.

Land includes those factors of production that have a fixed supply. The return to the productive services of land is rent. The term *economic rent* describes a payment to a factor in excess of the amount necessary to bring that factor into production. Land is in fixed supply, and rent is determined by the level of demand. These two facts led Henry George to suggest replacing all taxes with a single tax on land. George maintained that this single tax could raise money for government without affecting economic activity or the supply of land. However, such a tax would have a negative effect on the efficient allocation of land among competing uses.

Capital is a produced factor of production. Like the other factors, it is demanded by firms because it is productive. Capital receives the payment of interest. Because the marginal revenue product curve of capital is downward sloping, less capital is acquired when interest rates rise. Government entry into the market for loanable funds can drive up the interest rate. This is called crowding out, because the higher interest rates crowd households and businesses out of the market for loanable funds.

After labor, land, and capital have been paid, any remaining revenue is profit. Profit is the residual that goes to entrepreneurs. Entrepreneurs try to increase their profits by increasing their monopoly power, taking uninsurable risks, and introducing innovations. The presence or absence of profits acts as a signal for other firms to enter or leave certain industries.

Marginal productivity theory tells us that each factor of production will be paid according to its productivity. This market-determined distribution is the natural outcome of market forces, and it may or may not be considered fair.

Chapter 15   Rent, Interest, and Profit   221

TRYING OUT THE TERMS

Match each of the following terms with its definition, and then check your answers. If you are having trouble, go back to the text and find the definition there.

_____ 1. capitalized value   _____ 4. demand-determined price

_____ 2. roundabout production   _____ 5. distributive justice

_____ 3. functional distribution of income

A. A price that is determined solely by changes in demand because supply is perfectly inelastic.

B. The present value of a stream of future rent payments.

C. The creation of physical capital (such as tools) that enhances productive capacity and ultimately allows increased output of consumer goods and services.

D. A normative argument for a particular distribution of income.

E. The pattern of payments to the productive resources (rent, wages, interest, and profits).

TESTING YOURSELF

In the next three sections, you will answer questions and work problems that are based on information in the text. Master all of the terms before you begin these sections. Work each section without referring to your notes or the text, and then check your answers.

Part I: True or False

Mark each statement as true or false. Whenever you mark a statement as false, jot down a sentence stating why it is false.

_____ 1. Productive resources with a supply fixed by nature are called land.

_____ 2. When the supply curve is perfectly inelastic, a change in demand will affect only price.

_____ 3. Economic rent is a payment to a productive resource equal to the amount necessary to bring that resource into production.

222   *Chapter 15   Rent, Interest, and Profit*

_____ 4. If a person earns more in one job than she could in another equally attractive occupation, the difference between the two wages is economic rent.

_____ 5. Henry George suggested that a tax on land be used to augment the existing income and property taxes.

_____ 6. George maintained that if all of the unearned income associated with land were taxed away, the supply of land would diminish very little.

_____ 7. Increasing land prices can provide an incentive to make land more productive.

_____ 8. An important economic function of the price of land is allocating land to its most highly valued economic use.

_____ 9. The object of all production is to encourage saving and investment.

_____ 10. When a monkey pulls a stick out of a tree to use in extracting ants from an anthill, the monkey is engaging in roundabout production.

_____ 11. The risk premium is the difference between the nominal interest rate and the real interest rate.

_____ 12. If the government enters the market for loanable funds, it may drive up the interest rate and discourage business and consumer borrowing.

Chapter 15   Rent, Interest, and Profit   223

_____ 13. An increase in government borrowing will have no effect on a firm that represents only a miniscule part of the demand for loanable funds.

_____ 14. The presence of economic profits enhances the efficiency of the market.

_____ 15. Marginal productivity theory was developed by John Bates Clark.

_____ 16. The market will generate an even income distribution.

_____ 17. The statement "Corporate profits accounted for 11.9 percent of income in 1940" refers to the market-determined distribution of income.

Part II: Problems

1. Graph A below shows the marginal revenue product of capital (demand) curve for a single firm. Graph B shows the market for loanable funds. The firm is a very small part of the entire market for loanable funds.

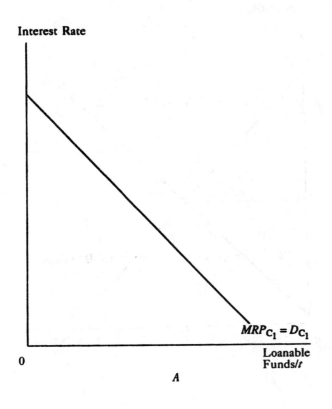
A

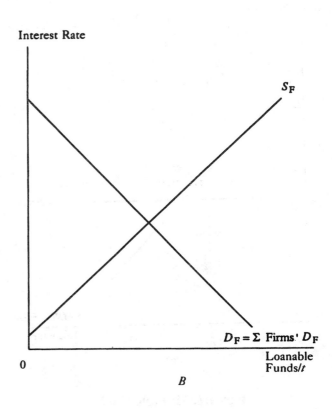
B

a. Draw the supply curve of loanable funds for this firm. Label the interest rate that it will pay and the quantity of funds that it will borrow.
b. Now suppose that this firm enrolls all of its factory employees in a training course that increases their productivity by 25 percent. What effect will this investment in human capital have on the firm's demand for and supply of loanable funds? Illustrate this on the graph.

Chapter 15 Rent, Interest, and Profit 225

2. The graphs below again illustrate the market for loanable funds for a firm and for the entire market. Suppose the government decides to fund its deficit by borrowing in the loanable funds market. What effect will this have on the market and the firm's demand for and supply of loanable funds? Illustrate these changes on the graphs.

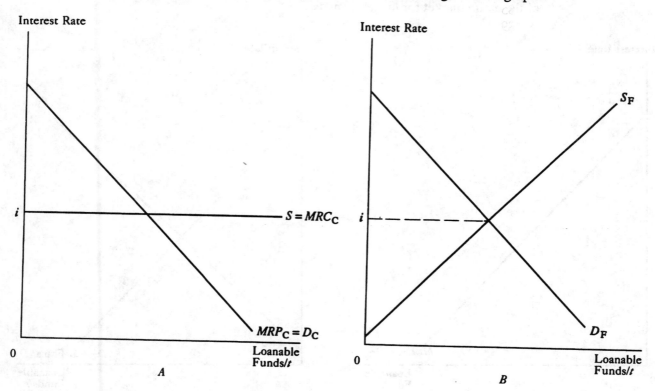

Part III: Multiple Choice

_____ 1. When people are willing to pay $15 for product Y, 200 units are sold. When people are willing to pay $6 for product Y, 200 units are sold. The price of product Y is
   a. not determined in the market.
   b. demand determined.
   c. fixed.
   d. not consistent with the law of demand.

_____ 2. The price of land is
   a. rent.
   b. surplus.
   c. the capitalized value of future rents.
   d. the capitalized value of historical rents.

_____ 3. James was earning $600 a week as a manager when he accepted a job as an investment banker for $300,000 a year. James is earning
   a. economic rent.
   b. more than his marginal revenue product.
   c. more than his marginal resource cost.
   d. an exploitative wage.

_____ 4. Mary Evans works as a secretary for $19,000 a year. She is offered a promotion to administrative assistant and a $10,000 raise. How much tax will Mary be willing to pay out of her raise if both jobs are equally attractive to her?
   a. $0.
   b. $5,000
   c. $9,999
   d. An amount that cannot be calculated from the information given

_____ 5. Henry George argued that a single tax on land would
   a. lead to greater income disparity between the rich and the poor.
   b. leave the supply of land unchanged.
   c. bring more land onto the market.
   d. encourage owners to make land more productive.

_____ 6. Economic rent
   a. serves no useful economic purpose.
   b. is paid only to land.
   c. is a short-run phenomenon.
   d. allocates land to its most highly valued use.

_____ 7. A good example of roundabout production would be
   a. hand-making a dress instead of using a sewing machine.
   b. producing goods for sale at home.
   c. making gardening tools in a factory.
   d. making dishes in a factory.

_____ 8. The market supply of loanable funds
   a. is upward sloping.
   b. comes from the personal savings of households.
   c. comes from businesses.
   d. is upward sloping and consists of funds from both businesses and households.

_____ 9. We observe a variety of interest rates because
   a. markets are imperfect.
   b. loans vary in both length and risk.
   c. both nominal and real rates are generally reported by the media.
   d. the Fed sets interest rates according to the type of market.

_____ 10. The real interest rate is the
   a. rate that is reported in the newspaper.
   b. rate given to a bank's best customers.
   c. nominal rate minus the expected rate of inflation.
   d. nominal rate plus the expected rate of inflation.

_____ 11. Whenever the government enters the market for loanable funds,
   a. private borrowing may be crowded out.
   b. the supply of loanable funds will increase.
   c. interest rates should fall.
   d. it can monopolize the market by prohibiting private borrowing.

Chapter 15   Rent, Interest, and Profit   227

_____ 12. All *except* which one of the following are ways an entrepreneur might seek to increase profits?
   a. Attempting to monopolize the industry
   b. Assuming only insurable risks
   c. Seeking innovative techniques and products
   d. Acquiring other firms

_____ 13. According to marginal productivity theory,
   a. income to a factor of production will increase as that factor's productivity increases.
   b. income will be distributed in proportion to the capital/labor/land ratio.
   c. profits should not be counted when income distribution is figured.
   d. income should be distributed according to law rather than market outcomes.

_____ 14. In 1990, the percentage of total U.S. income representing corporate profits was approximately
   a. 35 percent.
   b. 25 percent.
   c. 12 percent.
   d. 7 percent.

_____ 15. Since 1940, the smallest component of the functional distribution of income in the United States has been
   a. interest payments.
   b. rent.
   c. corporate profits.
   d. proprietors' income.

_____ 16. In a purely competitive factor market, the supply of and demand for productive resources will determine
   a. the functional distribution of income.
   b. a just distribution of income.
   c. the employment rate.
   d. the distributive justice rule.

TAKING ANOTHER LOOK

I.

Land can be in fixed supply even when it is underwater. Twenty-five years ago, about all you would see in the isolated waters off the coast of Maine were a few lonely lobster boats. Today, the same waters are jammed with the vessels of pleasure-seeking visitors. Moorings for boats are so scarce that some entrepreneurs are building marinas over prime lobster beds. The marina builders explain that a pleasure boater will be willing to pay $1,000 to tie up a boat for three months and that the pleasure boaters spend much more than the lobstermen. The lobstermen are angry and are calling for the city and state governments to limit the construction of marinas. If they are successful, what do you think will happen to the cost of mooring a boat in Maine for the summer?

228   *Chapter 15   Rent, Interest, and Profit*

II.

Iraq invaded Kuwait in the summer of 1990. The resulting fall in the oil supply caused the world price of oil, and gasoline, to increase dramatically. The OPEC countries faced a dilemma. They could increase the supply of oil to the world market and help maintain worldwide economic stability, or they could maintain the current level of production. Why would they want to do the latter? Because the new higher price was yielding them an economic rent (windfall profit) on each barrel of the fixed supply of oil that they chose to sell.

CHECKING OUT

Now that you have finished studying this chapter, you should be able to:

1. Describe the productive resource land and explain economic rent.

2. Explain the relationship between interest and capitalized value, crowding out, and roundabout production.

3. Itemize the sources of profit and the role that profit plays in a market economy.

4. Discuss and analyze the influences that help determine the distribution of income.

ANSWERS

Trying Out the Terms

1. B   4. A
2. C   5. D
3. E

Testing Yourself

Part I: True or False

1. true
2. true
3. false. Economic rent is a payment to a resource that is greater than the amount necessary to bring that resource into production.
4. true
5. false. He suggested that a tax on land be the only tax.
6. false. He believed that the supply of land was fixed and would be unaffected by a single tax.
7. true
8. true
9. false. The ultimate object of production is consumption.
10. true.
11. false. The risk premium is the difference between the T-bill interest rate and the interest rate to private borrowers for the same length of time.

Chapter 15 Rent, Interest, and Profit   229

12. true
13. false. A firm's supply curve of loanable funds is perfectly elastic (horizontal); therefore, when government borrowing causes market rates to increase, the firm's supply curve shifts up.
14. true
15. true
16. false. According to marginal productivity theory, factors are paid according to their productivity. This may produce a very unequal distribution of income.
17. true

Part II: Problems

1. a.

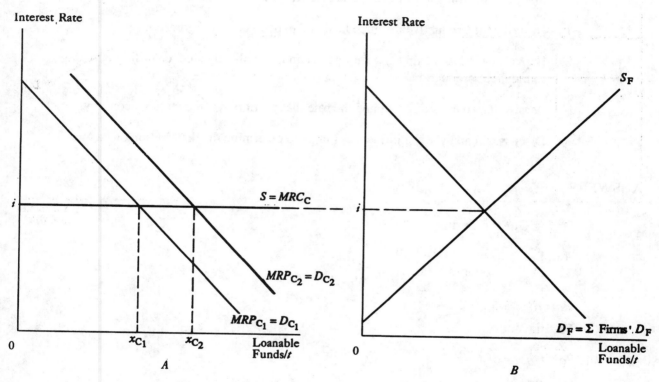

   b. The firm's MRP_c (demand curve) will shift to the right. The firm will obtain a greater quantity of loanable funds. The interest rate will not change. This firm is such a small part of the market that the shift of its demand curve will have no effect on the market. (See the graph above.)

2. The government's demand is huge, so it will shift the market demand curve and the interest rate will rise. This in turn will shift the firm's supply curve of loanable funds. The firm will now obtain fewer loanable funds at a higher interest rate. This is an example of crowding out. (See Figure below.)

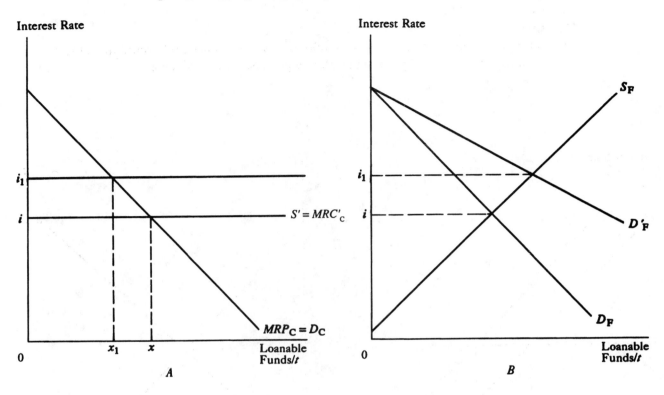

Part III: Multiple Choice

1. b
2. c
3. a
4. c
5. b
6. d
7. c
8. d
9. b
10. c
11. a
12. b
13. a
14. d
15. b
16. a

Chapter 15   Rent, Interest, and Profit

Name _____

CHAPTER 15 EXERCISES

The following table shows supply and demand data for a certain tract of land.

Price/Acre	S_0	D_0	D_1	D_2	D_3
$1,000	2,000	150	1,000	1,400	1,800
800	2,000	300	1,200	1,600	2,000
600	2,000	500	1,400	1,800	2,200
400	2,000	600	1,600	2,000	2,400
200	2,000	750	1,800	2,200	2,500
0	2,000	1,000	2,000	2,500	3,000

1. Graph and label the supply curve and the four demand curves.

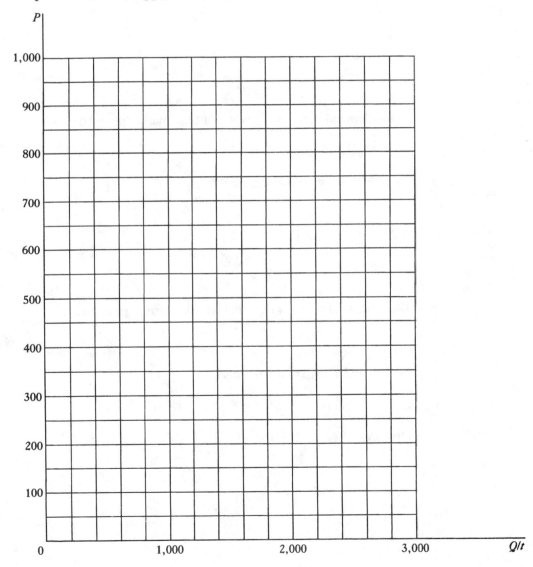

Chapter 15   Rent, Interest, and Profit   233

2. a. If the demand curve is D_0, what will the market price be?

Will there be any economic rent?

How much?

b. If the demand curve is D_1, what will the market price be?

Will there be any economic rent?

How much?

c. If the demand curve is D_2, what will the market price be?

Will there be any economic rent?

How much?

d. If the demand curve is D_3, what will the market price be?

Will there be any economic rent?

How much?

CHAPTER 16

POVERTY, INEQUALITY, AND INCOME REDISTRIBUTION POLICIES

CHECKING IN

Marginal productivity theory tells us that productive resources are paid according to the value placed on their productivity. To a large extent, this is true in the United States. This chapter discusses the nation's income distribution and then examines some instances when marginal productivity theory does not hold. Discrimination may prevent certain groups from earning the amounts the theory predicts. Sometimes individuals (or the nation as a whole) find the market distribution of income unsatisfactory and seek to change that distribution in a variety of ways.

Income distribution can be measured in two ways. The preceding chapter defined the functional distribution of income as the pattern of payments to the factors of production. In the United States, most income is in the form of wages and salaries. A personal distribution of income measures how income is divided among individuals or households. Personal income distributions are often illustrated with a Lorenz curve.

Discrimination occurs when equally productive individuals or groups of individuals are paid at different rates. Sometimes, what appears to be discrimination is really due to a difference in productivity or some objective choice. The existence of discrimination not only harms the individual worker but also impairs the economic efficiency of the entire nation. Market forces often eliminate discrimination, because it is costly to entrepreneurs. Profit-seeking employers can produce at a lower cost by not discriminating.

Many people view income redistribution as a public good and believe that the government must provide it. There are many reasons people support income redistribution: they may have interdependent utility functions; they may be insuring themselves against possible future poverty; they may view poverty as a negative externality; or they may want to transfer income to themselves through the political process. The United States has many income redistribution programs. Social Security is the largest. Some programs are aimed at equality of opportunity, whereas others seek equality of results. There is concern that redistribution programs may encourage people to not work. The negative income tax has often been suggested as a program that can provide a guaranteed minimum level of income without reducing the incentive to seek employment.

Chapter 16   Poverty, Inequality, and Income Redistribution Policies   235

TRYING OUT THE TERMS

Match each of the following terms with its definition, and then check your answers. If you are having trouble, go back to the text and find the definition there.

_____ 1. personal distribution of income   _____ 4. interdependent utility function

_____ 2. workfare   _____ 5. Gini coefficient

_____ 3. Lorenz curve

A. A measure of how total income is divided among individuals or households.

B. A graph showing the cumulative percentages of income received by various percentages of households.

C. A numerical measure of income equality equal to the area between the Lorenz curve and the diagonal divided by the area of the triangle below the diagonal on the Lorenz curve diagram.

D. Preference patterns in which the welfare of some individuals depends on the well-being of others.

E. State welfare programs requiring beneficiaries to take jobs or participate in training in order to remain eligible for benefits.

TESTING YOURSELF

In the next three sections, you will answer questions and work problems that are based on information in the text. Master all of the terms before you begin these sections. Work each section without referring to your notes or the text, and then check your answers.

Part I: True or False

Mark each statement as true or false. Whenever you mark a statement as false, jot down a sentence stating why it is false.

_____ 1. In the United States, income is primarily determined by productivity.

_____ 2. The statement "50 percent of the people in this country earn 80 percent of the income" refers to the personal distribution of income.

236   *Chapter 16   Poverty, Inequality, and Income Redistribution Policies*

_____ 3. If a country's Lorenz curve lies perfectly straight along the 45-degree line, income in that country is distributed in a perfectly even way.

_____ 4. Lorenz curves contain information about the absolute distribution of personal income.

_____ 5. Between 1980 and 1991, the poverty level in the United States remained relatively constant.

_____ 6. In the United States, measures of poverty include both cash and in-kind payments.

_____ 7. Thomas Sowell maintains that, because of discrimination, the monetary returns to education are less for members of minority groups than for the population at large.

_____ 8. One way of measuring discrimination against women is to compare the earnings of single men and single women.

_____ 9. Market forces should eliminate discrimination, because firms that hire women and minorities should be more profitable.

_____ 10. In the United States, most income redistribution comes from the private sector.

_____ 11. Redistribution policies designed to increase productivity have the goal of equality of results.

Chapter 16   Poverty, Inequality, and Income Redistribution Policies   237

_____ 12. Donations to a program that provides shoes for needy children are an example of specific egalitarianism.

_____ 13. George Stigler and Gordon Tullock argue that, because of political power, most income transfers go to the wealthy.

_____ 14. Transfers to the elderly have increased in the United States because the level of their wealth has fallen.

Part II: Problems

(The problems are based on material presented in Policy Focus.) Use the following equation in Problems 1-3:

$$W = IG - (t_n \times EI)$$

where W = welfare payment,
IG = income guarantee,
t_n = negative tax rate, and
EI = earned income.

1. Find t_n when

   a. $W = \$4,000$, $IG = \$20,000$, and $EI = \$40,000$.

   b. $W = \$10,000$, $IG = \$12,000$, and $EI = \$10,000$.

   c. $W = \$5,000$, $IG = \$8,000$, and $EI = \$5,000$.

2. Find W when

   a. $IG = \$5,000$, $t_n = 0.5$, and $EI = \$10,000$.

238   _Chapter 16   Poverty, Inequality, and Income Redistribution Policies_

b. $IG = \$5,000$, $t_n = 0.5$, and $EI = \$5,000$.

c. $IG = \$12,000$, $t_n = 0.333$, and $EI = \$9,000$.

d. $IG = \$12,000$, $t_n = 0.333$, and $EI = \$0$.

3. Find IG when

a. $W = \$5,000$, $t_n = 0.4$, and $EI = \$8,000$.

b. $W = \$12,000$, $t_n = 0.6$, and $EI = \$15,000$.

c. $W = \$10,000$, $t_n = 0.5$, and $EI = \$8,000$.

Part III: Multiple Choice

_____ 1. A Lorenz curve measures the _____ income distribution.
   a. functional
   b. personal
   c. absolute
   d. age-adjusted

_____ 2. The Lorenz curve of _____ would lie closest to the 45-degree line.
   a. Sweden
   b. the United States
   c. Mexico
   d. South Africa

_____ 3. If the personal income distribution of the United States is adjusted for life-cycle changes,
   a. the Lorenz curve becomes a straight line.
   b. the poverty rate increases.
   c. wealth effects dominate income effects.
   d. there is a trend toward a more equal distribution of income.

Chapter 16   Poverty, Inequality, and Income Redistribution Policies   239

4. According to Table 3 in the text chapter, in the United States the highest incidence of poverty is among
   a. all African-Americans.
   b. people over 65.
   c. households headed by African-Americans between 25 and 34.
   d. households headed by African-Americans over 65.

5. Wages may be higher in some occupations than in others if
   a. supply in the higher paying occupations is restricted by discriminatory practices.
   b. fewer workers have been channeled into the higher paying occupations.
   c. workers in the higher paying occupations are more productive.
   d. either supply in the higher paying occupations is restricted or fewer workers have been channeled into higher paying occupations.

6. Why may women and minorities earn less than white males?
   a. Less investment in human capital
   b. Channeling in specific occupations
   c. Lower productivity
   d. Discrimination
   e. All of the above

7. If paying for a foster child in New York City makes the Reynolds family of Cheyenne, Wyoming, feel better, they
   a. have interdependent utility functions.
   b. have regional interdependencies.
   c. have independent utility functions.
   d. are free riders.

8. When a person feels personal benefits from the reduction of poverty but refuses to participate to private redistribution, that person is
   a. a free rider.
   b. a general egalitarian.
   c. a specific egalitarian.
   d. irrational.

9. Private redistribution is more likely to take place if
   a. there is no public redistribution.
   b. it is done anonymously and in a large group.
   c. it is done in a small, homogeneous group.
   d. there are no externalities associated with poverty.

10. An elderly person living in poverty is more likely to benefit from a redistribution policy that
    a. seeks equality of opportunity.
    b. seeks equality of results.
    c. is based on productivity.
    d. encourages economic growth.

11. In the United States, income redistribution is carried out by
    a. the federal government.
    b. state and local governments.
    c. private organizations.
    d. all levels of government and private organizations.

12. The largest income redistribution program in the United States is
    a. Social Security.
    b. welfare.
    c. food stamps.
    d. agricultural supports.

13. Workfare programs require
    a. anyone who receives welfare to work.
    b. welfare recipients who are able to work to accept a job or enter a training program.
    c. welfare recipients to find jobs in the private sector.
    d. mothers of infants to work as day-care assistants.

14. A major attraction of the negative income tax is that
    a. it would cost less to implement than other types of distribution programs.
    b. the government could control the way recipients spend the money.
    c. it would not go to undeserving people.
    d. there is no income test involved.

15. The percentage of gross domestic product spent on social welfare programs is
    a. higher in the United States than in any other country.
    b. higher in the United States than in any other industrial country with the exception of Sweden.
    c. lower in the United States than in any other country.
    d. lower in the United States than in any other industrial country with the exception of Japan.

TAKING ANOTHER LOOK

It sometimes seems that those who live in poverty are condemned to continue there despite the best efforts of governments and individuals. Fortunately, this is not always the case; the market system and productivity-based distribution do produce happy endings—and beginnings.

In a recent *New York Times* column, Anthony Lewis recounts the story of a 10-year-old Vietnamese boy whose family arrived in the United States several years ago with only $200, which they spent on used winter coats. The family now owns a successful grocery store in Oregon, and the boy, now grown, is a graduate of Harvard Law School and clerks for Supreme Court Justice Sandra Day O'Connor.

Chapter 16   Poverty, Inequality, and Income Redistribution Policies

CHECKING OUT

Now that you have finished studying this chapter, you should be able to:

1. Describe the measurement of income distribution in the United States.

2. Explain how poverty is defined and the characteristics of those most likely to be poor.

3. Analyze the effects of discrimination on wage differences.

4. Summarize the arguments for and against the redistribution of income through government policy, and discuss the advantages and disadvantages of equality of opportunity versus equality of results strategies, and redistribution in kind versus in cash.

5. Describe current government transfer programs and proposals for policy reform.

ANSWERS

Trying Out the Terms

1.	A	4.	D
2.	E	5.	C
3.	B		

Testing Yourself

Part I: True or False

1. true
2. true
3. true
4. false. Lorenz curves provide information about the relative distribution of personal income.
5. true
6. false. They generally do not include in-kind payments and therefore overestimate the poverty rate.
7. false. Sowell argues that returns to education are higher for minority groups.
8. true
9. true
10. false. The public sector is responsible for most income redistribution in the United States.
11. false. The goal of these programs is equality of opportunity.
12. true
13. false. They maintain that, because of political power, most income transfers go to the middle class.
14. false. Although it is true that transfers to the elderly have increased, it is also true that their accumulated wealth has increased.

242   *Chapter 16   Poverty, Inequality, and Income Redistribution Policies*

Part II: Problems

1. a. $t_n = 0.4$
    b. $t_n = 0.2$
    c. $t_n = 0.6$
2. a. $W = \$0$
    b. $W = \$2,500$
    c. $W = \$9,003$
    d. $W = \$12,000$
3. a. $IG = \$8,200$
    b. $IG = \$21,000$
    c. $IG = \$14,000$

Part III: Multiple Choice

1. b	5. d	9. c	13. b
2. a	6. e	10. b	14. a
3. d	7. a	11. d	15. d
4. c	8. a	12. a	

Name _____

CHAPTER 16 EXERCISES

You are given the following income distribution information for the southern and western areas of the United States in 1985.

SOUTHERN UNITED STATES

Income Class	Upper Limit for Class	Percentage of Total Income	Cumulative Percentage
Lowest fifth	$11,795	4.5	_____
Second fifth	20,100	10.5	_____
Middle fifth	30,100	16.4	_____
Fourth fifth	45,119	24.1	_____
Highest fifth	73,847	44.6	_____

WESTERN UNITED STATES

Income Class	Upper Limit for Class	Percentage of Total Income	Cumulative Percentage
Lowest fifth	$14,592	4.9	_____
Second fifth	24,572	11.1	_____
Middle fifth	35,352	16.9	_____
Fourth fifth	50,900	24.0	_____
Highest fifth	82,742	43.1	_____

Source: U.S. Department of Commerce, *Statistical Abstract of the United States: 1989* (Washington DC: U.S. Government Printing Office, 1989).

1. a.   Calculate the cumulative percentage of income for each group.

Chapter 16   Poverty, Inequality, and Income Redistribution Policies

b. Graph each Lorenz curve.

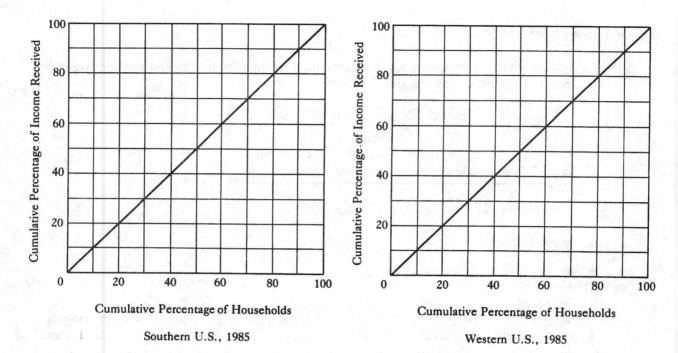

Southern U.S., 1985   Western U.S., 1985

2. a. In which region is there more relative poverty?

   b. In which region is there more absolute poverty?

   c. Which region will have a larger Gini coefficient?

CHAPTER 17

MARKET FAILURE AND GOVERNMENT INTERVENTION POLICIES

CHECKING IN

Markets *almost* always work. You have studied two instances of market failure: monopoly power and poverty. This chapter discusses what happens when markets don't work. Is there any way for society to produce a more desirable outcome? One way is to look to government to provide solutions. Government acts through its laws. As legislative bodies pass new laws and court decisions change existing laws, the economy is affected, sometimes intentionally, but sometimes as a side effect.

Externalities occur when some costs and/or benefits of production are not considered when economic decisions are made. Unrecognized social costs, or negative externalities, result in overproduction, whereas unrecognized social benefits, or positive externalities, result in underproduction. The Coase theorem suggests that market forces may resolve many externality problems when property rights are clearly defined and the number of people affected is small.

Because a public good is nonexcludable and nonrivalrous, the market will not provide enough of it; sometimes, the market will not provide a public good at all. Public goods are underproduced because some people, called free riders, will consume them without paying for them. Free-riding behavior means that a firm cannot expect to make a profit by producing a public good. Not all goods provided by the government are public goods; on the other hand, not all public goods are provided by the government.

The market does not solve the problems of monopoly, externalities, and public goods, so people often look to the government for solutions. The next chapter will discuss how the government deals with these situations.

Chapter 17   Market Failure and Government Intervention Policies   247

TRYING OUT THE TERMS

Match each of the following terms with its definition, and then check your answers. If you are having trouble, go back to the text and find the definition there.

_____ 1. Coase theorem   _____ 6. Clean Air Act

_____ 2. social costs   _____ 7. internalization

_____ 3. externalities   _____ 8. tort law

_____ 4. property law   _____ 9. eminent domain

_____ 5. tort   _____ 10. contract law

A. Law that concerns the enforcement of property rights.

B. Law that deals with intentional and unintentional wrongs inflicted by one party on another.

C. Law that deals with the enforcement of voluntary exchanges.

D. A doctrine that gives government the right to buy property at "fair market value" if the purchase is in the public interest.

E. A wrongful action (or failure to act) that causes damage to the person or property of another individual.

F. Costs or benefits associated with consumption or production that are not reflected in market prices and fall on parties other than the buyer or seller.

G. Costs that are borne by society or some group in society without compensation.

H. The incorporation of the social costs of negative external effects into the market price.

I. The idea that well-defined property rights are sufficient to internalize any external effect that is present, when there are small numbers of affected parties.

J. Federal law passed in 1970 that empowered the EPA to set emission standards and impose standards on polluters.

TESTING YOURSELF

In the next three sections, you will answer questions and work problems that are based on information in the text. Master all of the terms before you begin these sections. Work each section without referring to your notes or the text, and then check your answers.

248   *Chapter 17   Market Failure and Government Intervention Policies*

Part I: True or False

Mark each statement as true or false. Whenever you mark a statement as false, jot down a sentence stating why it is false.

_____ 1. Market failures frequently occur when property rights are not clearly defined.

_____ 2. Dandy Danny's sign reads "Money back if you are not satisfied." If Dandy Danny refuses to pay up when you are unhappy with one of his hamburgers, there may be a contract violation.

_____ 3. External costs cause underproduction.

_____ 4. Most economists agree that the market will eventually resolve the problems caused by externalities.

_____ 5. If firms properly internalized the costs of pollution, pollution levels would fall to zero.

_____ 6. Acid rain is a negative externality.

_____ 7. The Coase theorem holds that production can be increased if property rights are well defined.

_____ 8. If other store owners agree to pay to clean up an abandoned store front on Main Street, they are following the Coase theorem.

Chapter 17   Market Failure and Government Intervention Policies   249

_____ 9. When the government imposes a tax on individuals or firms that pollute the air, it is forcing cost internalization.

_____ 10. Public goods are goods provided by the government.

_____ 11. If Janie listens to the local public radio station without sending in a contribution, she is imposing an external cost.

_____ 12. If there were no public goods, there would be no free riders.

_____ 13. Although there is no market for public goods, the demand curve for these goods can easily be determined through the political process.

_____ 14. Governments provide both public and private goods.

_____ 15. Steven Cheung found that externalities may have more negative effects than had previously been supposed.

Part II: Problems

1. The following schedules show the private demand (D_p), external benefits (*EB*), and supply schedule for a product with substantial positive externalities. You should be aware of two things in working this problem. First, you must sum vertically (add the relevant price for each quantity). Second, in this case external benefits are constant.

250   *Chapter 17   Market Failure and Government Intervention Policies*

Quantity	Price/Private Demand (D_p)	Price/External Benefit (EB)	Price/Combined Demand ($D_p + EB$)	Price/Supply
2	$18	$8	_____	$10
4	16	8	_____	12
6	14	8	_____	14
8	12	8	_____	16
10	10	8	_____	18
12	8	8	_____	20

a. Complete the schedule for combined demand ($D_p + EB$), and graph all the schedules.

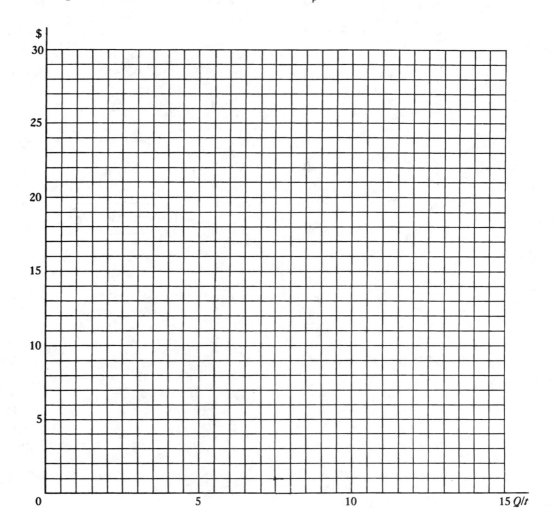

Chapter 17 *Market Failure and Government Intervention Policies*

b. When only private demand and supply interact, what price and quantity will prevail?

c. If external benefits are taken into account, what price and quantity will prevail?

2. The following schedules show the marginal costs (*MC*), the social costs (*SC*), and the demand for a product with substantial external costs.

Quantity	Price/Marginal Costs (*MC*)	Price/Social Costs (*SC*)	Price/Total Supply (*MC* + *SC*)	Price/ Demand
0	$0	$0	$0	$40
1	5	2	_____	37
2	10	4	_____	34
3	15	6	_____	31
4	20	8	_____	28
5	25	10	_____	25
6	30	12	_____	22

252   *Chapter 17   Market Failure and Government Intervention Policies*

a. Complete the schedule of the true supply curve (*MC* + *SC*), and graph all the schedules. Once again, you sum vertically.

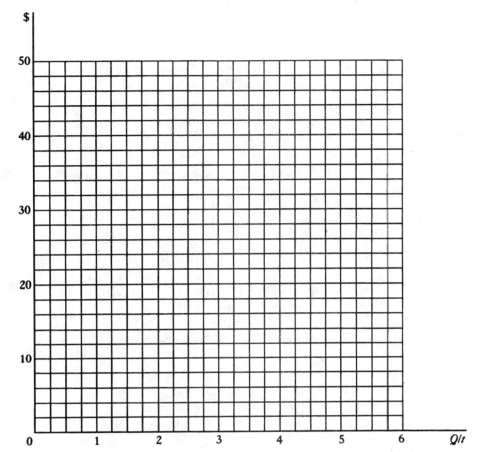

b. When only private demand and supply interact, what price and quantity will prevail?

c. If external costs are taken into account, what price and quantity will prevail?

Part III: Multiple Choice

_____ 1. Property law would be involved if
   a. a trespassing child fell into your beautiful Japanese fish pond.
   b. a careless waiter dumped orange juice down your back.
   c. a rock star failed to appear for a concert.
   d. your microwave oven wouldn't cook.

2. The inoculation of children against contagious diseases is an example of a
   a. private good with social benefits.
   b. private good with social costs.
   c. purely private good.
   d. purely public good.

3. When Mesa Petroleum built a park in front of its corporate office, it was
   a. imposing external costs on its shareholders.
   b. providing external benefits to the community.
   c. assuming some of the responsibilities of government.
   d. providing a purely public good.

4. When a negative externality is present, how do price and output compare to what they would be in an optimal solution?
   a. Price is the same, but output is too low.
   b. Price is too high, and output is too low.
   c. Price is too low, and output is too high.
   d. Price is too low, and output is the same.

5. A firm will take social costs into account if
   a. it is a good corporate citizen.
   b. the government forces it to internalize all costs.
   c. it is able to offer social benefits equal to the social costs.
   d. its product is a public good.

6. The pollution level would be reduced to zero if
   a. firms were forced to internalize their costs.
   b. the marginal social costs of pollution were equal to the marginal social benefits.
   c. the production process causing pollution was halted.
   d. either firms were forced to internalize their costs or the marginal social costs of pollution were equal to the marginal social benefits.

7. The government can force firms to internalize external costs by
   a. placing a tax on the firm equal to the external costs.
   b. charging the firm a fee equal to the external costs.
   c. paying the firm to correct the externality.
   d. either placing a tax or charging a fee that is equal to the external costs.

8. Firms impose external costs because
   a. they do not consider costs that they don't have to pay.
   b. they are unaware of them.
   c. production drops to zero if costs are internalized.
   d. All of the above

9. For the Coase theorem to apply,
   a. property rights must be clearly defined.
   b. a small number of individuals must be involved.

Chapter 17   *Market Failure and Government Intervention Policies*

    c.   there must be no external costs.

    d.   property rights must be clearly defined and also only a small number of individuals must be involved.

10. State Street Jazz Club has begun having post-lunch concerts in its building next door to Happy Hours Day Care. According to the Coase theorem,
    a.   Happy Hours can't do anything except switch naptime to before lunch.
    b.   Happy Hours can pay State Street to switch the concert to before lunch.
    c.   State Street can pay to soundproof a room for Happy Hours.
    d.   the room can be soundproofed or the concert switched, but who pays depends on how property rights are defined.

11. The Coase theorem states that
    a.   production will be the same, regardless of how property rights are defined.
    b.   income distribution will be the same, regardless of how property rights are defined.
    c.   property rights should be assigned to the party imposing the externality.
    d.   costs can never be fully internalized.

12. The government is often reluctant to impose controls on externalities because
    a.   it is hard to measure the true social costs.
    b.   it is easy to make a mistake.
    c.   enforcement is expensive.
    d.   All of the above

13. The free-rider problem occurs
    a.   only when people are excluded from consumption of a public good.
    b.   more often in large groups than in small groups.
    c.   when the government becomes involved in what is essentially a market problem.
    d.   when the government makes in-kind rather than cash distributions.

14. A good is considered a public good if it is
    a.   provided by the government.
    b.   nonrivalrous in consumption.
    c.   nonexcludable in consumption.
    d.   both nonrivalrous and nonexcludable.

15. Many economists regard education as
    a.   a purely private good.
    b.   a purely public good.
    c.   a private good with some characteristics of a public good.
    d.   most efficient when it is provided by the market.

16. Welfare economics deals with
    a.   normative policy prescriptions.
    b.   positive approaches to income redistribution.
    c.   statistically measuring levels of national well-being.
    d.   finding market solutions to both positive and negative externalities.

Chapter 17   Market Failure and Government Intervention Policies

TAKING ANOTHER LOOK

Free-riding keeps public goods from being provided by the market. Most people won't pay for something they can have at no cost. Why are most fireworks shows free? One way to avoid this problem is by tying the public good to the purchase of a private good. The fireworks show might follow a concert by a popular group. The ticket price would reflect both the performance and the fireworks. Of course, there would still be folks parked by the side of the road, but they didn't get to hear the concert.

CHECKING OUT

Now that you have finished studying this chapter, you should be able to:

1. Describe the economic and policy impact of property law, tort law, and contract law.

2. Define externalities and explain how the Coase theorem can resolve some externality problems.

3. Explain how free-riding behavior results in the underproduction of public goods.

4. Evaluate the public goods aspects of income redistribution and education.

5. Discuss welfare economics.

ANSWERS

Trying Out the Terms

1. I	4. A	7. H	10. C
2. G	5. E	8. B	
3. F	6. J	9. D	

Testing Yourself

Part I: True or False

1. true
2. true
3. false. External costs cause overproduction.
4. false. In the case of externalities, the majority of economists believes that there is a legitimate role for government in the market.
5. false. Pollution levels would fall to zero only if production of the good in question fell to zero.
6. true
7. false. The Coase theorem states that production will be the same regardless of who has the property rights, as long as the number of people affected is small and the property rights are clearly defined.
8. true
9. true
10. false. Public goods are goods that are nonexcludable and nonrivalrous. They are provided by government and the private sector.

256   *Chapter 17   Market Failure and Government Intervention Policies*

11. false. She is enjoying an external benefit. She is also a free rider.
12. true
13. false. Whenever there is a public good, there will be free riders who will hide their demand for the good. It is also very difficult for individuals to place a monetary value on such public goods as defense and police protection.
14. true
15. false. In studying bees and apple orchards, Cheung found that markets work very well in correcting externalities and that there may be fewer market failures than we thought.

Part II: Problems

1. a.

Quantity	Price/Private Demand (D_p)	Price/External Benefit (EB)	Price/Combined Demand ($D_p + EB$)	Price/ Supply
2	$18	$8	$26	$10
4	16	8	24	12
6	14	8	22	14
8	12	8	20	16
10	10	8	18	18
12	8	8	16	20

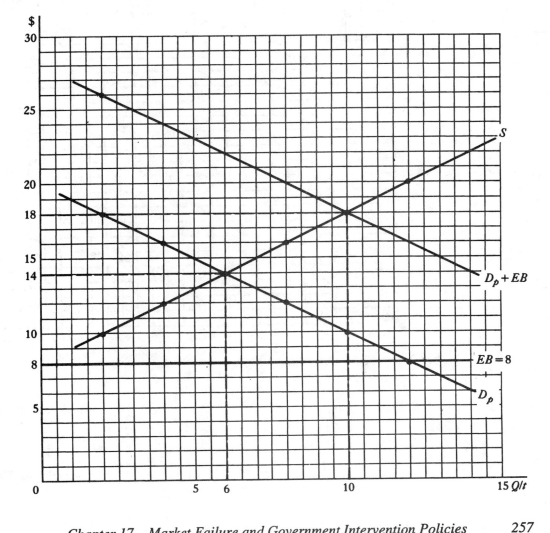

Chapter 17 Market Failure and Government Intervention Policies

b. price = $14; quantity = 6
   c. price = $18; quantity = 10

2. a.

Quantity	Price/Marginal Costs (MC)	Price/Social Costs (SC)	Price/Total Supply (MC + SC)	Price/ Demand
0	$ 0	$ 0	$ 0	$40
1	5	2	7	37
2	10	4	14	34
3	15	6	21	31
4	20	8	28	28
5	25	10	35	25
6	30	12	42	22

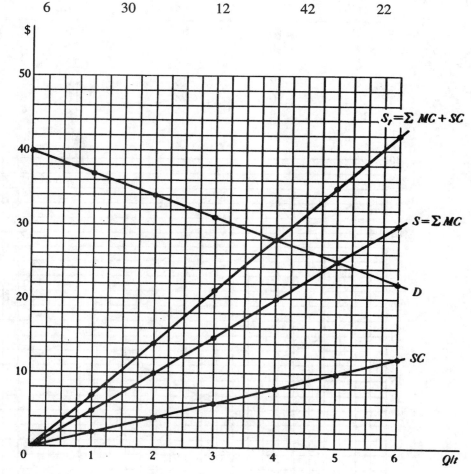

   b. price = $25; quantity = 5
   c. price = $28; quantity = 4

Part III: Multiple Choice

1. a   5. b   9. d   13. b
2. a   6. c   10. d   14. d
3. b   7. d   11. a   15. c
4. c   8. a   12. d   16. a

258   *Chapter 17   Market Failure and Government Intervention Policies*

Name _____

CHAPTER 17 EXERCISES

Joe and Carol own the only houses on an isolated road. They are considering hiring a private security service to drive by their houses on a regular basis. The firm charges $80 for each drive-by. Joe and Carol have the following demand schedule for this service:

	Quantity Demanded	
Price	By Carol	By Joe
$80	0	0
70	0	0
60	0	1
50	0	2
40	1	3
30	2	4
20	3	5
10	4	6

1. Clearly, neither of them will employ the service if he or she has to pay for it alone. Since they can use the service jointly (one drive-by will cover both houses), they can combine their demands. Fill in their combined demand schedule. (Note: This is rather tricky, since you are summing vertically. For each quantity, add the price Joe is willing to pay and the price Carol is willing to pay. Two entries have been made for you.)

Quantity	Price	
0		
1	100	($40 + $60)
2	80	($30 + $50)
3	_____	
4	_____	
5	_____	
6	_____	
7	_____	

Chapter 17   Market Failure and Government Intervention Policies   259

2. Graph their individual demand curves and their combined demand curve on the following graph.

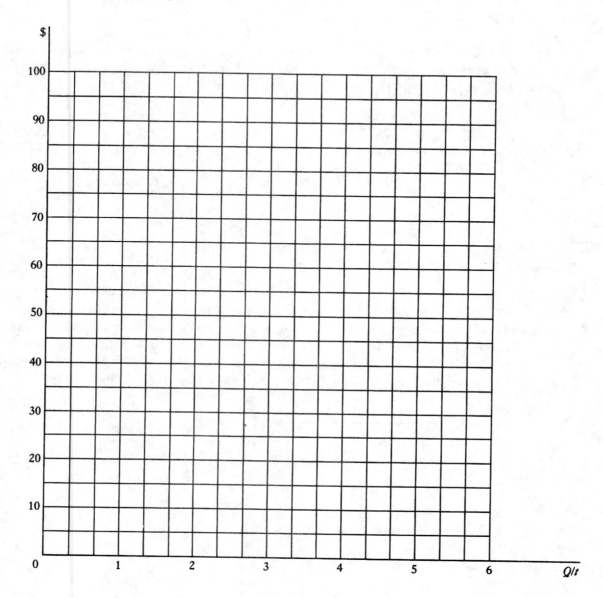

3. If they combine their demands, how many drive-bys will Joe and Carol purchase and what will their combined expenditures be?

260 Chapter 17 *Market Failure and Government Intervention Policies*

CHAPTER 18

GOVERNMENT FAILURE AND PUBLIC CHOICE

CHECKING IN

The preceding chapter discussed several ways in which markets can fail. It concluded by stating that many people look to the government to correct market failures. This chapter considers some of the ways governments attempt to correct market failures and the related costs. Public choice theory is one method of evaluating government provision of public and private goods.

When economic decisions are made through the political process, there are strong incentives for individuals and groups to attempt to affect the outcome. Rent seeking occurs when individuals or groups attempt to generate transfers to themselves. Politicians may respond by attempting to extract rent in exchange for legislation favorable to certain individuals or groups. Consumers' defense of their consumer surplus against rent seekers is called rent defending.

Many economists believe that political decision making and public provision of goods lead to an excessively large government. Logrolling, or vote trading, makes government too big, because the beneficiaries of government programs do not have to bear the entire costs of these programs. Bureaucracy and bureaucratic decision making lead to a large government because the system provides incentives to maximize budgets instead of minimizing costs. Although it is necessary to have some government involvement in a market economy, the degree of involvement varies. Sometimes a government function can be provided more efficiently by relying on the market. Privatization occurs when government activities and/or assets are transferred to the private sector.

Two additional approaches to explaining government failure come from the Austrian school of economic thought and radical economics. The Austrian economists assume that decision makers have incomplete information. They oppose economic planning by governments. Radical economics is based on the belief that government protects capitalist monopolies, which exploit workers and Third World countries.

Chapter 18   Government Failure and Public Choice   261

TRYING OUT THE TERMS

Match each of the following terms with its definition, and then check your answers. If you are having trouble, go back to the text and find the definition there.

_____ 1. rent seeking

_____ 2. dual labor markets

_____ 3. privatization

_____ 4. logrolling

_____ 5. rent defending

_____ 6. median voter theorem

A. The commitment of scarce resources to capture returns created artificially.

B. Actions by consumers to keep their consumer surplus from being captured by rent seekers.

C. A theorem that predicts that under majority rule, politicians will reflect the positions of voters near the center of the political spectrum.

D. Vote trading in the legislative process.

E. The transfer of governmental activities and/or assets to the private sector.

F. The radical economists' idea that there are two labor markets because of artificial barriers that keep some workers earning low wages.

TESTING YOURSELF

In the next three sections, you will answer questions and work problems that are based on information in the text. Master all of the terms before you begin these sections. Work each section without referring to your notes or the text, and then check your answers.

Part I: True or False

Mark each statement as true or false. Whenever you mark a statement as false, jot down a sentence stating why it is false.

_____ 1. Public choice economics combines economics and sociology.

_____ 2. According to public choice theory, politicians will usually vote for programs that benefit a few and distribute costs widely.

262   Chapter 18   Government Failure and Public Choice

_____ 3. William C. Mitchell argues that a proposal that taxes market efficiency stands a better chance of adoption than a proposal that rewards efficiency.

_____ 4. An important defense contractor takes a congressional representative to lunch and happens to discuss how a new contract could benefit her firm, she is extracting rent.

_____ 5. The congressional repeal of a law requiring warranties on used cars is a good example of a milker bill.

_____ 6. In W. C. Nicholson's campaign for mayor, he has taken the position that the local marina should be closed for the winter season. His opponent maintains that it should be open year round. Public opinion is mixed. According to the median voter theorem, as election day approaches, each candidate will continue to hold the same position.

_____ 7. If a senator from Arkansas votes for a bill to build a military base in Mississippi because he expects the senator from Mississippi to vote for a bill to build a new highway across Arkansas, they are conducting yellow-dog politics.

_____ 8. The efficiency of a bureau is usually evaluated in terms of some measurable output.

_____ 9. Because the U.S. economy is market-controlled, privatization is not an issue.

_____ 10. The basic premise of the Austrian school of economic thought is that markets are basically stable and operate with full information.

Chapter 18   Government Failure and Public Choice   263

_____ 11. The Austrian school of economics holds that many macroeconomic problems have their roots in microeconomic political maneuvering.

_____ 12. Radical economists base some of their thinking of the works of Karl Marx.

_____ 13. Radical economists view the state as the adversary of monopoly power.

_____ 14. Low voter turnout in the United States appears to be irrational and can be attributed primarily to voter apathy.

_____ 15. Because the government grants a monopoly to the mail service, it has no competition.

Part II: Problem

1. The following graph illustrates a monopoly market that is operating without government intervention.

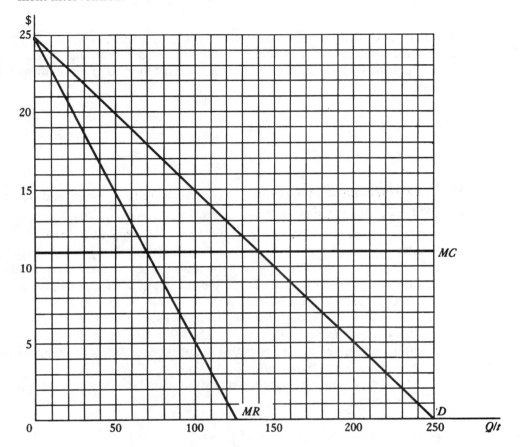

   a. What price will the monopolist charge? What quantity will be sold?

   b. What would the price and quantity be if this were a competitive market?

   c. What would the consumer surplus be in a competitive market?

   d. What would the consumer surplus be in a monopoly market?

_____ e. If the government seeks to regulate this market, how much will the monopolist be willing to spend on rent seeking?

_____ f. If consumers defend their consumer surplus (rent defending) and the monopolist counters with rent seeking, what is the most the two groups will spend?

Part III: Multiple Choice

_____ 1. Suppose Representative Tate proposes that the state fund college scholarships for all students who graduate from high school with an average of B or better, but that this scholarship not go into effect until the class entering first grade this year graduates (12 years from now). This proposal will have the best chance of being adopted if
   a. Representative Tate makes clear the amount of taxes that will have to be collected in order to fund the project.
   b. the proposal is accompanied by a clearly stated plan for an increase in the sales tax to fund the plan.
   c. Representative Tate suggests that the plan be funded only after the scholarships are in place, since it is difficult to predict what they will cost.
   d. the plan is contingent on funding by the school districts where the high schools are located.

_____ 2. A politician who attempts to build a coalition of rent-seeking groups by brokering transfers to those groups is
   a. rent seeking.
   b. acting like an entrepreneur.
   c. breaking the law.
   d. logrolling.

_____ 3. Consumers' use of political pressure to resist monopolies is called
   a. rent defending.
   b. rent extracting.
   c. applying the Tiebout solution.
   d. coalition monitoring.

_____ 4. Senator Jones accepts a campaign donation from the Association of Lady Bug Raisers. The next week he introduces a bill declaring the lady bug the national insect. This is called
   a. rent extracting.
   b. logrolling.
   c. pork-barrel politics.
   d. both logrolling and pork-barrel politics.

266   _Chapter 18   Government Failure and Public Choice_

5. Chip McGuire visits the courthouse to show the county commissioners his new jail-security system and to invite them all to a barbeque at his ranch. Chip is being a
   a. yellow dog.
   b. rent seeker.
   c. rent extractor.
   d. perfect competitor.

6. Logrolling tends to create an excessively large government because
   a. it results in many projects with dispersed benefits.
   b. that is the optimal level of public output.
   c. local beneficiaries of government projects believe that someone else is paying for them.
   d. projects are determined by bureaucrats rather than by a legislature.

7. The transfers of government assets and/or activities to the private sector is called
   a. pro-market implementation.
   b. deficit financing.
   c. privatization.
   d. private sector initiative.

8. Some social critics have suggested using a voucher system for public education because it would
   a. introduce competition into public education.
   b. improve the quality of public education.
   c. increase the quantity of public education.
   d. All of the above

9. The theories of the Austrian school of economics are very close to those of
   a. public choice economists.
   b. political scientists.
   c. libertarians.
   d. classical economists.

10. All *except* which one of the following is among Hayek's arguments against government planning?
    a. Planning results in more planning.
    b. No plan can cover all details.
    c. High morale destroys the planning process.
    d. Planning often leads to a dictatorship.

11. Economists of the Austrian school think that
    a. most problems can be solved by market forces.
    b. the economy would be improved by industrial restructuring.
    c. orthodox economic analysis is too narrow.
    d. All of the above

Chapter 18   Government Failure and Public Choice   267

_____ 12. Radical economists maintain that individuals in a capitalistic society
   a. feel alienated because they are prevented from purchasing a high level of consumption goods.
   b. are not able to participate in a dual labor market.
   c. feel alienated because they have little control over their own destinies.
   d. waste money on consumer goods because they are unemployed and have nothing else to do.

_____ 13. The most serious weakness of the modern radical critique is that
   a. industrial capitalism does not exist in the United States.
   b. their proposals for change are very costly.
   c. their proposals for change would lead to high levels of unemployment.
   d. they point out weaknesses without suggesting solutions.

_____ 14. In analyzing third-world development, radical economists
   a. follow traditional Marxist theory.
   b. assert that industrial capitalists export excessively complex technology to underdeveloped countries.
   c. assert that industrial capitalists drain capital from underdeveloped countries.
   d. oppose exporting luxuries to underdeveloped countries.

_____ 15. The theory of dual labor markets holds that
   a. marginal productivity theory mirrors reality.
   b. capitalists intentionally hold down the pay of certain groups.
   c. pay should accurately reflect the level of investment in human capital.
   d. markets provide different levels of pay arbitrarily.

TAKING ANOTHER LOOK

Behavior that supports the median voter theorem can be observed in the marketplace as well as the voting booth. Many times consumers are referred to as voters, with firms competing for their dollar "votes." Firms sometimes face the dilemma of having to choose between advertising to women who are full-time homemakers and advertising to women who are employed. Some believe that to target one group is to risk putting off the other. According to a _Wall Street Journal_ article, some markets resolve the dilemma by portraying women in their ads in a manner suggestive of either a professional women or a homemaker. For example, they might show a woman holding both a dust cloth and a cellular telephone. This attempt to avoid either extreme is similar to the political maneuvering described in the text.

CHECKING OUT

Now that you have finished studying this chapter, you should be able to:

1. Examine the implications of self-interested behavior in the public sector (public choice) as a cause of government failure.

2. Develop the concept of rent seeking.

3. Analyze the effects of rent defending.

4. Explain why government grows in terms of logrolling and bureaucratic incentives and why regulation creates a bias against new products and new technology.

5. List some of the methods of privatization.

6. Identify the contributions of the Austrian school and radical economics to understanding governmental failure.

ANSWERS

Trying Out the Terms

1. A   5. B
2. F   6. C
3. E
4. D

Testing Yourself

Part I: True or False

1. false. Public choice economics combines economics and political science.
2. true
3. true
4. false. She is rent seeking. The congressional representative may be extracting rent.
5. true
6. false. By election day they should both have moved toward the center. Mr. Nicholson will say it shouldn't be closed all season, and his opponent will suggest it not be open all the time.
7. false. They are logrolling.
8. false. Because bureaus produce activities rather than goods, they are usually evaluated on the basis of the size of expenditures on these activities.
9. false. Many goods and services provided by the government are candidates for privatization.
10. false. The Austrian school holds that individuals make economic decisions in a state of partial ignorance.
11. true
12. true
13. false. In the radical view, the state protects big business and monopolies.
14. false. Low voter turnout can be seen as a result of the determination by rational voters that the costs of voting outweigh the benefits.
15. false. The postal service is selling communication. While it may have a monopoly on one means of distribution, it still suffers competition from the telephone, faxes, and private delivery services.

Chapter 18   Government Failure and Public Choice   269

Part II: Problem

1. a. price = $18; quantity = 70
   b. price = $11; quantity = 140
   c. Consumer surplus is $980, which is the area of the triangle formed by the price axis above the competitive price, the demand curve, and the competitive quantity.
      1/2[($25 − $11) × 140] = $980
   d. Consumer surplus is $245, which is the area of the triangle formed by the price axis above the monopoly price, the demand curve, and the monopoly quantity.
      1/2[($25 − $18) × 70] = $245
   e. $490 = ($18 − $11) × 70
   f. $1,470 = $735 × 2. The area of rent defense is the surplus consumers stand to lose without regulation:
      [($18 − $11) × 70] + 1/2[($18 − $11) × 70] = $490 + $245 = $735

Part III: Multiple Choice

1. c	5. b	9. a	13. d
2. b	6. a	10. c	14. a
3. a	7. c	11. a	15. b
4. a	8. d	12. c	

Name _____

CHAPTER 18 EXERCISES

Recently, newspapers have reported that some drug addicts are so desperate for treatment that they commit crimes just so they can be sentenced to prison, where they can receive treatment. The reason they are doing this is that government-funded drug treatment centers are full and have long waiting lists, and these people do not have the money for private treatment.

Suppose the government decides to privatize the existing government-funded drug treatment centers in order to provide more efficient treatment. The text lists seven methods that governments can use to privatize a government service. Consider each of them, then select three of these methods that you think might provide a feasible solution. Give an example of how each could be implemented, and list some potential problems that might crop up.

1.

2.

3.

Chapter 18   Government Failure and Public Choice   271

CHAPTER 19

POLICY STUDIES: CITIES, THE ENVIRONMENT, AND HEALTH CARE

CHECKING IN

The two preceding chapters discussed a number of economic theories that address the problems of market and government failures. In this chapter, you will examine closely three areas in which such failures often occur: cities, the environment, and health care.

Cities come in an assortment of sizes. They are established and grow or stagnate because of the benefits and costs of living in groups. These benefits and costs are called economies of agglomeration and diseconomies of agglomeration, respectively. The best size for any particular city will be that size where the difference between the benefits and the costs of agglomeration is greatest.

One function of local government is to provide public goods of a local nature, such as police and fire protection. Often the correct level of services is difficult to determine because the benefits of the local public good may spill over into another jurisdiction that is not paying for it. Local governments may attempt to charge nonresidents user fees. Another solution, suggested by Tiebout, may be competition between adjacent cities, which will cause people to move to the location with the most desirable combination of taxes and services.

When a resource is a common access resource—one that is jointly owned by many people—it is often overused. The owners consider the benefits but not the cost of consuming it. This situation is called the tragedy of the commons. Overfishing of certain varieties of ocean fish and the disappearance of the American buffalo are examples of this situation. Governments can avert such tragedies by assigning property rights to the resource or by establishing regulations for the use of the resource. This problem is compounded when the resource is a global common, such as the oceans held in common by many nations.

In the past two decades, the health care industry has grown at an astonishing rate. Increasing costs coupled with increases in demand have created spiraling prices, which absorb an alarming share of GDP. The issue has become one of national importance and debate.

Chapter 19   Policy Studies: Cities, the Environment, and Health Care   273

TRYING OUT THE TERMS

Match each of the following terms with its definition, and then check your answers. If you are having trouble, go back to the text and find the definition there.

_____ 1. tragedy of the commons

_____ 2. diseconomies of agglomeration

_____ 3. Tiebout hypothesis

_____ 4. economies of agglomeration

_____ 5. common access resource

_____ 6. user charges

A. The cost savings that individuals enjoy when enough of them locate close together in or near a large city.

B. The additional costs that individuals must pay when too many of them locate in one city (thus creating negative external effects for one another).

C. Fees that cover part or all of the cost of a public service.

D. The idea that competition among local governments as suppliers of local public services will force them to offer the desired combination of spending and taxing to voters, who will migrate to those jurisdictions that produce that combination.

E. A resource that is not owned by any individual but is available for all to use.

F. The overuse of common access resources.

TESTING YOURSELF

In the next two sections, you will answer questions that are based on information in the text. Master all of the terms before you begin these sections. Work each section without referring to your notes or the text, and then check your answers.

Part I: True or False

Mark each statement as true or false. Whenever you mark a statement as false, jot down a sentence stating why it is false.

_____ 1. The many discount outlets clustered along interstate highways, such as I–75 in Georgia and Florida, are an example of economies of agglomeration.

_____ 2. Optimal city size is best determined by local zoning boards.

274   *Chapter 19   Policy Studies: Cities, the Environment, and Health Care*

_____ 3. When small towns lose population, they are usually able to maintain their downtown business and shopping districts.

_____ 4. When significant spillovers are present, crime prevention will be underprovided.

_____ 5. Revenue sharing is not effective in correcting interjurisdictional externalities.

_____ 6. The Tiebout hypothesis suggests that people will express their preference for local public goods by moving about until they find communities that offer what they are looking for.

_____ 7. Based on the example of mass transit, it appears that it is easier to measure the costs of providing a positive externality than to measure the benefits of that externality.

_____ 8. When shrimpers in the Gulf of Mexico continue to catch shrimp, even though they know they are exhausting the population, they are attempting to run the competition out of business.

_____ 9. Because the Brazilian rain forests represent a global commons, one approach to maintaining them would be for other countries to pay Brazil to restrict deforestation.

_____ 10. The use of high-sulfur coal in electrical generation is a source of acid rain.

_____ 11. Most hazardous waste problems are the result of surreptitious dumping.

Chapter 19   Policy Studies: Cities, the Environment, and Health Care

_____ 12. In the United States, spending on health care tripled between 1985 and 1995.

_____ 13. The increasing cost of health care would have been even greater had not supply increased as demand increased.

_____ 14. Improved levels of health care should lead to a fall in demand for health care because people are heathier.

_____ 15. Under the Clinton plan, rich people will pay more for health care and poor people won't pay at all.

Part II: Multiple Choice

_____ 1. The growth of suburban governments surrounding large cities may
   a. cause needless duplication of government services.
   b. make governments more sensitive to voter demands.
   c. contribute to the free-rider problem.
   d. both make governments more sensitive to voter demands and contribute to the free-rider problem.

_____ 2. Fiscal conservatives argue against grants from higher levels of government to lower levels on the grounds that
   a. they are an ineffective method of transferring income between jurisdictions with different levels of wealth.
   b. cities would not provide positive externalities to surrounding suburbs with this funding.
   c. local politicians find it easier to spend money when they don't have to pay for it by raising taxes.
   d. they lead to diseconomies of agglomeration.

_____ 3. Spruce City has the only swimming pool in the county, and many county residents who do not pay city taxes swim there. How can Spruce City discourage these free riders?
   a. It can charge everyone who comes to the pool an admission fee.
   b. It can charge only nonresidents an admission fee.
   c. It can have special hours for nonresidents.
   d. It cannot overcome the free-rider problem.

276   Chapter 19   _Policy Studies: Cities, the Environment, and Health Care_

4. Marshall and Agatha recently retired; they are very concerned about health care and security. The Tiebout hypothesis suggests that they
   a. will have to choose between health care and security.
   b. should arrange for private provision of health care.
   c. will move to a community that provides both and pay the higher taxes involved.
   d. will move closer to an urban center.

5. Proponents of public mass transit systems argue that these systems
   a. have many characteristics of public goods.
   b. will not be provided unless the government does it.
   c. will eliminate many areas of high population density.
   d. have negative externalities that only the government can correct.

6. When resources are held in common, users will
   a. use the resources on a rotation basis.
   b. overuse the resources.
   c. underuse the resources.
   d. assign property rights to the resources.

7. The tragedy of the commons can be averted by
   a. allowing market forces to replace government regulation.
   b. having government assign property rights to the common resource.
   c. having government impose regulations on the use of the resource.
   d. having government either assign property rights or impose regulations.

8. The problem of acid rain is distinctive because
   a. the source of the pollution is fairly easy to identify.
   b. there are no spillovers associated with acid rain.
   c. pollution associated with acid rain is mainly a local problem.
   d. we do not understand the source of acid rain.

9. When a local government imposes a fine on households that refuse to recycle their newspapers and aluminum cans, that government is
   a. using the Tiebout hypothesis.
   b. using a market incentive to regulate a local common resource.
   c. circumventing a market solution.
   d. privatizing garbage collection.

10. Past problems with hazardous waste were the result of
    a. a refusal by local governments to accept responsibility for a national problem.
    b. a lack of information and government regulation.
    c. too much regulation.
    d. a failure to employ adequate user fees.

Chapter 19   Policy Studies: Cities, the Environment, and Health Care

11. Which of the following did *not* cause the demand curve for health care to shift to the right over the last three decades?
    a.   Technological advances in medical treatment
    b.   Higher income for U.S. citizens
    c.   Government- and employer-provided health insurance
    d.   Longer life expectancies.

12. As a result of rising incomes during the 1960s and 1970s,
    a.   the supply curve of physicians shifted to the right.
    b.   the quantity of physicians supplied increased.
    c.   medical school applications began to increase during the 1980s.
    d.   the law of supply was violated.

13. Under the Clinton health plan,
    a.   employers and employees would split the cost of health care.
    b.   employers would pay 80 percent of health costs and employees would pay 20 percent.
    c.   employers would pay all of the cost of health care.
    d.   employees could choose between employer-paid care and paying for their own insurance.

14. In the United States, 25 percent of spinal injuries are the result of
    a.   medical malpractice.
    b.   automobile accidents.
    c.   automobile accidents involving drinking drivers.
    d.   assaults.

15. Which group would *not* be against the Clinton health care plan?
    a.   Trial lawyers
    b.   The tobacco lobby
    c.   Major insurance companies
    d.   Small insurance companies

TAKING ANOTHER LOOK

What can a small town do when the merchants move out to the regional mall? Some folks in Havana, Florida, used economies of agglomeration to turn their town around. They persuaded three antique dealers to move into vacant downtown stores. Soon, several other dealers opened shops, and one entrepreneur moved into an old house to house her expensive antiques. Before long, there were two art galleries, a rare book dealer, several restaurants, and bed and breakfast inns. Then some out-of-town dealers got together and opened an antique mall housing about twenty boutiques in the closed Ford dealership. Now Havana is a popular North Florida weekend destination instead of a town to speed through on the way to Panama City or Atlanta.

278   *Chapter 19   Policy Studies: Cities, the Environment, and Health Care*

CHECKING OUT

Now that you have finished studying this chapter, you should be able to:

1. Explain optimal city size in terms of economies and diseconomies of agglomeration, and demonstrate how the provision of local public goods is complicated by spillovers.

2. Use housing and transportation to explore various blends of private and public roles in the provision of urban services.

3. Explain the role of the tragedy of the commons, inadequate information, and sovereignty issues in making some kinds of environmental issues difficult to address and solve.

4. Identify the economic issues in the health care crisis.

5. Evaluate the Clinton proposal for policy reform of health care.

ANSWERS

Trying Out the Terms

1. F   4. A
2. B   5. E
3. D   6. C

Testing Yourself

Part I: True or False

1. true
2. false. It is best determined by the individuals who live in the city.
3. false. Even when small towns are not losing people, the shopping may be largely abandoned as regional malls serving several towns spring up.
4. true
5. false. It is very effective because it offers external funding to assist in solving a local problem.
6. true
7. true
8. false. They are enacting the tragedy of the commons. They realize that if they don't go out and catch the shrimp, other shrimpers will.
9. true
10. true
11. false. Most hazardous waste problems stem from dumping in the past, when there was less knowledge about its dangers.
12. true
13. false. One reason health care costs are so high is that supply fell at the same time that demand was increasing.

Chapter 19   Policy Studies: Cities, the Environment, and Health Care   279

14. false. Improved health care means more people grow up and live longer, and old people have more health problems; demand will increase.
15. false. Under this plan everybody, even the poor, pay something.

Part II: Multiple Choice

1. d	5. a	9. b	13. b
2. c	6. b	10. b	14. d
3. b	7. d	11. a	15. c
4. c	8. a	12. b	

Name _____

CHAPTER 19 EXERCISES

Each of the following statements is false. In the space provided, rewrite each statement so that it is true.

1. Economies of agglomeration cause urban firms to face higher average cost curves.

2. The optimal size for a U.S. city is a population between 500,000 and 800,000.

3. Barbara Boggs Sigmund believes that the growth of new suburbs may offer the solution to many urban problems.

4. A city can determine the optimal level of crime prevention by vertically summing the demand curves of its citizens. This eliminates the demand of nonresidents.

5. The Reagan administration encouraged cities to solve the spillover problem by offering them intergovernmental grants.

6. The Tiebout hypothesis calls for federal standards for local public goods.

7. The Local Initiative Support Corporation provides low-cost housing, using only private funds.

Chapter 19   Policy Studies: Cities, the Environment, and Health Care   *281*

8. Proponents of public mass transportation maintain that an adequate system reduces population density.

9. User charges are not effective in controlling spillovers because they are hard to collect.

10. Because they involve common access resources, pollution problems can never be solved by rigid assignment of property rights.

11. Scientists are able to predict where the greenhouse effect will be harmful but not when.

12. The tragedy of the commons represents a market failure.

13. Because people only go to the doctor when they have to, an increase in third-party payments will not cause an increase in demand for health care.

14. Life expectancy is lower in the United States than in many other countries because medical care is not as good as it is in those countries.

15. The present system of medical care in the United States is a purely market-based system.

CHAPTER 20

TRADE AMONG NATIONS

CHECKING IN

Most countries engage in substantial trade with other nations. In the United States, international trade accounts for between 10 and 12 percent of GNP. The percentage is much higher in many other countries.

Trade between two countries is very much like trade between two individuals. It occurs when both parties benefit from the exchange. International trade is based on comparative advantage. A country produces those goods with low opportunity costs and exchanges them for goods with higher domestic opportunity costs. Such specialization increases total output with the same amount of resources. Other benefits from trade are increased competition and economies of scale.

In spite of the advantages international trade can bring to a nation, it is often opposed by many groups that are hurt by imports. For example, producers and workers in domestic industries that compete with imports often seek protective legislation. Tariffs, quotas, and nontariff barriers are all ways of interfering with free trade. For most of its history, the United States had high tariffs. However, since 1934, U.S. tariffs have been dramatically reduced. Advocates of protectionism have several arguments supporting their case. Although most of these arguments (balance of payments, employment, and cheap foreign labor) have weak economic foundations, the infant industry and national defense arguments are valid under certain restricted circumstances. The optimal tariff argument and the theory of the second best are more sophisticated rationales for protectionism. Nevertheless, the goal of most calls for protection is really income redistribution.

Multinational corporations operate in many countries. These firms may either increase or decrease competition, depending on the specific circumstances. They increase the transfer of technology between countries. If the company is very large and the country is small, the company may have too much power compared to the government of the host country.

Chapter 20   Trade Among Nations   283

TRYING OUT THE TERMS

Match each of the following terms with its definition, and then check your answers. If you are having trouble, go back to the text and find the definition there.

_____ 1. gains from trade   _____ 10. trade diversion

_____ 2. consumption possibilities curve   _____ 11. commercial policy

_____ 3. terms of trade   _____ 12. quota

_____ 4. multinational corporation   _____ 13. comparative advantage

_____ 5. nontariff barriers   _____ 14. common market

_____ 6. tariff   _____ 15. free trade area

_____ 7. trade creation   _____ 16. tariff quota

_____ 8. absolute advantage   _____ 17. fair trade

_____ 9. product cycle

A. The increase in economic well-being resulting from specialization and trade.

B. The ability to produce something using fewer resources than other producers use.

C. The ability to produce something at a lower opportunity cost than other producers face.

D. The ratio at which one product is exchanged for another.

E. A line showing the consumption combinations attainable through trade.

F. A series of stages, from development to standardization, through which a new product passes.

G. A tax on imported goods or services.

H. A limit on the amount of a good or service that can be imported during a given time period.

I. Trade restrictions other than tariffs and quotas.

J. The set of actions that a country undertakes to deliberately influence trade in goods and services.

K. An agreement between two or more countries to eliminate tariffs and other trade barriers on trade among themselves, while each country maintains its existing trade barriers to outside countries.

284   *Chapter 20   Trade Among Nations*

L. A free trade area with a common external tariff, free movement of capital and labor, and harmonization of social and economic policies.

M. Shifting from a higher-cost supplier to a lower cost supplier as a result of forming a free trade area or common market.

N. Shifting from a lower cost supplier to a higher cost supplier as a result of forming a free trade area or common market.

O. A combination of a quota and a tariff that allows a certain amount of a good or service to be imported without paying a tariff and imposes the tariff on further imparts.

P. A firm with headquarters in one country and plants in one or more subsidiaries in other countries.

Q. The idea that the United States should impose trade barriers equivalent to those that its trading partners place on U.S. exports.

TESTING YOURSELF

In the next three sections, you will answer questions and work problems that are based on information in the text. Master all of the terms before you begin these sections. Work each section without referring to your notes or the text, and then check your answers.

Part I: True or False

Mark each statement as true or false. Whenever you mark a statement as false, jot down a sentence stating why it is false.

_____ 1. Trade will take place if one party to the transaction gains from the trade.

_____ 2. Mercantilists discouraged imports and encouraged exports.

_____ 3. A country with an absolute advantage in a product should produce that product for export.

_____ 4. If all countries specialized and traded, world output would increase without an increase in the use of resources.

Chapter 20   Trade Among Nations   285

_____ 5. A country's comparative advantage is fixed and will not change over time.

_____ 6. The production of low-cost cotton textiles is concentrated in England.

_____ 7. Trade increases the number of choices available to consumers.

_____ 8. If the U.S. government imposes a $6 import fee on every lamb imported from New Zealand, it has imposed a specific tariff.

_____ 9. No one gains from protectionist policies.

_____ 10. If a quota is in place, an increase in demand will cause both price and quantity to increase.

_____ 11. Dumping can be a form of price discrimination.

_____ 12. The Smoot-Hawley Act enacted the highest tariff ever imposed in the United States.

_____ 13. Political support for protectionism should come from an alliance of consumers and exporters.

_____ 14. If market externalities distort opportunity costs, then the theory of the second best holds that a tariff may be appropriate.

_____ 15. Strict immigration laws are a form of employment protection.

Part II: Problems

1. Each of the states in the following table is using one-half of its resources on the production of each good.

	Output/Hour	
	Bread	Cheese
Kansas	150	300
Missouri	300	900

a. If these states specialized in the production of either cheese or bread, how much could each produce?

b. Which state has an absolute advantage in bread and in cheese?

c. What is the opportunity cost of cheese in Kansas and in Missouri?

d. What is the opportunity cost of bread in Kansas and in Missouri?

e. Which state should specialize in bread?

Chapter 20   Trade Among Nations   287

2. The country of Arcadia represents a very small part of the world market for cut flowers. The figure below shows the demand and supply curves for Arcadia.

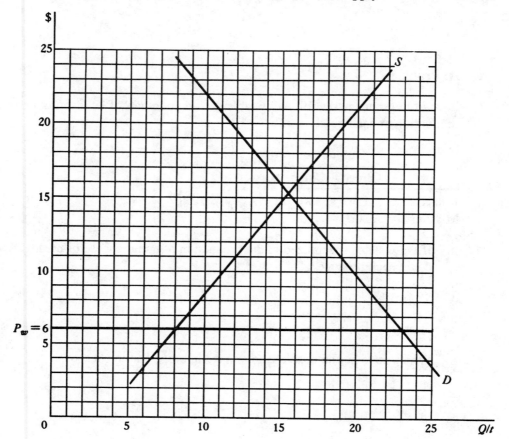

a. If there is free trade, how many boxes of flowers will be bought and at what price?

How many will be produced domestically?

How many will be imported?

b. If Arcadia imposes a tariff of $5 on each box of flowers, what will happen to the price and quantity?

How many will be produced domestically?

288   Chapter 20   Trade Among Nations

How many will be imported?

c.   What size quota would Arcadia have to impose to achieve the same results?

Part III: Multiple Choice

_____ 1.   In the United States, trade represents about _____ percent of GDP.
a.   3 to 5
b.   10 to 12
c.   15 to 18
d.   25 to 30

_____ 2.   International trade occurs
a.   for the same reasons that domestic trade occurs.
b.   only between countries in the same common market.
c.   even when there is no opportunity for profit.
d.   only when exchange rates are flexible.

For Questions 3–6, use the following information: In one hour, Lester can peel 10 potatoes or make 50 cookies. In one hour, James can peel 15 potatoes or make 60 cookies.

_____ 3.   Lester has an absolute
a.   advantage in cookies.
b.   advantage in both potatoes and cookies.
c.   disadvantage in both potatoes and cookies.
d.   advantage in potatoes.

_____ 4.   For Lester, the opportunity cost of 1 potato is
a.   1 cookie.
b.   5 cookies.
c.   10 cookies.
d.   50 cookies.

_____ 5.   James has
a.   a comparative advantage in cookies.
b.   a comparative advantage in potatoes.
c.   an absolute advantage in both potatoes and cookies.
d.   a comparative advantage in potatoes and an absolute advantage in both potatoes and cookies.

_____ 6.   If they are going to specialize,
a.   James should peel potatoes.
b.   James should make cookies.
c.   Lester should make cookies.
d.   James should peel potatoes and Lester should make cookies.

Chapter 20   Trade Among Nations   289

7. If Canada can produce 1 steer for 6 bushels of corn and France can produce 1 steer for 8 bushels of corn, then
   a. the two countries will not trade.
   b. Canada will be willing to trade 1 steer to France for 6 bushels of corn.
   c. France will be willing to trade 1 bushel of corn to Canada for one-eighth of a steer.
   d. the terms of trade will be somewhere between 1 steer for 6 bushels and 1 steer for 8 bushels.

8. If one nation's productivity or potential level of output for a certain product is greater than that of another nation, it has
   a. an absolute advantage.
   b. a comparative advantage.
   c. a productive advantage.
   d. excess capacity.

9. The first nation to produce a product is likely to
   a. maintain the comparative advantage in that product if the world market is large.
   b. maintain the comparative advantage in that product if the world market is small.
   c. lose the comparative advantage quickly, even if it has the technology and skills needed in production.
   d. be immune to the product cycle.

10. When a tariff is imposed,
    a. the total quantity sold increases, while the quantity imported decreases.
    b. both the quantity sold and the quantity imported decreases.
    c. the quantity produced domestically increases.
    d. the quantity sold and the quantity imported decrease and the quantity produced domestically increases.

11. If a quota is imposed, the winners are
    a. the producers and workers in the country that is exporting.
    b. the exporter, producers, and workers in the country that is importing.
    c. the government of the importing country, since a quota works like a tax.
    d. the importer and the producers and workers in the country that is importing.

12. Domestic preference laws act as
    a. a tariff.
    b. a quota.
    c. a nontariff barrier.
    d. free-trade legislation.

13. An infant industry argument for protection may be economically valid if the industry
    a. will eventually be able to compete in the world market.
    b. generates substantial external benefits.
    c. is financed with imported capital.
    d. will eventually be able to compete in the world market or generates substantial external benefits.
    e. generates substantial external benefits and is financed with imported capital.

14. The national defense argument for protection
    a. is more valid now than it was before World War II.
    b. would be valid if an extensive nuclear war was anticipated.
    c. would be valid if a nonnuclear war of attrition was anticipated.
    d. has no economic validity.

15. The concept of fair trade calls for
    a. arbitrary tariffs.
    b. a "level playing field."
    c. across-the-board tariff reductions.
    d. the abolition of all nontariff barriers.

16. A country that is poor in raw materials, capital, or skilled labor
    a. has no comparative advantage.
    b. cannot gain from trade.
    c. can import inputs and produce its own final goods.
    d. can import but not export.

CHECKING OUT

Now that you have finished studying this chapter, you should be able to:

1. Describe the benefits of free trade based on comparative advantage.

2. Analyze the effects of tariffs, quotas, and other trade restrictions.

3. Evaluate the arguments for tariff protection.

4. Discuss the costs and benefits of forming free trade areas and common markets.

5. Evaluate the impact of immigration and direct foreign investment.

ANSWERS

Trying Out the Terms

1. A	5. I	9. F	13. C	17. Q
2. E	6. G	10. N	14. L	
3. D	7. M	11. J	15. K	
4. P	8. B	12. H	16. O	

Testing Yourself

Part I: True or False

1. false. Both parties must gain from trade.
2. true

Chapter 20 Trade Among Nations   291

3. false. A country should specialize in and export products in which it has a comparative advantage.
4. true
5. false. Comparative advantage may change if there is a change in resources or technology.
6. false. It is concentrated in countries with low-cost, low-skill labor, though it was developed in England.
7. true
8. true
9. false. Domestic producers, their workers, and their suppliers gain, but consumers and workers in export industries lose.
10. false. Only price will increase, since the quantity is fixed by the government.
11. true
12. true
13. false. These groups should support free trade.
14. true
15. true

Part II: Problems

1. a. Kansas could produce either 300 units of bread or 600 units of cheese. Missouri could produce either 600 units of bread or 1,800 units of cheese.
   b. Missouri has an absolute advantage in both bread and cheese.
   c. The opportunity cost of cheese in Kansas is 1/2 unit of bread. In Missouri, it is 1/3 unit of bread.
   d. The opportunity cost of bread in Kansas is 2 units of cheese. In Missouri, it is 3 units of cheese.
   e. Kansas should specialize in bread.
2. a. Twenty-three boxes of flowers will be bought at $6. Eight boxes will be produced domestically. Fifteen boxes will be imported.
   b. Nineteen boxes of flowers will be bought at $11. Twelve boxes will be produced domestically. Seven boxes will be imported.
   c. Arcadia would have to impose a quota of seven boxes to have the same results.

Part III: Multiple Choice

1. b	5. d	9. b	13. d
2. a	6. d	10. d	14. c
3. c	7. d	11. d	15. b
4. b	8. a	12. c	16. c

292   *Chapter 20   Trade Among Nations*

Name _____

CHAPTER 20 EXERCISES

Mark each statement as true or false. If you mark a statement as false, write a sentence that makes the statement true.

_____ 1. If Chile can produce a maximum of 25 units of grapes or 30 units of beef and Argentina can produce a maximum of 25 units of grapes or 35 units of beef, Chile should produce grapes and trade with Argentina for beef.

_____ 2. Specialization and trade can result in an increase in total world output without an increase in the use of world resources.

_____ 3. The theory of comparative advantage was set forth by John Stuart Mills.

_____ 4. Gains from trade are always equal.

_____ 5. According to the product cycle, when the market for a product is strong, wealthy countries will produce it, but when the market begins to weaken, only developing nations will produce it.

_____ 6. A quota is a tax on imported goods.

_____ 7. A tariff quota is a tariff placed on imports above a fixed quantity or quota.

_____ 8. Most economists prefer tariffs to free trade.

Chapter 20   Trade Among Nations   293

_____ 9. A monopolist is likely to be in favor of international trade.

_____ 10. Foreign competition is unpopular with owners of resources only when the competition is in the resource market.

_____ 11. The increased output from comparative advantage is the sole benefit of international trade.

_____ 12. The United States puts fewer restrictions on the inflow or outflow of capital than most other countries.

_____ 13. Organized labor generally opposes liberal immigration legislation.

_____ 14. Multinational firms impede trade.

CHAPTER 21

INTERNATIONAL FINANCE AND EXCHANGE RATES

CHECKING IN

International trade, which you studied in the preceding chapter, involves not only the exchange of goods and services but also the exchange of payment. This exchange can be complicated, because most countries have their own currencies. This chapter discusses the financing of international transactions.

Currencies are exchanged in foreign exchange markets. The demand for foreign exchange is a reflection of the demand for foreign goods, services, and financial assets that must be paid for in the foreign currency. The supply of foreign exchange is determined by the desire of foreigners to buy domestic goods, services, and financial assets. The foreign exchange market can involve a lot of risk. Participating in the forward market is one way to reduce the risk of foreign exchange.

As in all markets, the supply and demand curves for foreign exchange will shift when something other than price changes. Changes in relative prices, incomes, interest rates, tastes, population, technology, and input cost and availability may cause these curves to shift. Surpluses and shortages often occur in foreign exchange markets. One way to eliminate these surpluses and shortages is to change the price, but it is also possible to shift supply and demand curves, ration foreign exchange, or draw on accumulated reserves.

The United States summarizes the transactions between its residents and foreigners in its balance of payments. This statement is composed of four accounts: the current account, the capital account, a statistical discrepancy, and the settlement account. The sum of the current and capital accounts and the statistical discrepancy is the balance of payments surplus or deficit. The settlement account shows how this surplus or deficit was financed.

There are four different international monetary systems. Under the gold standard, all currencies can be redeemed for a fixed amount of gold. The movements of gold ensure balance of payments equilibrium. This flow of gold between countries leaves a nation with little power to control its money supply. This is a major drawback of the gold standard.

Between 1945 and 1973, the Bretton Woods system governed international transactions. It provided fairly stable exchange rates and relied on international reserves to settle deficits. This system failed because it was too dependent on the U.S. dollar as a reserve.

Since 1973, most foreign exchange markets have depended on floating rates that are set by the interaction of supply and demand. Under floating rates, changes in the value of

Chapter 21   International Finance and Exchange Rates   295

currency solve the deficit problem. Countries can control their own money supplies separately from the foreign exchange market. Floating rates can be very volatile.

Under exchange control, all foreign exchange passes through the government. This system gives government the power to ration foreign exchange. The government may also have different rates for different uses of foreign exchange. Black markets for currency usually develop under an exchange control system.

TRYING OUT THE TERMS

Match each of the following terms with its definition, and then check your answers. If you are having trouble, go back to the text and find the definition there.

_____ 1. statistical discrepancy

_____ 2. appreciation

_____ 3. balance of payments

_____ 4. gold standard

_____ 5. International Monetary Fund (IMF)

_____ 6. European Monetary Union (EMU)

_____ 7. foreign exchange market

_____ 8. depreciation

_____ 9. trade weighted dollar

_____ 10. forward market

_____ 11. capital account

_____ 12. speculators

_____ 13. current account

_____ 14. balance of trade

_____ 15. balance of payments deficit

_____ 16. hedgers

_____ 17. real exchange rate

_____ 18. Bretton Woods System

_____ 19. international monetary reserves

_____ 20. key currency

A. Difference between the value of a country's merchandise exports and imports.

B. The foreign currency exchange rate after adjustment for changes in relative price levels.

C. An annual summary of transactions between residents of one country and residents of the rest of the world.

D. The part of the balance of payments that summarizes transactions in currently produced goods and services.

E. The currency that serves as a major reserve asset and is used in transactions between third-party nations.

F. The part of the balance of payments that summarizes purchases and sales of financial assets.

296   *Chapter 21   International Finance and Exchange Rates*

G. The part of the balance of payments that reflects unrecorded transactions and inaccurate estimates of spending by tourists.

H. An excess of a country's foreign spending over its foreign earnings for a given year.

I. The network of banks and financial institutions through which buyers and sellers exchange national currencies.

J. The market in which contracts are made for future deliveries of specific amounts of a currency at a specified price.

K. A price index for the dollar that measures changes in its value in terms of a market basket of currencies of major trading partners.

L. The pool of gold and major currencies created under the Bretton Woods system, from which countries could borrow to settle deficits and replenish from surpluses.

M. The international monetary system in effect from 1945 to 1973, based on infrequent changes in currency prices, ample reserves, and the dollar as key currency.

N. People who try to reduce their risk by buying or selling contracts in the forward market for currency.

O. People who asssume risk in the forward market for currency in return for a chance of a profit.

P. A market-determined increase in a currency's price.

Q. A market-determined decrease in a currency's price.

R. An international monetary system in which currencies were defined in terms of gold, money supplies were linked to gold, and balance of payments deficits were settled in gold.

S. The agency that supervised the operation of the Bretton Woods system and maintained a reserve pool, and which continues to assist countries with currency and monetary management problems.

T. A currency area of members of the European Community in which exchange rates are fixed among members within narrow bonds, but float together with respect to other currencies; broke up in 1993.

TESTING YOURSELF

In the next three sections, you will answer questions and work problems that are based on information in the text. Master all of the terms before you begin these sections. Work each section without referring to your notes or the text, and then check your answers.

Chapter 21   International Finance and Exchange Rates   297

Part I: True or False

Mark each statement as true or false. Whenever you mark a statement as false, jot down a sentence stating why it is false.

_____ 1. A balance of payments deficit puts downward pressure on the price of a nation's currency.

_____ 2. A transaction that involves a payment from someone in the United States to someone in another country will be recorded as an addition to the U.S. balance of payments.

_____ 3. In recent years, foreign investment in the United States has decreased.

_____ 4. The recent increase in the statistical discrepancy in the balance of payments accounts indicates that there may have been an increase in unrecorded capital inflows into the United States.

_____ 5. If Americans decide to invest more in Brazil, the demand for Brazilian cruzados (currency) will increase.

_____ 6. Interest rates are the most significant determinant of demand for foreign exchange.

_____ 7. If the United States imposed a tariff on sweaters imported from Peru, the demand for Peruvian soles (currency) would increase.

_____ 8. If a country that is experiencing inflation increases its imports, this will have a dampening effect on the inflation.

298   *Chapter 21   International Finance and Exchange Rates*

_____ 9. If Morris, Inc. buys a forward contract for Colombian pesos in June to pay for the coffee delivery it will accept in December, it has avoided the risk of fluctuating exchange rates.

_____ 10. The forward markets were more active in the 1950s and 1960s than they are today.

_____ 11. When a government interferes in a foreign exchange market with floating exchange rates, there is a dirty float.

_____ 12. If there is a balance of payments deficit in a country operating on the gold standard, gold will flow into the country.

_____ 13. Operating on the gold standard gives a nation more control over its macroeconomic policy tools.

_____ 14. Under the Bretton Woods system, exchange rates were neither fully fixed nor truly floating.

_____ 15. Exchange control inhibits free international trade.

Chapter 21   International Finance and Exchange Rates   299

Part II: Problems

1. The following graphs show the foreign exchange market for Danish kroner in equilibrium. Show the effect that each of the following events would have on the market.

   a. Denmark begins to subsidize the Danish cheese industry.

   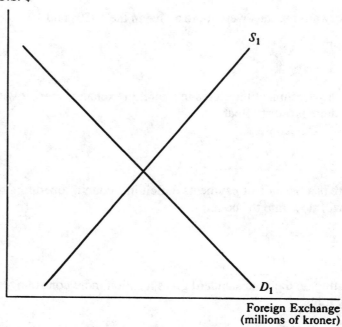

   b. Prices in the United States fall, relative to prices in Denmark.

   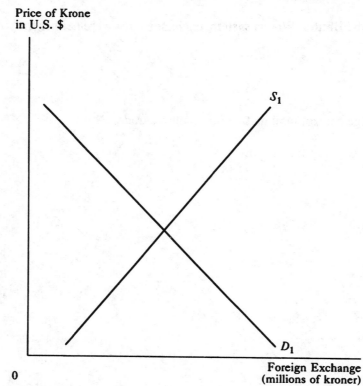

300   Chapter 21   International Finance and Exchange Rates

c. The price of wool used in Danish-made sweaters increases.

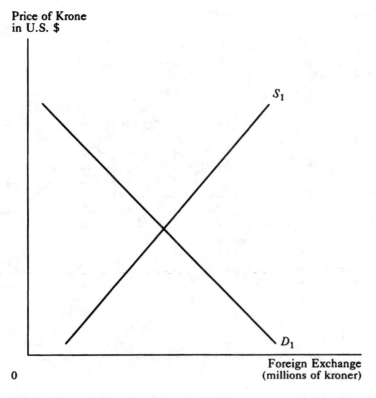

d. Danish interest rates fall, relative to those in the United States.

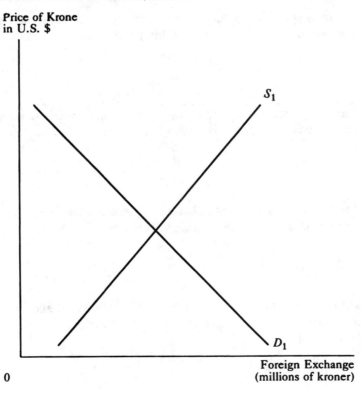

Chapter 21   International Finance and Exchange Rates   301

2. The graph below shows the foreign exchange market for Swiss francs.

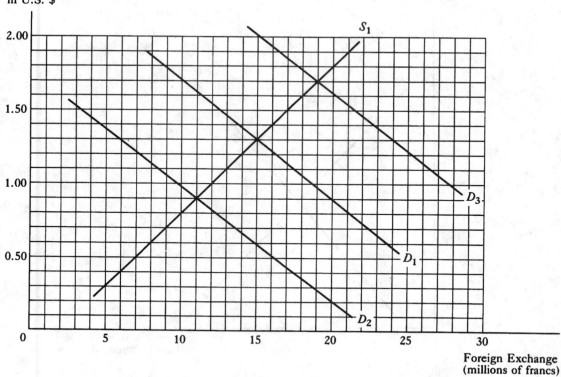

a. If the market reflects S_1 and D_3 and exchange rates are floating, what is the exchange rate? How many francs will be exchanged for dollars?

b. If the market reflects S_1 and D_3 and the exchange rate is fixed at $1.30, will there be a surplus or a shortage of francs? How large?

c. If the market reflects S_1 and D_2 and the exchange rate is fixed at $1.30, will there be a surplus or a shortage of francs? How large?

d. If the exchange rate is allowed to float between $1.10 and $1.50 and the demand curve shifts from D_1 to D_2, what will happen to the exchange rate and the quantity of francs exchanged?

e. If the exchange rate is allowed to float between $1.10 and $1.50 and the demand curve shifts from D_3 to D_1, what will happen to the exchange rate and the quantity of francs exchanged?

f. If the exchange rate is allowed to float between $1.10 and $1.50 and the market reflects S_1 and D_1, what will happen to the exchange rate? Will there be a surplus or a shortage of francs? How large?

Part III: Multiple Choice

_____ 1. A U.S. balance of payments surplus would be decreased by all *except* which one of the following?
a. Mexican citizens buy condominiums in Texas.
b. U.S. residents spend their vacations in Cancun.
c. A U.S. factory buys a new lathe from Poland.
d. A U.S. developer builds a shopping center in Montreal.

_____ 2. Which of the following would be included in the balance of trade?
a. Investment by foreign citizens in U.S. corporations
b. A dividend from a French firm received by a U.S. citizen
c. The sale of a large machine to an Italian corporation by a U.S. firm
d. Unreported income from drug smuggling

_____ 3. If the dollar price of the Venezuelan bolivar (currency) decreases, there will be
a. an increase in the supply of U.S. dollars.
b. a decrease in the supply of the bolivar.
c. an increase in the bolivar price for dollars.
d. a decrease in the bolivar price for dollars.

_____ 4. Suppose the price of the Canadian dollar is $0.80. What is the price of the U.S. dollar in Canadian dollars?
a. $8.00
b. $1.25
c. $0.80
d. An amount that cannot be determined.

_____ 5. If interest rates in the United States rose relative to those in the rest of the world, we would expect
a. the supply of dollars to increase.
b. the demand for dollars to increase.
c. foreign investment in the United States to increase.
d. U.S. investment abroad to increase.
e. the demand for dollars to increase as foreign investment in the United States increased.

Chapter 21   International Finance and Exchange Rates   303

6. Which of the following would *not* cause the demand curve for Mexican pesos to shift?
   a. A change in the U.S. tariff structure
   b. A change in export subsidies in Mexico
   c. A change in population in the United States
   d. A change in preferences of Mexicans for U.S.-made goods

7. A country has a dirty float when
   a. black markets develop under exchange control.
   b. the government announces different exchange rates for industrial firms and individuals.
   c. the government enters the exchange market when rates are not fixed.
   d. a country with fixed rates unexpectedly devalues its currency.

8. Which of the following is a goal of an ideal international monetary system?
   a. Stable exchange rates
   b. Control over macroeconomic policy tools
   c. A self-correction mechanism for balance of payments surpluses and deficits
   d. All of the above

9. When a country is on the gold standard,
   a. its exchange rate is determined in market exchanges with other currencies that are also tied to gold.
   b. balance of payment deficits will be corrected as gold leaves the country.
   c. monetary policy is made stronger.
   d. exchange rates are flexible within a narrow range.

10. One drawback to the gold standard is that
    a. no one really knows what gold is worth.
    b. the money supply cannot be determined by the government.
    c. there is not enough gold in the world to support the U.S. money supply.
    d. gold cannot serve as an international reserve.

11. Under the Bretton Woods system, each country
    a. agreed to let its exchange rate float in the world market.
    b. set a par value for its currency in gold.
    c. agreed to buy and sell its own currency in gold alone.
    d. set a fixed rate for its currency in either U.S. dollars or British pounds.

12. Under the Bretton Woods system, a country that ran consistent balance of payments deficits could
    a. borrow from the international reserves at the International Monetary Fund.
    b. change the price of its currency.
    c. agree to let its currency float against the key currencies.
    d. either borrow from the international reserves at the IMF or change the price of its currency.

304   *Chapter 21   International Finance and Exchange Rates*

_____ 13. The Bretton Woods system failed because
     a.   it did not provide enough acceptable international reserves.
     b.   Great Britain refused to let the British pound serve as a key currency.
     c.   higher prices brought a great deal more gold onto the market and the value of all currencies depreciated.
     d.   the International Monetary Fund closed its "gold window."

_____ 14. Floating exchange rates work
     a.   because the IMF guarantees a minimum level for key currencies.
     b.   by curing the problem of overshooting.
     c.   on the principles of supply and demand.
     d.   because it is possible for foreign exchange markets to sustain a prolonged equilibrium.

_____ 15. Exchange control is practiced
     a.   only when exchange rates are fixed.
     b.   primarily by less developed countries.
     c.   primarily by the highly industrialized nations.
     d.   primarily by the International Monetary Fund.

CHECKING OUT

Now that you have finished studying this chapter, you should be able to:

1. Identify the components of the balance of payments accounts and discuss the uses of balance of payments information.

2. Explain the relationship between the foreign exchange market and the trade and capital flows on the balance of payments.

3. Explain how the foreign exchange market works and how the market for currencies is different from other kinds of markets.

4. Discuss the operation of floating rates since 1973.

5. Analyze the advantages and disadvantages of various types of fixed exchange rate systems, including the gold standard, Bretton Woods, and the European Monetary Union.

ANSWERS

Trying Out the Terms

1. G	5. S	9. K	13. D	17. B
2. P	6. T	10. J	14. A	18. M
3. C	7. I	11. F	15. H	19. L
4. R	8. Q	12. O	16. N	20. E

Chapter 21   International Finance and Exchange Rates   305

Testing Yourself

Part I: True or False

1. true
2. false. It will be a deduction.
3. false. It has increased.
4. true
5. true
6. false. Changes in relative price levels are the most significant determinant.
7. false. The demand would fall as importers bought fewer of the now more costly sweaters.
8. true
9. true
10. false. Forward markets are more active when exchange rates float, as they have in the United States since 1973.
11. true
12. false. Gold will flow out. People will exchange domestic currency for gold, which they will then use to buy foreign currency.
13. false. A nation loses control of these tools on the gold standard.
14. true
15. true

Part II: Problems

1. a. Cheese becomes cheaper and exports increase; the demand for kroner increases.

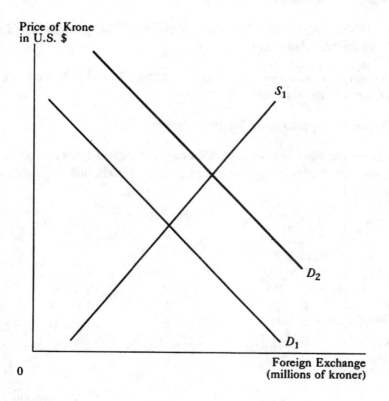

306 Chapter 21 International Finance and Exchange Rates

b. U.S. citizens buy fewer Danish imports; the demand for kroner decreases. At the same time, Danes demand more dollars to purchase U.S. goods; the supply of kroner increases.

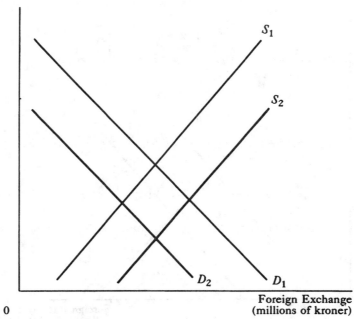

c. Sweaters become more expensive and fewer are exported; the demand for kroner decreases.

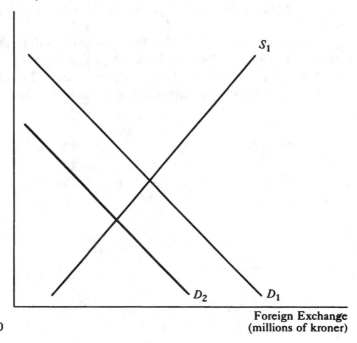

d. Danes want to purchase more dollars to invest in the United States; the supply of kroner increases.

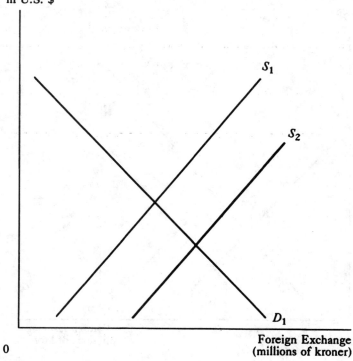

2. a. The exchange rate will be $1.70; 19 million francs will be exchanged.
   b. There will be a shortage of 9 million francs.
   c. There will be a surplus of 9 million francs.
   d. The exchange rate will be $1.10; there will be a surplus of approximately 4 million francs.
   e. The exchange rate will be $1.30; 15 million francs will be exchanged. The market will clear, so there will be neither a shortage nor a surplus.
   f. The exchange rate will be $1.30; 15 million francs will be exchanged. The market will clear, so there will be neither a shortage nor a surplus.

Part III: Multiple Choice

1. a
2. c
3. c
4. b

5. e
6. d
7. c
8. d

9. b
10. b
11. b
12. d

13. a
14. c
15. b

Name _____

CHAPTER 21 EXERCISES

Correctly arrange the following entries in a hypothetical balance of payments statement (next page) for the United States. Calculate the value of the balance of trade, the current account, the value of the capital account, and the statistical discrepancy.

U.S. private investment abroad	−46,172
Service transactions (net)	+2,400
Foreign private investment in the U.S.	+152,376
Merchandise imports	−315,235
Investment income, (net)	+11,294
Change in U.S. government assets abroad	−1,758
Transfers, public and private	−10,331
Change in foreign government asset in U.S	+17,974
Merchandise exports	+185,105

Chapter 21   International Finance and Exchange Rates   *309*

U.S. BALANCE OF PAYMENTS (HYPOTHETICAL)
(millions of dollars)

CURRENT ACCOUNT

      Balance of trade   _____

      Balance on current account   _____

CAPITAL ACCOUNT

      Balance on capital account   _____

STATISTICAL DISCREPANCY

CHAPTER 22

ECONOMIES IN TRANSITION

CHECKING IN

All countries must contend with similar economic problems. Opportunity costs and the law of demand exist under all economic systems. However, economic systems operate in a variety of ways. This chapter describes the most prevalent economic systems and examines the economies of several countries. Economists use comparative economics to analyze various institutions and determine how they affect economic outcomes.

Economic systems are often classified by ideology. Most economic systems fall into the categories of capitalism or socialism. These categories are so broad, however, that the usefulness of this approach is limited. Communist countries belong in the category of socialism. These countries all considered themselves Marxist, yet their economic systems were quite different. Many of these countries developed their economic systems under dominant leaders Lenin, Stalin, Mao, and Castro.

All economies engage in planning, but different systems plan at different levels. If planning takes place at a high level (as in many socialist countries), much more information is required by the planners. Central planning is the determination of national output. The Soviet Union experienced high industrial growth in the early twentieth century because of a central decision not to produce consumer goods. Plans have to be implemented. Workers and managers must be provided with adequate incentives if planned production levels are to be reached.

During the past twenty years, the Soviet Union and other Eastern and Central European countries began to adopt economic reforms leading toward a market system. These reforms have accelerated with the dissolution of the Soviet Union. The transition to a market economy is made more difficult by the lack of basic capitalistic institutions such as banking systems and stock markets.

Economic reforms have occurred in other parts of the world as China, too, has moved to a stronger reliance on markets and Mexico has restructured its economy, reducing its strong reliance on government market activities.

Chapter 22   Economies in Transition   *311*

TRYING OUT THE TERMS

Match each of the following terms with its definition, and then check your answers. If you are having trouble, go back to the text and find the definition there.

_____ 1. socialism

_____ 4. privatization

_____ 2. capitalism

_____ 5. communism

_____ 3. perestroika

_____ 6. glasnost

A. An economic system in which private individuals own the means of production and are free to use them in response to economic incentives.

B. An economic system in which the nonhuman means of production are owned by the state.

C. The final stage of social evolution according to Marx, in which the state has withered away and economic goods are distributed according to need.

D. Political reforms involving free speech and tolerance of dissent in the former Soviet Union in the Gorbachev era.

E. Economic reforms in the former Soviet Union in the Gorbachev era.

F. Transferring assets from public to private ownership in order to increase the share of economic decisions made through the market.

TESTING YOURSELF

In the next two sections, you will answer questions that are based on information in the text. Master all of the terms before you begin these sections. Work each section without referring to your notes or the text, and then check your answers.

Part I: True or False

Mark each statement as true or false. Whenever you mark a statement as false, jot down a sentence stating why it is false.

_____ 1. The process which enables societies to answer the basic economic questions is determined by the ownership of productive resources and the political organization of the society.

_____ 2. The percentage of GDP passing through the government is a good measure of the degree to which government is involved in economic decision making.

312   *Chapter 22   Economies in Transition*

_____ 3. Tax systems can be designed to encourage or discourage particular economic activities.

_____ 4. Government intervention does not occur in a capitalist economy.

_____ 5. Marx predicted that communism would be established first in industrialized countries.

_____ 6. In Marxist theory, socialism is the final stage in historical development.

_____ 7. Lenin's model for revolution has been fulfilled in several countries, such as Vietnam and Cuba.

_____ 8. The development of socialism in Yugoslavia was carried out under the direction of Stalin.

_____ 9. Under the five-year plans, money did not exist in the Soviet Union.

_____ 10. Between the 1930s and the 1970s, the Soviet Union enhanced its growth by borrowing ideas and technology.

_____ 11. By using internal rate of return calculations, the Soviet Union was able to achieve an efficient allocation of capital.

_____ 12. Gorbachev introduced the socialist solution to the Soviet Union.

Chapter 22   Economies in Transition   _313_

_____ 13. Privatization is observed only as socialist countries move toward market decision making.

_____ 14. As nations move from socialism to capitalism, there is a marked increase in income inequality.

_____ 15. Since 1976, China has greatly expanded trade with the rest of the world.

_____ 16. Reformed production incentives allowed Chinese enterprises to increase production of consumer goods.

_____ 17. The recent growth in Mexico is at least partially attributable to increased public spending to create employment opportunities.

_____ 18. In Japan, taxes are considerably higher than they are in the United States.

_____ 19. Under Castro, Cuba remained reliant on agriculture.

_____ 20. F.A. Hayek demonstrated that properly estimated shadow prices will allow a planned economy to reach the same level of efficiency as a market system.

Part II: Multiple Choice

_____ 1. An essential similarity between capitalism and socialism is
a. the ownership of nonhuman resources.
b. the ownership of human resources.
c. the determination of income distribution.
d. None of the above

314   Chapter 22   Economies in Transition

2. Under socialism, the decision-making process centers on
   a. the private property owner.
   b. the owners of capital.
   c. a planning organization.
   d. elected officials.

3. Marx predicted that all *except* which one of the following would occur under communism?
   a. An end to scarcity
   b. A new social order
   c. Increased class conflict
   d. The withering away of the state

4. Countries that consider themselves Marxist
   a. believe that capitalism exploits workers.
   b. deplore the presence of profits in an economy.
   c. tend to have strong-willed leaders.
   d. All of the above

5. During the period of the New Economic Policy
   a. planning was instituted for all sectors of the Soviet economy.
   b. parts of the economy operated with markets and other parts operated with economic planning.
   c. many industries in the Soviet Union were nationalized.
   d. planning was instituted for all sectors of the Soviet economy and many industries in the Soviet Union were nationalized.

6. Forced collectivization and rapid industrialization occurred in the Soviet Union during
   a. the Cultural Revolution.
   b. the period of five-year plans.
   c. perestroika.
   d. the New Economic Policy.

7. Under the leadership of Gorbachev, the Soviet Union
   a. moved into a more solidly Marxist stance.
   b. placed planning on a local level rather than a national level.
   c. moved away from central planning and toward market solutions.
   d. became an economic ally of China.

8. The simplest enterprises to privatize are
   a. farms.
   b. utilities.
   c. retail establishments.
   d. manufacturers.

Chapter 22   Economies in Transition   315

_____ 9. Countries that have been most successful in either development or rebuilding have
    a. relied mainly on domestic savings.
    b. received substantial loans from industrialized countries.
    c. developed export subsidies to attract foreign capital.
    d. reduced reliance on imported technical aid.

_____ 10. The revolution in China under the leadership of Mao
    a. took place at the direction of Stalin.
    b. followed the model established by the Soviet Union.
    c. occurred just after the Korean War.
    d. preceded the period of War Communism.

_____ 11. The Cultural Revolution was based on the
    a. radical restructuring of the economy.
    b. emphasizing the role of the worker.
    c. revolutionary values of Mao.
    d. All of the above

_____ 12. During the reforms led by Deng in China,
    a. economic incentives were offered in the form of higher wages.
    b. more consumer goods were produced.
    c. international trade was discouraged.
    d. economic incentives were offered in the form of higher wages and more consumer goods were produced.

_____ 13. In Mexico, the revenues from privatization were used to
    a. pay benefits to displaced workers.
    b. subsidize exports.
    c. reduce the budget deficit.
    d. enforce environmental standards.

_____ 14. Japan's recent economic success is due in part to
    a. the devastation of World War II.
    b. a changing social structure.
    c. high rates of saving.
    d. All of the above

_____ 15. In Cuba, after the establishment of the Castro regime,
    a. the economy became dependent on Soviet aid.
    b. market capitalism was used for consumer goods and central planning was used for heavy industry.
    c. industrialization was the first national priority.
    d. the principle of self-reliance was the foreign policy rule.

_____ 16. Lange argued that a socialist economy could be as efficient as a competitive economy if
    a. there were centrally established shadow prices.
    b. local managers were allowed to keep a percentage of the profits.
    c. there was a combination of central and local decision making.
    d. all economic calculations were rational.

316   *Chapter 22 Economies in Transition*

CHECKING OUT

Now that you have finished studying this chapter, you should be able to:

1. List the factors used to classify economies as market-oriented, socialist, and hybrid.

2. Distinguish among capitalism, socialism, and communism as theoretical economic systems and discuss the advantages and disadvantages of each.

3. Describe the events leading up to the collapse of communism in the former Soviet Union and Central Europe.

4. Discuss the process of transition from a centrally planned to a market economy and the difficulties being encountered in Eastern and Central Europe.

5. Evaluate the changes currently taking place in China, Japan, and Mexico as examples of economies in transition.

ANSWERS

Trying Out the Terms

1. B   5. C
2. A   6. D
3. E
4. F

Testing Yourself

Part I: True or False

1. false. The two factors determining how the economic questions are answered are ownership of resources and locus of economic decision making.
2. false. In many countries this pass-through may be a transfer of income with decision making being retained in the private sector.
3. true
4. false. Government intervention usually occurs to some degree in all economies.
5. true
6. false. Socialism is an intermediate stage; communism is the final stage.
7. true
8. false. Stalin's direction was in the Soviet Union.
9. false. Money played a small role, but it did exist to permit payment for consumer goods and wages.
10. true
11. false. Although there were some internal rate of return calculations, they were poor approximations of market rates; allocation of capital was inefficient.
12. false. Gorbachev introduced *glasnost* and its economic reform program, *perestroika*.
13. false. Privatization is an important move toward a market economy, but it has also taken place in Western industrial countries such as France and the United States.

Chapter 22   Economies in Transition   *317*

14. true
15. true
16. true
17. false. The transition is mainly due to reduced public spending and increased privatization.
18. false. They are much lower.
19. true
20. false. Hayek maintained that central planning would always be less efficient than a market system since it deflects many resources into information creation.

Part II: Multiple Choice

1. d	5. b	9. a	13. c
2. c	6. b	10. b	14. d
3. c	7. c	11. d	15. a
4. d	8. c	12. d	16. a

318   *Chapter 22   Economies in Transition*

Name _____

CHAPTER 22 EXERCISES

Mark each statement as true or false. Whenever you mark a statement as false, jot down a sentence stating why it is false.

_____   1. All economies are mixed, although the degree may vary.

_____   2. The general pattern is the lower the income of a country the higher the degree of government consumption.

_____   3. Planning does not occur in capitalist economies.

_____   4. Capitalism and communism are the extremes of economic systems.

_____   5. Capitalistic countries tend to be politically democratic.

_____   6. Any economic system must depend on wages, prices, and profits to provide incentives.

_____   7. Under the New Economic Policy, the Soviet Union virtually eliminated the market system.

_____   8. In the last fifteen years, Western (nonsocialist) countries have moved toward a higher degree of centralization.

Chapter 22   Economies in Transition   *319*

_____ 9. One benefit of private ownership of resources is the presence of incentives, such as profit, that reward efficiency.

_____ 10. Perestroika represented efforts to reorganize planning and produce more consumer goods.

_____ 11. The usual measure of national economic performance is per capita GDP.

_____ 12. The current inflation in the former Soviet Union is largely due to consumers spending their new, higher wages.

_____ 13. The Cultural Revolution emphasized education and a move to a freer market system in China.

_____ 14. Mexico's economic success has been accompanied by a move from communism to a market economy.

_____ 15. Since 1990, Japan's rapid economic growth has become the Japanese "miracle."